Workbook I

ATHENAZE

An Introduction to Ancient Greek

SECOND EDITION

Gilbert Lawall

James F. Johnson

Luigi Miraglia

New York   Oxford

OXFORD UNIVERSITY PRESS

2004

Oxford University Press

Oxford   New York
Auckland   Bangkok   Buenos Aires   Cape Town   Chennai
Dar es Salaam   Delhi   Hong Kong   Istanbul   Karachi   Kolkata
Kuala Lumpur   Madrid   Melbourne   Mexico City   Mumbai
Nairobi   São Paulo   Shanghai   Taipei   Tokyo   Toronto

Published by Oxford University Press, Inc.
198 Madison Avenue, New York, New York, 10016
http://www.oup-usa.org

Oxford is a registered trademark of Oxford University Press

ISBN: 0–19–514954–8

Printing number: 9 8 7 6 5 4 3 2 1

Printed in the United States of America
on acid-free paper

PREFACE

The authors are grateful to the following for proofreading the manuscript for this book: Elizabeth Baer of the Berkshire Country Day School, Lenox, Massachusetts; Maurice Balme of York, England; Cynthia King of Wright State University, Dayton, Ohio; and Kolbeinn Sæmundsson of the Menntaskólinn í Reykjavík, Iceland.

The stories included in this workbook are taken from the Italian edition of *Athenaze* prepared by Luigi Miraglia and T. F. Bórri, *Athenaze: Introduzione al greco antico*, Volume I, Accademia Vivarium Novum, Montella, Italy, 1999. The story for Chapter 10β was written for this workbook by Luigi Miraglia.

James Johnson
Gilbert Lawall
Luigi Miraglia

CONTENTS

INTRODUCTION

To Students Using This Workbook:

This Workbook accompanies Book I of *Athenaze: An Introduction to Ancient Greek*, Second Edition. It provides exercises covering all the grammar sections in the textbook and all the vocabulary lists at the beginnings of the chapters in the textbook. It also provides periodic cumulative vocabulary lists arranged by parts of speech, covering chapters 1–5, 6–9, 10–13, and 14–16. Also included is material for grammatical review and consolidation.

Each chapter of the Workbook contains at least one reading passage, short at first and becoming longer in the later chapters. Some readings in the later chapters focus on social and political conditions in Athens just prior to the outbreak of the Peloponnesian War, and some reflect on the pride of the Athenians in their defeat of the Persians and the philosophical and religious implications of the inspiring victory of a democratic people, few in number, but fighting for a just cause, over vast numbers of invaders seeking to enslave them. The final readings round out the story of Odysseus that begins in Chapter 7 of the textbook.

All words in the reading passages that have not occurred in chapter vocabulary lists prior to the reading are glossed below the paragraphs of the readings. These glosses include words that have been used in the stories in the textbook but are glossed there because they have not occurred in vocabulary lists. Even for subsequent paragraphs of the readings in this book we continue to gloss words that have not occurred in the chapter vocabulary lists, even though they have been glossed earlier in the story. You will therefore be familiar with many of the words that are glossed in the readings in this book. Our aim has been to include as much help as needed to enable rapid comprehension and translation of the readings. We recommend that you read through the glosses beneath each paragraph before reading the paragraph itself. Remember that if you find words in the readings that are not glossed and for which you do not recall the meanings, you can find the words in the cumulative vocabulary lists in this book or in the Greek to English Vocabulary at the end of the textbook.

Answers for all the exercises and translations of all the readings are given in the Answer Key at the back of this book, so that you can check all your answers and translations. You can write your answers in the slots provided in each exercise, and you can write translations of the readings on separate sheets of paper. Some of you will prefer, however, to write answers to the exercises on separate sheets of paper rather than in the workbook itself. This will allow you to use the exercises more than once. We would, in fact, recommend that you use these exercises several times—first after completing the work in the textbook for each half of a chapter, then as review prior to quizzes on chapters or groups of chapters, then as review prior to tests such as midterms, and finally as review prior to the final examination. If you do not write in the book, you will find yourself freshly challenged each time you use these exercises for review.

When using the cumulative vocabulary lists, we recommend that you cut a small notch in a piece of paper and cover the column of English equivalents and test your knowledge of the Greek word before moving your notched paper down to reveal the English. Do this in reverse to test your knowledge of the vocabulary from English to Greek.

One final helpful suggestion: The readings systematically incorporate forms of nouns, verbs, and other parts of speech presented in the corresponding chapters of the textbook. We suggest that you locate and underline these forms in the stories in the workbook so that you can focus on the forms themselves and how they are used in their sentences. This conscious attention to individual forms will enable you to master them more readily.

We hope that you will find the material in this book useful. Always be honest with yourself; do not use the Answer Key until you have completed the exercises. Don't cheat on yourself; use the Answer Key to check yourself; use it as a learning tool; use it to your benefit!

1
Ο ΔΙΚΑΙΟΠΟΛΙΣ (α)

Exercise 1α

Circle the noun form that goes with the article:

1. ὁ: κλῆρον (κλῆρος) 2. τὸν: (ἄνθρωπον) ἄνθρωπος. 3. τὸν: ἀγρός (ἀγρόν.) 4. ὁ: (σῖτος) σῖτον. 5. ὁ: (οἶκος) οἶκον. 6. τὸν: (πόνον) πόνος. 7. ὁ: (αὐτουργός) αὐτουργόν. 8. ὁ: (ἀγρός) ἀγρόν.

Exercise 1β

Fill in the blank with the word or phrase that correctly completes the sentence:

1. ὁ οἶκός ἐστι ___μῑκρός___ .   μῑκρόν   μῑκρός

2. ὁ ἄνθρωπός ἐστι ___μακρός___ .   μακρός   μακρόν

3. ὁ ἀγρὸς παρέχει ___πολὺν σῖτον___ .   πολὺς σῖτος   πολὺν σῖτον

4. ὁ ἄνθρωπος ___τὸν οἶκον___ φιλεῖ.   τὸν οἶκον   ὁ οἶκος

5. ___μῑκρός___ ἐστιν ὁ πόνος.   μῑκρόν   μῑκρός

Exercise 1γ

Identify the functions of the words or phrases in the completed sentences in the exercise above by writing S, C, DO, LV, or TV above the appropriate words or phrases.

Exercise 1δ

Give an English equivalent of:

1.	ὁ πόνος	work	7.	ὁ ἀγρός	the farm
2.	πολύς	much	8.	φιλεῖ	he loves
3.	ὁ οἶκος	house	9.	ἀλλά	but
4.	λέγει	he says	10.	δέ	and, but
5.	χαίρει	she rejoices	11.	καλός	beautiful
6.	πονεῖ	he works	12.	καί	and

1

Exercise 1ε

Give the Greek equivalent of:

1. he/she lives   οἰκεῖ
2. grain, food   ὁ σῖτος
3. for   γάρ
4. long, large   μάκρος
5. he/she works   πονεῖ
6. not   οὐ
7. then   οὖν

8. farmer   ὁ αὐτουργός
9. small   μικρός
10. so   οὖν
11. human being   ὁ ἄνθρωπος
12. he/she/it is   ἐστί(ν)
13. he/she says   λέγει
14. in Athens   ἐν ταῖς Ἀθήναις

(β)

Exercise 1ζ

Put the proper accents on the following words, phrases, and sentences:
1. ἀγρός. 2. βαδίζει. 3. μακρός ἐστι. 4. πολύς. 5. οἶκος. 6. οἰκεῖ. 7. χρόνος πολύς. 8. ὁ αὐτουργός ἰσχυρός ἐστίν. 9. μακρός. 10. ἥλιος. 11. ἀγρός μῑκρός. 12. ὁ Δικαιόπολίς ἐστιν αὐτουργός. 13. ὁ χρόνος ἐστι μακρός. 14. ὁ σῖτός ἐστι πολύς.

Exercise 1η

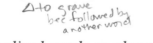
Δ το grave
bec followed by
another word

Identify the functions of the underlined words or phrases in the following passage by writing S, C, DO, LV, TV, or IV above the underlined words or phrases:

¹ὁ Δικαιόπολις ἐν τῷ ἀγρῷ ²πονεῖ· τὸν γὰρ ³ἀγρὸν ⁴σκάπτει. ⁵μακρός ⁶ἐστιν ⁷ὁ πόνος καὶ ⁸χαλεπός· ⁹τοὺς γὰρ λίθους ἐκ τοῦ ἀγροῦ ¹⁰φέρει. ¹¹μέγαν λίθον ¹²αἴρει καὶ ¹³φέρει πρὸς τὸ ἕρμα. ¹⁴ἰσχῡρός ἐστιν ¹⁵ὁ ἄνθρωπος ἀλλὰ πολὺν χρόνον πονεῖ καὶ μάλα ¹⁶κάμνει. ¹⁷φλέγει γὰρ ¹⁸ὁ ἥλιος καὶ ¹⁹κατατρίβει ²⁰αὐτόν. ²¹καθίζει οὖν ὑπὸ τῷ δένδρῳ καὶ ²²ἡσυχάζει οὐ πολὺν χρόνον. δι' ὀλίγου γὰρ ²³ἐπαίρει ²⁴ἑαυτὸν καὶ ²⁵πονεῖ. τέλος δὲ ²⁶καταδύνει ²⁷ὁ ἥλιος. οὐκέτι οὖν ²⁸πονεῖ ²⁹ὁ Δικαιόπολις ἀλλὰ πρὸς τὸν οἶκον ³⁰βαδίζει.

Exercise 1θ

Give an English equivalent of:

1. ὁ χρόνος   *time*
2. φέρει   *he carries*
3. αὐτόν   *him*

4. πρός   *toward*
5. αἴρει   *he lifts*
6. πρὸς τὸν ἥλιον   *toward the sun*

Exercise 1ι

Give the Greek equivalent of:

1. difficult   χαλερός
2. he/she walks   βαδίζει
3. he/she sits   καθίζει

4. sun   ὁ ἥλιος
5. strong   ἰσχυρός
6. he/she goes   βαδίζει

Exercise 1κ

Translate into English on a separate sheet of paper:

Ο ΟΙΚΟΣ

ὁ οἶκος μῑκρός ἐστιν ἀλλὰ καλός. ὁ οὖν ἄνθρωπος τὸν οἶκον φιλεῖ. ἐν τῷ ἀγρῷ ὁ πόνος χαλεπός ἐστιν, καὶ ὁ Δικαιόπολις ἀεὶ μάλα κάμνει. μῑκρὸς γάρ ἐστιν ὁ ἀγρός, μακρὸς δὲ ὁ πόνος. σκάπτει γὰρ τὸν ἀγρὸν ὁ ἄνθρωπος καὶ πονεῖ πολὺν χρόνον. ἐν τῷ οἴκῳ δὲ ἡσυχάζει καὶ οὐκέτι πονεῖ. ὁ οὖν Δικαιόπολις ἐν τῷ οἴκῳ χαίρει.

[ἀεὶ, *always* μάλα κάμνει, *is very tired* σκάπτει, *digs* ἡσυχάζει, *he rests* οὐκέτι, *no longer*]

2
Ο ΞΑΝΘΙΑΣ (α)

Exercise 2α

Circle the correct translation of the English phrase:

1. He/She loosens: λύεις, (λύει,) λύω. 2. I love: φιλεῖ, (φιλῶ,) φιλεῖς. 3. You are:
ἐστί(ν), (εἶ,) εἰμί. 4. He/She calls: καλεῖς, (καλεῖ,) καλῶ. 5. Come out!: ἐκβαίνω,
(ἔκβαινε,) ἐκβαίνεις. 6. He/She hurries: (σπεύδει,) σπεύδεις, σπεύδω. 7. You sleep:
καθεύδει, καθεύδω, (καθεύδεις.) 8. I drive: ἐλαύνεις, (ἐλαύνω,) ἐλαύνει.
9. He/She/It is here: πάρειμι, (πάρεστι(ν),) πάρει. 10. Call!: καλῶ, καλεῖ, (κάλει.)
11. I step out: ἐκβαίνεις, ἐκβαίνει, (ἐκβαίνω.) 12. Drive!: ἐλαύνω, ἐλαύνει,
(ἔλαυνε.) 13. Don't hurry!: οὐ σπεύδει, (μὴ σπεῦδε,) σπεῦδε.

Exercise 2β

Fill in the blank with the verb that correctly completes the sentence:

1. ὁ Δικαιόπολις __ἐκβαίνει__ ἐκ τοῦ οἴκου.   ἐκβαίνω   ἐκβαίνει
   ἐκβαίνεις

2. ὦ Ξανθία, __σπεῦδε__ (hurry!) πρὸς τὸν ἀγρόν.   σπεύδεις   σπεύδει
   σπεῦδε *spay-oo-de*

3. ὁ Ξανθίας δοῦλός __ἐστιν__.   ἐστιν   εἶ   εἰμί

4. (ἐγὼ) τοὺς βοῦς εἰς τὸν ἀγρὸν __ἐλαύνω__.   ἐλαύνει   ἐλαύνω
   ἐλαύνεις

5. μὴ __φέρε__ τὸ ἄροτρον, ὦ δέσποτα.   φέρει   φέρεις   φέρε

6. ὁ δοῦλος τοὺς λίθους ἐκ τοῦ ἀγροῦ __φέρει__.   φέρε   φέρει   φέρεις

7. μὴ __ἔλαυνε__ τοὺς βοῦς.   ἔλαυνε   ἐλαύνεις   ἐλαύνει

8. ὁ αὐτουργὸς ἐν τῷ οἴκῳ οὐ __πονεῖ__.   πονεῖς   πονῶ   πονεῖ

only used for emphasis

Exercise 2γ

Circle the correct Greek translation of the underlined phrase:

1. Dicaeopolis <u>is not</u> lazy.   οὔκ ἐστιν   οὔκ ἐστιν   (οὐκ ἔστιν)
2. <u>I am not</u> a slave.   (οὐκ εἰμί)   οὔκ εἰμί   οὐκ εἰμί
3. Why <u>am I not</u> happy?   οὔκ εἰμί   (οὐκ εἰμί)   οὐκ εἰμί
4. Why <u>are you not working</u>?   οὐ πονεῖς   οὔ πονεῖς   (οὐ πονεῖς)
5. The slave <u>is not</u> strong.   οὔκ ἐστιν   (οὐκ ἔστιν)   οὐκ ἐστίν

4

Exercise 2δ

Give an English translation of the following phrases:

1. ὁ ἰσχῡρὸς ἄνθρωπος.   the strong man
2. ὁ μακρὸς χρόνος.   the long time
3. ὁ ἀργὸς δοῦλος.   the lazy slave
4. τὸ μῑκρὸν ἄροτρον.   the small plow
5. ὁ χαλεπὸς πόνος.   the difficult work
6. ὁ μῑκρὸς οἶκος.   the small home

Exercise 2ε

Give an English equivalent of:

1. ἀργός   lazy
2. τὸ ἄροτρον   the plow
3. μή   not (cannot)
4. οὕτως   thus, so
5. ἐλαύνει   he drives
6. ἐγώ   I
7. μέν . . . δέ . . .   on the one/other
8. καθεύδει   he sleeps

Exercise 2ζ

Give the Greek equivalent of:

1. he/she is present   πάρεστι(ν)
2. he/she calls   καλεῖ
3. why?   τί
4. slave   ὁ δοῦλος
5. it is there   πάρεστιν
6. come!   ἐλθέ
7. he/she hurries   σπεύδει
8. he/she steps out   ἐκβαίνει

(β)

Exercise 2η

Transform to the accusative, dative, genitive, and vocative cases:

1. ὁ μακρὸς χρόνος   Acc.   τὸν μακρὸν χρόνον
2.   Gen.   τοῦ μακροῦ χρόνου
3.   Dat.   τῷ μακρῷ χρόνῳ
4.   Voc.   ὦ μακρὲ χρόνε

5. τὸ ἰσχῡρὸν δένδρον   Acc.   _τὸ ἰσχῡρὸν δένδρον_
6.   Gen.   _τοῦ ἰσχῡροῦ δένδρου_
7.   Dat.   _τῷ ἰσχῡρῷ δένδρῳ_
8.   Voc.   _τὸ ἰσχῦρὸν δένδρον_
                                 _ὦ_

Exercise 2θ

Fill in the blanks with the correct endings; be sure to apply the correct accents where needed:

ὁ Δικαιόπολις ἐκβαίνει ἐκ τ__οῦ__[1] οἴκ__ου__[2] καὶ καλεῖ τὸν Ξανθίᾱν. ὁ Ξανθίᾱς δοῦλ__ος__[3] ἐστιν, ἰσχῡρ__ὸς__[4] μὲν ἄνθρωπ__ος__,[5] ἀργ__ὸς__[6] δέ· οὐ γὰρ πονεῖ, εἰ μὴ πάρεστιν ὁ Δικαιόπολις. νῦν δὲ καθεύδει ἐν τ__ῷ__[7] οἴκ__ῳ__.[8] ὁ οὖν Δικαιόπολις καλεῖ αὐτ__ὸν__[9] καὶ λέγει· "ἐλθὲ δεῦρο, ὦ δοῦλ__ε__.[10] τί καθεύδεις; μὴ οὕτως ἀργὸς ἴσθι ἀλλὰ σπεῦδε." ὁ οὖν Ξανθίᾱς βραδέως ἐκβαίνει ἐκ τ__οῦ__[11] οἴκ__ου__[12] καὶ λέγει· "τί εἶ οὕτω χαλεπ__ός__,[13] ὦ δέσποτα; οὐ γὰρ ἀργ__ός__[14] εἰμι ἀλλὰ ἤδη σπεύδω." ὁ δὲ Δικαιόπολις λέγει· "ἐλθὲ δεῦρο καὶ συλλάμβανε· αἶρε γὰρ τὸ ἄροτρον καὶ φέρε αὐτὸ πρὸς τ__ὸν__[15] ἀγρ__όν__.[16] ἐγὼ γὰρ ἐλαύνω τοὺς βοῦς. ἀλλὰ σπεῦδε· μῑκρ__ός__[17] μὲν γάρ ἐστιν ὁ ἀγρ__ός__,[18] μακρὸς δὲ ὁ πόν__ος__."[19]

before enclitic — (margin note)

Exercise 2ι

Put acute accents on the proper syllables of the following words:

1. καθίζεις.   2. φέρει.   3. βαδίζω.   4. λέγεις.   5. φέρω.   6. βάδιζε.   7. λέγε.
8. βαδίζεις.   9. καθίζω.   10. ἐκβαίνεις.   11. λέγει.   12. φέρεις.   13. ἐκβαίνω.   14.
λέγω.   15. ἐκβαίνει.   16. καθίζει.   17. κάθιζε.   18. καθεύδω.   19. φέρε.   20. ἔκβαινε.

Exercise 2κ

Give an English equivalent of:

1. βλέπω   _I look_   4. τὸ δένδρον   _the tree_
2. βραδέως   _slowly_   5. ἄγω   _I lead_
3. ὁ βοῦς   _the oxen_   6. ἔπειτα   _then_

Exercise 2λ

Give the Greek equivalent of:

1. already   *ἤδη*   5. master   *ὁ δεσπότης*
2. I step   *βαίνω*   6. I lead   *ἄγω*
3. I lead in   *εἰσάγω*   7. into   *πρός*
4. I help   *συλλαμβάνω*   8. I take   *λαμβάνω*

Exercise 2μ

Translate into English on a separate sheet of paper:

ΜΕΤΑ ΜΕΣΗΜΒΡΙΑΝ

[1] μετὰ δὲ μεσημβρίᾱν ὁ Δικαιόπολις λέγει· "ἐγὼ μὲν πρὸς τὸν οἶκον βαδίζω· μάλα γὰρ κάμνω. σὺ δέ, ὦ Ξανθίᾱ, ἐν τῷ ἀγρῷ μένε καὶ τοὺς λίθους αἶρε." ὁ μὲν οὖν Δικαιόπολις πρὸς τὸν οἶκον βαδίζει καὶ καθεύδει. ὁ δὲ Ξανθίᾱς μένει ἐν τῷ ἀγρῷ καὶ τοὺς λίθους αἴρει.

[ΜΕΤΑ ΜΕΣΗΜΒΡΙΑΝ, *After Noontime*   **μάλα . . . κάμνω,** *I am very tired*   **σὺ,** *you*   **μένε,** *stay*   **τοὺς λίθους,** *the stones*]

[2] ὁ δὲ ἥλιος φλέγει καὶ κατατρίβει τὸν δοῦλον. ἐν δὲ τῷ ἀγρῷ δένδρον μακρόν ἐστιν. τὸ δὲ δένδρον σκιὰν παρέχει. ὁ οὖν δοῦλος πρὸς τὸ μακρὸν δένδρον βλέπει. ἔπειτα δὲ βραδέως πρὸς τὸ δένδρον βαδίζει· ὁ Δικαιόπολις γὰρ οὐ πάρεστιν. ὁ οὖν Ξανθίᾱς ὑπὸ τῷ δένδρῳ καθίζει. ὁ δὲ δοῦλος οὐ πονεῖ ἀλλὰ καθεύδει ὑπὸ τῷ δένδρῳ. ὁ δὲ Δικαιόπολις ἐκ τοῦ οἴκου ἐκβαίνει καὶ τοὺς βοῦς ἐλαύνει πρὸς τὸν ἀγρόν. ἐν δὲ τῷ ἀγρῷ τὸν δοῦλον ὑπὸ τῷ δένδρῳ καθεύδοντα βλέπει. λέγει οὖν· "ὦ κατάρᾱτε δοῦλε, τί ἤδη ὑπὸ τῷ δένδρῳ καθεύδεις; τί οὐκ αἴρεις τοὺς λίθους; τί οὐ φέρεις τοὺς λίθους ἐκ τοῦ ἀγροῦ; ὦ Ξανθίᾱ, ἰσχῡρὸς μὲν εἶ, μάλα ἀργὸς δέ, καὶ οὐ φιλεῖς τὸν πόνον." ὁ δὲ Ξανθίᾱς ἐπαίρει ἑαυτὸν καὶ λέγει· "ἐγὼ ἀργὸς μὲν οὐκ εἰμί, κάμνω δὲ μάλα· ὁ γὰρ πόνος μακρός ἐστιν, φλέγει δὲ ὁ ἥλιος. σὺ δὲ δεσπότης χαλεπὸς εἶ. ὁ μὲν γὰρ ἀγρὸς καλός ἐστι καὶ πολὺν σῖτον παρέχει. σὺ οὖν σπεύδεις πρὸς τὸν ἀγρόν, καὶ τοὺς βοῦς ἐλαύνεις, καὶ τὸ ἄροτρον λαμβάνεις. σὺ μὲν γὰρ εἶ δεσπότης, καὶ τὸν ἀγρὸν μάλα φιλεῖς· ἐγὼ δὲ δοῦλός εἰμι, καὶ οὐ μάλα φιλῶ τὸν ἀγρόν. μὴ χαλεπὸς ἴσθι, ὦ δέσποτα· ἰδού, τοὺς λίθους αἴρω."

[**φλέγει,** *is blazing*   **κατατρίβει,** *wears out*   **σκιὰν,** *shade*   **παρέχει,** *provides*   **ὑπὸ,** *under*   **ἐκ,** *out of*   **καθεύδοντα,** *sleeping*   **κατάρᾱτε,** *cursed*   **μάλα,** *very*   **ἐπαίρει ἑαυτὸν,** *lifts himself, gets up*   **κάμνω,** *I am tired*   **σὺ,** *you*   **ἰδού,** *look!*]

3
Ο ΑΡΟΤΟΣ (α)

Exercise 3α

Translate the English words and phrases with the correct form of the Greek verb supplied:

1. λύω: he/she loosens — λύει
2. λύω: they loosen — λύουσι
3. φιλέω: I love — φιλῶ
4. λύω: loosen! (pl.) — λύετε
5. εἰμί: you (sing.) are — εἶ
6. προσχωρέω: to approach — προσχωρεῖν
7. καθεύδω: sleep! (sing.) — κάθευδε
8. προσχωρέω: they approach — προσχωροῦσι(ν)
9. καλέω: he/she calls — καλεῖ
10. φιλέω: love! (pl.) — φιλεῖτε
11. λαμβάνω: take! (sing.) — λάμβανε
12. φιλέω: to love — φιλεῖν
13. σπεύδω: he/she hurries — σπεύδει
14. πίπτω: they are falling — πίπτουσι(ν)
15. καθεύδω: you (sing.) sleep — καθεύδεις
16. πίπτω: to fall — πίπτειν
17. ἐλαύνω: I drive — ἐλαύνω
18. πίπτω: fall! (pl.) — πίπτετε
19. πάρειμι: he/she/it is here — πάρεστι(ν)
20. μένω: they are waiting — μένουσι(ν)
21. καλέω: call! (sing.) — κάλει
22. μένω: to wait — μένειν
23. ἐκβαίνω: I step out — ἐκβαίνω
24. εἰμί: they are — εἰσι(ν)

8

Exercise 3β

Write the form of the verb supplied that correctly completes the sentence:

1. οἱ αὐτουργοὶ τοὺς φίλους (μένω) _μένουσι_ .
2. ὦ φίλοι, δεῦρο (hurry!: σπεύδω) _σπεύδετε_ .
3. οἱ δοῦλοι τοὺς λίθους ἐκ τοῦ ἀγροῦ (ἐκφέρω) _ἐκφέρουσι_ .
4. λίθος δὲ μέγας ἐν τῷ ἀγρῷ (εἰμί) _ἐστίν_ .
5. οὐ δυνατόν ἐστιν (ἐκφέρω) _ἐκφέρειν_ τοσοῦτον λίθον.
6. πρὸς τὸν ἀγρὸν (drive!: ἐλαύνω) _ἐλαύνετε_ τοὺς βοῦς, ὦ δοῦλοι.
7. οἱ βόες τὴν ἅμαξαν (*wagon*) (ἕλκω) _ἕλκουσι_ .
8. δυνατόν ἐστιν εἰς τὴν ἅμαξαν τὸν λίθον (αἴρω) _αἴρειν_ .
   into + acc (wagon)

Exercise 3γ

Give an English equivalent of:

1. πίπτω — _I fall_
2. μέγας — _great_
3. οὐκέτι — _no longer_
4. ἐκ τοῦ οἴκου — _in the house_
5. ὁ λίθος — _the stone_
6. προσχωρέω — _approach_
7. δεῦρο — _here_
8. τε καί — _both - and_
9. αἴτιος — _responsible_
10. ὦ Ζεῦ — _O Zeus_

Exercise 3δ

Give the Greek equivalent of:

1. I wait for _____
2. again _____
3. possible _____
4. O Zeus _____
5. he/she says _____
6. him _____
7. still _____
8. it _____
   or _____

(β)

Exercise 3ε

Place the correct accents on the following Greek nouns:

1. τὸν ἄνθρωπον
2. τῶν ἀνθρώπων
3. τοὺς οἴκους
4. οἱ οἶκοι
5. τὸν δοῦλον
6. τῷ δούλῳ

Exercise 3ζ

Give an English translation of the following phrases:

1. οἱ καλοὶ ἀγροί   _____
2. οἱ μακροὶ πόνοι   _____
3. οἱ ἀργοὶ δοῦλοι   _____
4. τὰ καλὰ δεῖπνα   _____
5. οἱ ἀνδρεῖοι αὐτουργοί   _____
6. οἱ μῑκροὶ οἶκοι   _____

Exercise 3η

Transform to the accusative, dative, genitive, and vocative cases:

1.	τὸ ἰσχῡρὸν ἄροτρον	Acc.	τὸ ἰσχῡρὸν ἄροτρον
2.		Dat.	τοῦ ἰσχῡροῦ ἀρότρου
3.	Dat	Gen.	τῷ ἰσχῡρῷ ἀρότρω
4.		Voc.	ὢ ἰσχῡρὸν ἄροτρον
5.	οἱ ἀνδρεῖοι ἄνθρωποι	Acc.	τοὺς ἀνδρείους ἀνθρώπους
6.		Dat.	τοῖς ἀνδρείοις ἀνθρώποις
7.		Gen.	τῶν ἀνδρείων ἀνθρώπων
8.		Voc.	ὢ ἀνδρεῖοι ἄνθρωποι
9.	τὰ καλὰ δεῖπνα	Acc.	τὰ καλὰ δένδρα
10.		Dat.	τοῖς καλοῖς δείπνοις
11.		Gen.	τῶν καλῶν δείπνων
12.		Voc.	τὰ καλὰ δεῖπνα
13.	ὁ ἀργὸς δοῦλος	Acc.	τὸν ἀργὸν δοῦλον
14.		Dat.	τῷ ἀργῷ δούλω
15.		Gen.	τοῦ ἀργοῦ δούλου
16.		Voc.	ὢ ἀργὰ δοῦλα

Exercise 3θ

Give an English equivalent of:

1. λύω   _____   5. ὁ παῖς   _____
2. σύ   _____   6. ἐπεί   _____
3. τοσοῦτος   _____   7. ἐν τῷ ἀγρῷ   _____
4. ὁ Φίλιππος   _____   8. τοσοῦτοι λίθοι   _____

Exercise 3ι

Give the Greek equivalent of:

1. girl   _____
2. dinner   _____
3. brave   _____
4. don't wait (sing.) any longer _____

5. I leave   _____
6. many   _____
7. father   _____

Exercise 3κ

Translate into English on a separate sheet of paper:

Ο ΦΙΛΙΠΠΟΣ ΑΠΟ ΤΟΥ ΔΕΝΔΡΟΥ ΠΙΠΤΕΙ

πολὺν χρόνον ἐν τῷ ἀγρῷ πονοῦσιν ὅ τε πατὴρ καὶ ὁ παῖς. ὁ μὲν οὖν Φίλιππος ἐπὶ πολλὰ δένδρα ἀναβαίνει καὶ τοὺς καρποὺς κατασείει· οἱ δὲ καρποὶ ἀπὸ τῶν δένδρων πίπτουσιν, καὶ ὁ Δικαιόπολις αὐτοὺς συλλέγει. τέλος δὲ ὁ Δικαιόπολις τὸν Φίλιππον πρὸς δένδρον μάλα μακρὸν ἄγει καί, "ἰδού, ὦ Φίλιππε," φησίν, "τοῦτο τὸ δένδρον πολὺν καρπὸν ἔχει. ἀνάβαινε οὖν καὶ κατάσειε τὸν καρπόν." ὁ δὲ Φίλιππος, "οὐ δυνατόν ἐστιν, ὦ πάτερ," φησίν, "ἐπὶ τοσοῦτον δένδρον ἀναβαίνειν. ἐγὼ γὰρ μάλα κάμνω." ὁ δὲ Δικαιόπολις, "μὴ ἀργὸς ἴσθι, ὦ παῖ," φησίν, "δυνατὸν γάρ ἐστιν ἐπὶ τὸ δένδρον ἀναβαίνειν. σπεῦδε." ὁ οὖν Φίλιππος τῷ δένδρῳ προσχωρεῖ καὶ βραδέως ἀναβαίνει. ἐξαίφνης δὲ ὀλισθάνει καὶ πίπτει πρὸς τὴν γῆν καὶ μένει ἐκεῖ ἀκίνητος. φόβος οὖν τὸν Δικαιόπολιν λαμβάνει. ἐπαίρει δὲ ἑαυτὸν ὁ Φίλιππος καί, "μὴ φόβον ἔχε," φησίν· "ἐγὼ γὰρ καλῶς ἔχω." ὁ δὲ Δικαιόπολις, "μάλα ἀνδρεῖος εἶ," φησίν, "ὦ παῖ. νῦν δὲ μηκέτι πόνει· κάμνεις γάρ. καιρός ἐστιν οἴκαδε βαδίζειν καὶ ἡσυχάζειν." ἐπεὶ δὲ εἰς τὸν οἶκον εἰσβαίνουσιν, ἡσυχάζουσι καὶ δειπνοῦσιν.

[ΑΠΟ + gen., *from*   ἐπὶ, *onto*   ἀναβαίνει, *climbs up*   τοὺς καρποὺς, *the fruits* κατασείει, *shakes down*   ἀπὸ, *from*   συλλέγει, *collects*   τέλος, *finally*   μάλα, *very*   ἰδού, *look!* τοῦτο τὸ, *this*   ἔχει, *has*   κάμνω, *I am tired*   ἐξαίφνης, *suddenly*   ὀλισθάνει, *he slips*   τὴν γῆν, *the ground*   μένει, *he stays*   ἐκεῖ, *there* ἀκίνητος, *motionless*   φόβος, *fear*   ἐπαίρει... ἑαυτὸν, *lifts himself, gets up*   μὴ φόβον ἔχε, *Don't be afraid (Don't have fear)*   καλῶς ἔχω, *I am well*   νῦν, *now* καιρός, *time*   οἴκαδε, *to home*   ἡσυχάζειν, *to rest*   δειπνοῦσιν: *deduce from* τὸ δεῖπνον]

4
ΠΡΟΣ ΤΗΙ ΚΡΗΝΗΙ (α)

Exercise 4α

Translate the English phrases and verbs with the correct form of the Greek verb supplied:

1. λύω: I loosen — λύω
2. φιλέω: they love — φιλοῦσι
3. εἰμί: we are — ἐσμέν
4. ἐθέλω: you (sing.) are willing — ἐθέλεις
5. χαίρω: greetings, friends! — χαίρετε
6. ἔχω: they have — ἔχουσι(ν)
7. θεωρέω: he/she is watching — θεωρεῖ
8. ποιέω: we make — ποιοῦμεν
9. ἀκούω: you (pl.) hear — ἀκούετε
10. ἔχω: I have — ἔχω
11. ἐθέλω: we wish — ἐθέλομεν
12. ἀκούω: he/she listens — ἀκούει
13. χαίρω: we rejoice — χαίρομεν
14. ἔχω: he/she has — ἔχει
15. ποιέω: they make — ποιοῦσι(ν)
16. ἐθέλω: you (pl.) are willing — ἐθέλετε
17. φιλέω: you (pl.) love — φιλεῖτε
18. λύω: you (sing.) loosen — λύεις
19. θεωρέω: you (sing.) watch — θεωρεῖς
20. εἰμί: be! (sing.) — ἴσθι
21. ἀκούω: listen! (sing.) — ἄκουε
22. χαίρω: to rejoice — χαίρειν
23. φιλέω: I love — φιλῶ
24. πονέω: work! (pl.) — πονεῖτε
25. οἰκέω: to dwell — οἰκεῖν
26. προσχωρέω: approach! (sing.) — προσχώρει
27. εἰμί: be! (pl.) — ἔστε

28.   εἰμί: you (sing.) are   _εἶ_
29.   εἰμί: to be   _εἶναι_
30.   εἰμί: you (pl.) are   _ἐστέ_

Exercise 4β

Transform each phrase to the plural, keeping it in the same case:

1.   τὴν θάλατταν   _τὰς θαλάττας_
2.   ἡ μέλιττα   _αἱ μέλιτται_
3.   τῆς μαχαίρᾱς   _τῶν μαχαιρῶν_
4.   τὸ ἄροτρον   _τὰ ἄροτρα_
5.   ἡ οἰκίᾱ   _αἱ οἰκίαι_
6.   τὴν κρήνην   _τὰς κρήνας_
7.   τῇ ὑδρίᾳ   _ταῖς ὑδρίαις_
8.   τοῦ καιροῦ   _τῶν καιρῶν_
9.   ἡ ἑορτή   _αἱ ἑορταί_
10. τῷ φίλῳ   _τοῖς φίλοις_
11. ἡ μάχαιρα   _αἱ μάχαιραι_

Transform each phrase to the singular, keeping it in the same case:

12. ταῖς μελίτταις   _τῇ μελίττη_
13. τῶν ὑδριῶν   _τῆς ὑδρίας_
14. τοὺς καιρούς   _τὸν καιρόν_
15. ταῖς ἑορταῖς   _τῇ ἑορτῇ_
16. τῶν φίλων   _τοῦ φίλου_
17. τὰς θαλάττᾱς   _τὴν θάλατταν_
18. τῶν μελιττῶν   _τῆς μελίττης_
19. ταῖς μαχαίραις   _τῇ μαχαίρᾳ_
20. τοῖς ἀρότροις   _τῷ ἀρότρῳ_
21. τὰς οἰκίᾱς   _τὴν οἰκίαν_
22. τῶν ἑορτῶν   _τῆς ἑορτῆς_

Exercise 4γ

Give an English equivalent of:

1. ἀκούω — *I hear*
2. ὁ ἀνήρ — *husband*
3. ἰδού — *look*
4. μάλα — *very*
5. ὁ χορός — *dance*
6. ἡ γυνή — *woman*
7. χαίρετε (imper.) — *greeting*
8. ἡ μήτηρ — *mother*
9. ἀργός — *lazy*
10. ἀπὸ τοῦ ἀγροῦ — *from the field*
11. ἆρα καθεύδεις; — *why are you sleeping*
12. ἡ ἑορτή — *festival*
13. καί (adv.) — *even*
14. ἔχω — *I have*
15. θεωρέω — *I watch*
16. τὰ Διονύσια — *festival of Dionysus*

Exercise 4δ

Give the Greek equivalent of:

1. first (adv.) _____
2. dear _____
3. spring _____
4. I am willing _____
5. I listen _____
6. I intend _____
7. man _____
8. friend (f.) _____
9. swiftly _____
10. I do _____
11. the right time _____
12. water jar _____
13. with difficulty _____
14. messenger _____
15. daughter _____
16. I rejoice _____

(β)

Exercise 4ε

Transform to the accusative case:

1. ἡ θάλαττα — τὴν θάλατταν
2. ὁ δεσπότης — τὸν δεσπότην
3. ἡ μάχαιρα — τὴν μάχαιραν
4. ὁ νεᾱνίας — τὸν νεᾱνίαν
5. ἡ ὁδός — τὴν ὁδόν
6. οἱ νεᾱνίαι — τοὺς νεᾱνίᾱς

7. αἱ ὑδρίαι   τὰς ὑδρίας
8. οἱ καιροί   τοὺς καιρούς
9. αἱ ἑορταί   τὰς ἑορτάς
10. οἱ δεσπόται   τοὺς δεσπότας

Transform to the dative case:

11. ὁ Ξανθίας   τῷ Ξανθίᾳ
12. ἡ ὑδρίᾱ   τῇ ὑδρίᾳ
13. ὁ πολίτης   τῷ πολίτη
14. ἡ ἑορτή   τῇ ἑορτῇ
15. ὁ φίλος   τῷ φίλω
16. αἱ θάλατται   ταῖς θαλάτταις
17. οἱ δεσπόται   τοῖς δεσπόταις
18. αἱ μάχαιραι   ταῖς μαχαίραις
19. οἱ νεᾱνίαι   τοῖς νεανίαις
20. αἱ νῆσοι   ταῖς νήσοις

Transform to the genitive case:

21. ἡ θάλαττα   τῆς θαλάττης
22. ὁ δεσπότης   τοῦ δεσπότου
23. ἡ μάχαιρα   τῆς μαχαίρας
24. ὁ Ξανθίας   τοῦ Ξανθίου
25. ἡ ὁδός   τῆς ὁδοῦ
26. οἱ δεσπόται   τῶν δεσποτῶν
27. αἱ ὑδρίαι   τῶν ὑδριῶν
28. οἱ καιροί   τῶν καιρῶν
29. αἱ ἑορταί   τῶν ἑορτῶν
30. οἱ φίλοι   τῶν φίλων

Exercise 4ζ

Give the corresponding plural forms:

1. πολλῇ   πολλαῖς
2. μέγαν   μεγάλους
3. πολλῆς   πολλῶν
4. ῥᾳδίῳ   ῥᾳδίοις
5. μεγάλου   μεγάλων

6. καλός   καλοί
7. ῥᾳδίᾳ   ῥᾳδίαι   ✳
8. πολλοῦ   πολλῶν
9. πολλῷ   πολλοῖς
10. καλόν   καλά
   or   καλούς

Exercise 4η

Write the form of the word supplied that correctly completes the phrase:

1. ἡ ___καλὴ___ ὑδρίᾱ (καλός)
2. αἱ ___καλαί___ ὑδρίαι (καλός)
3. ἡ ___μεγάλη___ ὑδρίᾱ (μέγας)
4. αἱ ___μεγάλαι___ ὑδρίαι (μέγας)
5. τῆς ___μακρᾶς___ ὁδοῦ (μακρός)
6. τῶν ___μακρῶν___ ὁδῶν (μακρός)
7. τῆς ___φίλης___ μητρός (φίλος)
8. τῶν ___φίλων___ μητέρων (φίλος)
9. τὴν ___ῥᾳδίαν___ ὁδόν (ῥᾴδιος)
10. τὰς ___ῥᾳδίας___ ὁδούς (ῥᾴδιος)
11. τὰς ___μεγάλας___ ἑορτᾱς (μέγας)
12. ___πολλαί___ κρῆναι (πολύς)
13. τῆς ___μεγάλης___ γυναικός (μέγας)

14. ταῖς _____ κρήναις (μέγας)
15. τῇ _____ κρήνῃ (μέγας)
16. τὴν _____ ὑδρίᾱν (μέγας)
17. _____ χρόνον (πολύς)
18. _____ δένδρα (πολύς)
19. τοῦ _____ πόνου (ῥᾴδιος)
20. τῶν _____ πόνων (ῥᾴδιος)
21. τῶν _____ πόνων (πολύς)
22. τῷ _____ ἀνδρί (φίλος)
23. τοῖς _____ νεᾱνίαις (καλός)
24. τὰ _____ δένδρα (πολύς)

Exercise 4θ

Give an English equivalent of:

1. στενάζω   I groan
2. ῥᾴδιος   easy
3. μάλιστα   very much
4. ἀεί   always
5. οἴκαδε   to the house
6. ἀληθῶς   truly
7. ἀργῶς   lazily

Give the Greek equivalent of:

8. road _____
9. why? _____
10. I persuade _____
11. well _____
12. other _____
13. land _____
14. what? _____

Exercise 4κ

Translate into English on a separate sheet of paper:

Η ΔΕΣΠΟΙΝΑ ΚΑΙ Η ΔΟΥΛΗ

[1] γυνή τις ὀνόματι Φαίδρᾱ τῇ κρήνῃ προσχωρεῖ. δούλη δὲ ἀκολουθεῖ. ἡ δὲ δούλη μεγάλην ὑδρίᾱν φέρει. κάμνει δὲ ἡ δούλη καί, "ὦ δέσποινα," φησίν, "μὴ οὕτω ταχέως βάδιζε· μεγάλη γάρ ἐστιν ἡ ὑδρίᾱ, καὶ οὐ ῥᾴδιόν ἐστι σπεύδειν." ἡ δὲ Φαίδρᾱ, "μὴ φλυᾱ́ρει, ὦ δούλη," φησίν, "ἀλλὰ σπεῦδε. ὥρᾱ γάρ ἐστί σοι βαδίζειν πρὸς τὸν δεσπότην καὶ ὕδωρ φέρειν αὐτῷ."

[Η ΔΕΣΠΟΙΝΑ, *The Mistress*　Η ΔΟΥΛΗ: deduce from ὁ δοῦλος　**γυνή τις**, *a certain woman*　**ὀνόματι**, *by name*　**Φαίδρᾱ**, *Phaedra*　**ἀκολουθεῖ**, *follows*　**κάμνει**, *is tired*　**φλυᾱ́ρει**, *talk nonsense!*　**ὥρᾱ...ἐστί**, *it is time*　**σοι**, *for you*　**ὕδωρ**, *water*]

[2] ἡ μὲν οὖν δούλη βραδέως βαδίζει πρὸς τὴν κρήνην. ἡ δὲ δέσποινα—μέγας γὰρ λίθος ἐστὶν ἐν τῇ ὁδῷ—προσχωρεῖ καὶ ἐπὶ τῷ μεγάλῳ λίθῳ καθίζει. ἔπειτα δὲ ἀπὸ τοῦ μεγάλου λίθου πρὸς τὴν δούλην βλέπει. ἡ δὲ οὐκέτι πρὸς τὴν κρήνην βαδίζει ἀλλὰ πρὸς μέγα δένδρον. ἡ οὖν δέσποινα καλεῖ αὐτὴν καί, "τί ποιεῖς, ἀργέ;" φησίν. "τί οὐ σπεύδεις πρὸς τὴν κρήνην; ἆρα ἐν νῷ ἔχεις ὑπὸ τῷ μεγάλῳ δένδρῳ καθίζειν καὶ καθεύδειν;" ἡ δὲ δούλη πρὸς τὴν δέσποιναν βλέπει καί, "μὴ οὕτω χαλεπὴ ἴσθι, ὦ δέσποινα," φησίν· "πολὺς γάρ ἐστιν ὁ πόνος, ἐγὼ δὲ οὐ πολὺν χρόνον ἐν νῷ ἔχω καθίζειν. ἰδού, ὁ ἥλιος φλέγει τε καὶ κατατρῑ́βει με."

[ἡ...δέσποινα, *the mistress*　ἐπί, *on*　αὐτήν: deduce from αὐτόν　ὑπό, *under*　φλέγει, *is blazing*　κατατρῑ́βει, *wears X down*　με, *me*]

[3] ἡ δὲ δέσποινα, "μὴ φλυᾱ́ρει," φησίν· "οὐ καιρός ἐστιν ἡσυχάζειν. οὐδὲν γὰρ ὕδωρ ἐστὶν ἐν τῇ οἰκίᾳ, ἐγὼ δὲ μέλλω οἴκαδε σπεύδειν καὶ δεῖπνον παρασκευάζειν τῷ δεσπότῃ. σπεῦδε οὖν." ἡ δὲ Μυρρίνη, "μὴ χαλεπὴ ἴσθι, ὦ Φαίδρᾱ," φησίν· "κάμνει γὰρ ἡ δούλη. ὁ γὰρ ἥλιος φλέγει καὶ κατατρῑ́βει αὐτήν. ἆρ' ἀγνοεῖς ὅτι πολλαί τε δοῦλαι καὶ πολλοὶ δοῦλοι κάμνουσιν, ὅτε φλέγει ὁ ἥλιος, καὶ οὐκ ἐθέλουσι πονεῖν; ἔᾱ οὖν αὐτὴν ἡσυχάζειν ὀλίγον χρόνον ἐν τῇ σκιᾷ."

[ἡ...δέσποινα, *the mistress*　φλυᾱ́ρει, *talk nonsense!*　ἡσυχάζειν, *to rest*　οὐδέν, *no*　ὕδωρ, *water*　τῇ οἰκίᾳ, *the house*　μέλλω + infin., *I am about* (to)　παρασκευάζειν, *to prepare*　κάμνει, *is tired*　φλέγει, *is blazing*　κατατρῑ́βει, *wears X down*　ἀγνοεῖς, *don't you know*　ὅτι, *that*　ὅτε, *when*　ἔᾱ, *allow!*　ὀλίγον, *short (small)*　τῇ σκιᾷ, *the shade*]

5
Ο ΛΥΚΟΣ (α)

Exercise 5α

Translate the English phrases with the correct form of the Greek verb supplied:

1. τῑμάω: you (pl.) honor — *τῑμᾶτε*
2. ζητέω: they seek — *ζητοῦσι*
3. ζητέω: to seek — *ζητεῖν*
4. βοάω: we shout — *βοῶσι(ν)*
5. τῑμάω: honor! (sing.) — *τίμα*
6. ὁράω: I see — *ὁρῶ*
7. φιλέω: you (sing.) love — *φιλεῖς*
8. τῑμάω: they honor — *τῑμῶσι(ν)*
9. τῑμάω: to honor — *τῑμᾶν*
10. ὁράω: we see — *ὁρῶμεν*
11. τῑμάω: he/she honors — *τῑμᾷ*
12. ζητέω: seek! (pl.) — *ζητει*
13. βοάω: you (sing.) shout — *βοᾷ*
14. φιλέω: they love — *φιλοῦσι(ν)*
15. τῑμάω: honor! (pl.) — *τῑμᾶτα*
16. βοάω: I shout — *βοῶ*
17. οἰκέω: he/she lives — *οἰκει*
18. ζητέω: seek! (sing.) — *ζητει*

Exercise 5β

Place accents on all the following verb forms:

1. λύει
2. φιλε-ε > φιλει
3. φευγουσι(ν)
4. φιλε-ει > φιλεῖ
5. λύετε
6. ποιε-ομεν > ποιοῦμεν
7. τῑμα-ετε > τῑμᾶτε
8. ὁρα-εις > ὁρᾷς
9. τῑμα-ε > τῑμᾶ
10. διωκε

Exercise 5γ

Write the correct form of the article to indicate a change of subject:

1. ὁ πατὴρ τὴν κόρην ζητεῖ, _____ δὲ ἐν τῇ οἰκίᾳ οὐ πάρεστιν.

2. ὁ αὐτουργὸς τοὺς δούλους καλεῖ, _____ δὲ οὐκ ἀκούουσιν.

3. ὁ Φίλιππος τὸν Ἄργον καλεῖ, _____ δὲ τὸν λαγὼν διώκει ἀνὰ τὸ ὄρος.

4. ὁ Φίλιππος τὰς κόρας ὁρᾷ, _____ δὲ ἀποτρέχουσιν.

Exercise 5δ

Rewrite the following phrases using elision:

1. ἆρα ἀκούεις   _____

2. κατὰ ὁδόν   _____

3. ἀλλὰ ἐθέλουσιν   _____

4. μετὰ ὑμῶν (*with you*)   _____

Exercise 5ε

Give an English equivalent of:

1. βοάω	_____	8. τά πρόβατα	_____
2. ἀνὰ τὸ ὄρος	_____	9. οὔτε . . . οὔτε	_____
3. ὁ λύκος	_____	10. τρέχω	_____
4. ῥᾴθῡμος	_____	11. ὁ λαγώς	_____
5. φυλάττω	_____	12. ἄκρος	_____
6. ὥστε	_____	13. ζητέω	_____
7. ὁράω	_____	14. δι' ὀλίγου	_____

Exercise 5ζ

Give the Greek equivalent of:

1. I am away	_____	7. down the hill	_____
2. I pursue	_____	8. grandfather	_____
3. go! (sing.)	_____	9. where?	_____
4. dog	_____	10. I flee	_____
5. nor	_____	11. dwelling	_____
6. I honor	_____	12. the top of the hill	_____

Grammar

Clauses of Result with ὥστε

The word ὥστε (see Vocabulary 5α) introduces clauses that express result; the verb in the result clause may be either indicative (negative οὐ) or an infinitive (negative μή), e.g.:

οὕτω ταχέως ὅ τε Ἄργος καὶ ὁ λαγὼς τρέχουσιν **ὥστε** δι' ὀλίγου **οὐ** δυνατόν **ἐστιν** ὁρᾶν οὔτε τὸν κύνα οὔτε τὸν λαγών. (See 5α:7–8.)
*Both Argus and the hare run so quickly **that** soon **it is not** possible to see either the dog or the hare.*

The distinction in meaning is as follows: ὥστε + indicative is used where the result is an actual fact, as in the sentence above (this is called *actual result*); ὥστε + an infinitive (negative μή) is used where the consequence is a tendency or possibility or where there is an expression of purpose as well as result (this is called *natural result*), e.g.:

οὕτως ἀνδρεῖός ἐστιν **ὥστε μὴ ἀποφεύγειν**.
*He is so brave **as not to flee away**.*

Some grammarians think that this distinction between actual and natural result is artificial and that the distinction is simply that when one wanted to specify person and number one used the indicative and when person and number were of no concern one used the infinitive.

It is important to note that result clauses are often anticipated in the main clause by some word such as οὕτω(ς) (underlined in the sentences above).

Exercise 5η

Granting a distinction between actual and natural result, indicate whether the following sentences would use ὥστε with the indicative or ὥστε with the infinitive by writing Ind. or Inf. in the blank:

1. He always runs so fast that (ὥστε) the enemy cannot catch him.   _____

2. She was so afraid that (ὥστε) she hurriedly left the building.   _____

3. She was brave enough as (ὥστε) to have no fear.   _____

4. He saw such good friends that (ὥστε) he asked them to stay for dinner.   _____

5. She is always so worried that (ὥστε) she doesn't travel.   _____

6. They went so far that (ὥστε) they missed what they were looking for.   _____

7. He guarded the gate so well that (ὥστε) the enemy did not enter.   _____

(β)

Exercise 5θ

Write the form of the verb εἰμί that correctly completes the sentence (see page 285 of the textbook for accenting enclitics):

1. ὁ ἀνὴρ σοφός _____.

2. τὰ πρόβατα μακρά _____.

3. αἱ ὑδρίαι μεγάλαι _____.

4. τὸ ἄροτρον μέγα _____.

5. οἱ μῦθοί _____ μῑκροί.

6. τὰ δένδρα ἀγαθά _____ .

7. οἱ λύκοι ἄγριοί _____.

8. καλά _____ τὰ πρόβατα.

Exercise 5ι

Give the Greek equivalent of the underlined English word or phrase; be sure to use the correct gender, number, and case:

1. I see <u>him</u>. _____

2. I see <u>them</u> (i.e., those men). _____

3. They saw <u>me</u>. _____ or _____

4. They saw <u>us</u>. _____

5. They <u>themselves</u> (m.) tried to prevent it. _____

6. I saw <u>them</u> (f.) coming through the door. _____

7. I saw <u>them</u> (m.) coming through the door. _____

8. Give the scroll <u>to me</u>, please. _____ or _____

9. You took <u>their</u> money and ran. _____

10. You took <u>her</u> money and ran. _____

11. You took <u>his</u> money and ran. _____

12. <u>Her</u> brother did not like the idea. _____

13. <u>You</u> (sing.) should have known better! _____

14. <u>We</u> fell asleep, while <u>you</u> (pl.) stayed awake. _____ _____

15. They called grandfather <u>himself</u>. _____

16. We gave it <u>to them</u>. _____ or _____

17. <u>My</u> good friend Lysistrata is coming to see me. _____

18. I'm listening to (ἀκούω + gen.) <u>you</u> (sing.) now. _____ or _____

19. I'm listening to (ἀκούω + gen.) <u>you</u> (pl.) now. _____

20. Listen to (ἄκουέ + gen.) <u>me</u>. _____

21. Listen to (ἄκουε + gen.) <u>us</u>. _____

22. I hear (ἀκούω + gen.) <u>them</u>. _____

23. I hear (ἀκούω + gen.) <u>him</u>. _____

24. I hear (ἀκούω + gen.) <u>her</u>. _____

25. They are doing these things <u>for you</u>, friends. _____

26. They are doing these things <u>for you</u>, my friend. _____or _____

27. <u>Our</u> house (οἰκίᾱ) just burned down. _____

28. <u>Your</u> (sing.) house (οἰκίᾱ) just burned down. _____

29. I made this bread <u>for her</u>. _____

30. I made this bread <u>for them</u> (i.e., for those women). _____

31. She <u>herself</u> said it was so. _____

32. He <u>himself</u> said it was so. _____

33. <u>The same</u> man brought it back. _____

34. <u>Your</u> (pl.) mother should know. _____

35. I saw the woman <u>herself</u>. _____

36. I saw the women <u>themselves</u>. _____

37. We went to <u>the same</u> spring. _____

38. She saw <u>you</u> (sing.). _____

39. They saw <u>you</u> (pl.). _____

40. I gave it to <u>them</u> (i.e., to those boys). _____

41. I gave it to <u>him</u>. _____

Exercise 5κ

Put the number of the English phrase in column A in front of the corresponding Greek phrase in column B:

A	B
1. The house is big.	____ ὁ οἶκος ὁ μέγας
2. The friend is good.	____ μέγας ὁ οἶκος
3. The tree is beautiful	____ ὁ ἀγαθὸς φίλος
4. The good friend	____ ὁ φίλος ἀγαθός
5. <u>The beautiful tree</u> is just outside my window.	____ καλὸν τὸ δένδρον
6. <u>The house, the big one</u>, is mine.	____ τὸ καλὸν δένδρον

Exercise 5λ

Single underline the Greek adjectives in the exercise above that are in the attributive position; double underline the Greek adjectives that are in the predicate position.

Exercise 5μ

Circle "attributive" or "predicate" as appropriate:

1. In the Greek for *your dog is lazy*, the possessive adjective σός or σή would occupy the attributive/predicate position.
2. The possessive genitives αὐτοῦ, *his*, αὐτῆς, *her*, and αὐτῶν, *their*, occupy the attributive/predicate position.
3. When αὐτός, -ή, -ό means *same*, it occupies the attributive/predicate position.
4. When αὐτός, -ή, -ό means *-self, -selves*, it occupies the attributive/predicate position.

Exercise 5ν

Give an English equivalent of:

1.	ἥκω	_____	6.	ἐπὶ τῇ ὁδῷ	_____
2.	ἐνταῦθα δή	_____	7.	νῦν	_____
3.	ἀγαθός	_____	8.	πάσχω	_____
4.	καί . . . καί	_____	9.	πρῶτος	_____
5.	ἀποφεύγω	_____	10.	ἡ αὐτὴ γυνή	_____

Exercise 5ξ

Give the Greek equivalent of:

1.	I learn	_____	6.	we	_____
2.	under the tree	_____	7.	I wonder at	_____
3.	I strike	_____	8.	you (pl.)	_____
4.	that (conj.)	_____	9.	savage	_____
5.	story	_____	10.	-self	_____

Exercise 5o

Translate into English on a separate sheet of paper:

Ο ΔΟΥΛΟΣ ΤΟΝ ΚΥΝΑ ΟΥ ΦΙΛΕΙ

[1] ὁ μὲν οὖν Φίλιππος καὶ ἡ Μέλιττα μῦθον ἀπὸ τῆς Μυρρίνης ἀκούειν ἐθέλουσιν. ἡ δὲ μήτηρ λέγει· "τί δέ; ποῖον μῦθον ἐθέλετε ἀκούειν;" ὁ δὲ Φίλιππος· "ἐγὼ μὲν μῦθον περὶ δεινοῦ καὶ μεγάλου θηρίου ἀκούειν ἐθέλω." ἡ δὲ Μέλιττα· "τί περὶ δεινοῦ καὶ μεγάλου θηρίου; τί οὐ περὶ καλῆς κόρης; ἆρ' οὐκ ἐθέλεις σὺ ἡμῖν λέγειν τοιοῦτον μῦθον, ὦ μῆτερ;"

[ποῖον, *what kind of?*   περὶ, *about*   δεινοῦ, *terrible*   θηρίου, *wild beast*   κόρης, *girl*   τοιοῦτον, *such a*]

[2] ἡ δὲ μήτηρ· "μὴ βοᾶτε· ὁ γὰρ πάππος καθεύδει. παρ' ἐμὲ δὲ ἔλθετε καὶ πρὸς ἐμοὶ καθίζετε· ἐγὼ μὲν γὰρ ὑμῖν καλὸν μῦθον λέγειν μέλλω· ἐν δὲ τῷ μύθῳ καὶ καλὴ γυνὴ ἔνεστιν καὶ ἀνδρεῖος ἀνὴρ καὶ θηρίον μέγα καὶ δεινόν. μὴ οὖν θορυβεῖτε ἀλλ' ἀκούετε."

[παρ(ὰ), *to*   μέλλω, *I am about* (to)   ἔνεστιν: *deduce from* ἐν *and* ἐστίν   θηρίον, *wild beast*   δεινόν, *terrible*   θορυβεῖτε, *make a commotion!*]

[3] ἐν δὲ τούτῳ ὁ Φίλιππος, "παῦε, ὦ μῆτερ," φησίν· "ὁ γὰρ Ξανθίας πρὸς ἡμᾶς τρέχει. ἀλλὰ τί ποιεῖ ὁ ἄνθρωπος; λίθους λαμβάνει καὶ τὸν κύνα βάλλει. ὦ Ζεῦ. ὦ ἀνόητε, τί ποιεῖς; μὴ βάλλε τὸν κύνα."

[ἐν . . . τούτῳ, *meanwhile*   παῦε, *stop!*   βάλλει, *is pelting*   ὦ ἀνόητε, *you fool*]

[4] ὁ δὲ δοῦλος λέγει· "ἆρ' ἐμὲ καλεῖς, ὦ παῖ; ἀλλ' ἐγὼ τὸν κύνα ἀπ' ἐμοῦ ἀπελαύνω. ὁ γὰρ κύων ἀεὶ πρὸς ἐμοὶ μένει καὶ ὑλακτεῖ· εἰ δὲ βαδίζω, ἐμὲ διώκει καὶ ἐπ' ἐμὲ ὁρμᾷ. πολλάκις δέ με δάκνειν ἐπιθῡμεῖ. τί οὖν ποιῶ; κάλει οὖν τὸν κύνα πρὸς σέ." ὁ οὖν Φίλιππος τὸν Ἄργον καλεῖ· "Ἄργε, δεῦρ' ἐλθὲ πρὸς ἡμᾶς. κάθιζε ἐνταῦθα μεθ' ἡμῶν. μὴ ἀποχώρει ἀφ' ἡμῶν ἀλλ' ἄκουε καὶ σὺ τὸν μῦθον. ἡ γὰρ μήτηρ ἀεὶ καλοὺς μύθους ἡμῖν λέγει. σὺ δέ, ὦ Ξανθίᾱ, ἄπιθι πρὸς τὸν ἀγρὸν καὶ πόνει." ἡ δὲ μήτηρ· "ἀλλὰ νῦν σῑγᾶτε, ὦ παῖδες, καὶ ἀκούετε τὸν μῦθον."

[ἀπελαύνω: *deduce from* ἀπο- *and* ἐλαύνω   ὑλακτεῖ, *barks*   εἰ, *if*   ὁρμᾷ, *he rushes*   πολλάκις, *often*   δάκνειν, *to bite*   ἐπιθῡμεῖ, *he desires*   ἐνταῦθα, *here*   μεθ' = μετά + *gen.*, *with*   ἀποχώρει, *go away!*   ἄπιθι: *deduce from* ἀπο- + ἴθι   σῑγᾶτε, *be silent!*]

VOCABULARY
CHAPTERS 1–5

VERBS

-ω Verbs

ἄγω	*I lead; I take*
αἴρω	*I lift*
ἀκούω	*I listen; I listen to; I hear*
ἀποφεύγω	*I flee away, escape*
βαδίζω	*I walk; I go*
βαίνω	*I step; I walk; I go*
βλέπω	*I look; I see*
γιγνώσκω	*I get to know, learn*
διώκω	*I pursue, chase*
ἐθέλω	*I am willing; I wish*
εἰσάγω	*I lead in; I take in*
ἐκβαίνω	*I step out; I come out*
ἐλαύνω	*I drive*
ἔχω	*I have; I hold*
ἥκω	*I have come*
θαυμάζω	*I am amazed; I wonder at; I admire*
καθεύδω	*I sleep*
καθίζω	*I sit*
λαμβάνω	*I take*
λέγω	*I say; I tell; I speak*
λείπω	*I leave*
λύω	*I loosen, loose*
μένω	*I stay; I wait; I wait for*
πάσχω	*I suffer; I experience*
πείθω	*I persuade*
πίπτω	*I fall*
σπεύδω	*I hurry*
στενάζω	*I groan*
συλλαμβάνω	*I help*
τρέχω	*I run*
τύπτω	*I strike, hit*
φέρω	*I carry*
φεύγω	*I flee; I escape*
φυλάττω	*I guard*
χαίρω	*I rejoice*

-άω Contract Verbs

βοάω	*I shout*
ὁράω	*I see*
τῑμάω	*I honor*

-έω Contract Verbs

ζητέω	*I seek, look for*
θεωρέω	*I watch; I see*
καλέω	*I call*
οἰκέω	*I live; I dwell*
ποιέω	*I make; I do*
πονέω	*I work*
προσχωρέω	*I go toward, approach*
φιλέω	*I love*

Imperatives

ἐλθέ	*come!*
ἴθι/ἴτε	*go!*

-μι Verbs

ἄπειμι	*I am away (from)*
εἰμί	*I am*
πάρειμι	*I am present; I am here; I am there*
φημί	*I say*

NOUNS

1st Declension

γῆ, γῆς, ἡ	*land; earth; ground*
δεσπότης, -ου, ὁ	*master*
ἑορτή, -ῆς, ἡ	*festival*
κόρη, -ης, ἡ	*girl*
κρήνη, -ης, ἡ	*spring*
μάχαιρα, -ᾱς, ἡ	*knife*
μέλιττα, -ης, ἡ	*bee*
νεᾱνίᾱς, -ου, ὁ	*young man*
οἰκίᾱ, -ᾱς, ἡ	*house; home; dwelling*
πολῑτης, -ου, ὁ	*citizen*
ὑδρίᾱ, -ᾱς, ἡ	*water jar*
φίλη, -ης, ἡ	*friend*

2nd Declension

ἄγγελος, -ου, ὁ	*messenger*
ἀγρός, -οῦ, ὁ	*field*
ἄνθρωπος, -ου, ὁ	*man; human being; person*

ἄροτρον, -ου, τό   plow
αὐτουργός, -οῦ, ὁ   farmer
δεῖπνον, -ου, τό   dinner
δένδρον, -ου, τό   tree
δοῦλος, -ου, ὁ   slave
ἥλιος, -ου, ὁ   sun
καιρός, -οῦ, ὁ   time; right time
λαγώς, -ώ, ὁ   hare
λίθος, -ου, ὁ   stone
λύκος, -ου, ὁ   wolf
μῦθος, -ου, ὁ   story
νῆσος, -ου, ἡ   island
ὁδός, -οῦ, ἡ   road; way; journey
οἶκος, -ου, ὁ   house; home;
                    dwelling
πάππος, -ου, ὁ   grandfather
πόνος, -ου, ὁ   toil, work
πρόβατα, -ων, τά   sheep
σῖτος, -ου, ὁ   grain; food
φίλος, -ου, ὁ   friend
χορός, -οῦ, ὁ   dance; chorus
χρόνος, -ου, ὁ   time

3rd Declension
ἀνήρ, ἀνδρός, ὁ   man; husband
βοῦς, βοός, ὁ   ox
γυνή, γυναικός, ἡ   woman; wife
θυγάτηρ, θυγα-
    τρός, ἡ   daughter
κύων, κυνός, ὁ/ἡ   dog
μήτηρ, μητρός, ἡ   mother
ὄρος, ὄρους, τό   mountain; hill
παῖς, παιδός, ὁ/ἡ   boy; girl; son;
                    daughter; child
πατήρ, πατρός, ὁ   father

PRONOUNS

αὐτά   them
αὐτάς   them
αὐτήν   her; it
αὐτῆς   of her, her; of it, its
αὐτό   it
αὐτόν   him; it
αὐτοῦ   of him, his; of it, its
αὐτούς   them
αὐτῶν   of them; their
ἐγώ   I
ἡμεῖς   we
σύ   you
τί;   what?

ὑμεῖς   you (pl.)

ADJECTIVES

1st/2nd Declension
ἀγαθός, -ή, -όν   good
ἄγριος, ᾱ, -ον   savage; wild; fierce
αἴτιος, -ᾱ, -ον   responsible (for); to
                    blame
ἄκρος, -ᾱ, -ον   top (of)
ἄλλος, -η, -ο   other, another
ἀνδρεῖος, -ᾱ, -ον   brave
αὐτός, -ή, -ό   -self, -selves
δυνατός, -ή, -όν   possible
ἐμός, -ή, -όν   my; mine
ἡμέτερος, -ᾱ, -ον   our; ours
ἰσχῡρός, -ά, -όν   strong
καλός, -ή, -όν   beautiful
μακρός, -ά, -όν   long; large
μέγας, μεγάλη,
    μέγα   big, large; great
μῑκρός, -ά, -όν   small
πολλοί, -αί, -ά   many
πολύς, πολλή,
    πολύ   much
πρῶτος, -η, -ον   first
ῥάδιος, -ᾱ, -ον   easy
σός, -ή, -όν   your; yours (sing.)
τοσοῦτος, τοσαύτη,
    τοσοῦτο   so great; pl., so great;
                    so many
ὑμέτερος, -ᾱ, -ον   your; yours (pl.)
φίλος, -η, -ον   dear
χαλεπός, -ή, -όν   difficult

2nd Declension
ἀργός, -όν   not working, idle,
                    lazy
ῥάθῡμος, -ον   careless

PREPOSITIONS

ἀνά   + acc., up
ἀπό   + gen., from
κατά   + acc., down
πρός   + dat., at, near, by;
        + acc., to, toward
εἰς   + acc., into; to; at
ἐκ, ἐξ   + gen., out of
ἐν   + dat., in; on
ἐπί   + dat., upon, on;
        + acc., at; against

ὑπό	+ dat., *under;* + acc., *under*

PREFIX

ἀπο-	*away*

ADVERBS

ἀεί	*always*
αὖθις	*again*
βραδέως	*slowly*
δεῦρο	*here, hither*
ἐνταῦθα	*then; here; hither; there; thither*
ἔπειτα	*then, thereafter*
ἔτι	*still*
ἤδη	*already; now*
ἰδού	*look!*
καί	*even; also, too*
μάλα	*very*
μάλιστα	*most, most of all; very much; especially*
μή	*not; don't . . . !*
μηκέτι	*don't . . . any longer!*
μόλις	*with difficulty; scarcely; reluctantly*
νῦν	*now*
οἴκαδε	*homeward, to home*
οὐ, οὐκ, οὐχ	*not*
οὐκέτι	*no longer*
οὖν	*so; then*
οὕτω(ς)	*so, thus*
ποῦ;	*where?*
πρῶτον	*first*
ταχέως	*quickly, swiftly*
τί;	*why?*

CONJUNCTIONS

ἀλλά	*but*
γάρ	*for*
ἐπεί	*when*
καί	*and*
καί . . . καί	*both . . . and*
ὅτι	*that*

οὐδέ	*and . . . not; nor; not even*
οὔτε . . . οὔτε	*neither . . . nor*
ὥστε	*so that, that, so as to*

PARTICLES

ἆρα	*introduces a question*
δέ	*and, but*
μέν . . . δέ . . .	*on the one hand . . . and on the other hand; on the one hand . . . but on the other hand*
τε . . . καί	*both . . . and*

EXPRESSIONS

ἄκρον τὸ ὄρος	*the top of the mountain / hill*
δι' ὀλίγου	*soon*
ἐν νῷ ἔχω	*I have in mind; I intend*
ἐν ταῖς 'Αθήναις	*in Athens*
ἐνταῦθα δή	*at that very moment, then*
ἑορτὴν ποιῶ	*I celebrate a festival*
ἴθι δή	*go on!*
τὰ Διονύσια ποιῶ	*I celebrate the festival of Dionysus*
χαῖρε/χαίρετε	*greetings!*
ὦ Ζεῦ	*O Zeus*

PROPER NAMES & ADJECTIVES

'Αθηναῖος, -ᾱ, -ον	*Athenian*
"Αργος, ὁ	*Argus*
Δικαιόπολις, ὁ	*Dicaeopolis*
Διονύσια, τά	*the festival of Dionysus*
Μέλιττα, ἡ	*Melissa*
Μυρρίνη, ἡ	*Myrrhine*
Ξανθίᾱς, -ου	*Xanthias*
Φίλιππος, ὁ	*Philip*

6
Ο ΜΥΘΟΣ (α)

Exercise 6α

Give the equivalent Greek forms of πλέω:

1. he sails   _____
2. you (pl.) sail   _____
3. you (sing.) sail   _____
4. to sail   _____
5. we sail   _____
6. they sail   _____
7. I sail   _____
8. sail! (sing.)   _____

Exercise 6β

Translate the English phrases with the correct form of the Greek verb supplied:

1. δέχομαι: he/she receives   _____
2. ἔρχομαι: they come   _____
3. ἔρχομαι: we go   _____
4. δέχομαι: receive! (sing.)   _____
5. πείθομαι: you (sing.) obey   _____ or
                                      _____
6. ἀφικνέομαι: you (pl.) arrive   _____
7. γίγνομαι: they become   _____
8. ἀφικνέομαι: arrive! (sing.)   _____
9. ἀφικνέομαι: I arrive   _____
10. φοβέομαι: fear! (pl.)   _____
11. φοβέομαι: he/she fears   _____
12. φοβέομαι: fear! (sing.)   _____
13. βούλομαι: you (pl.) wish   _____
14. ἀφικνέομαι: to arrive   _____
15. ἀφικνέομαι: they arrive   _____
16. ἀπέρχομαι: he/she goes away   _____
17. ἀφικνέομαι: we arrive   _____
18. λύομαι: to ransom   _____
19. λύομαι: you (sing.) ransom   _____ or
                                      _____
20. δέχομαι: receive! (pl.)   _____

Exercise 6γ

Give the forms of τῑμάομαι that correspond to the forms you gave for nos. 5, 6, 8, 9, 10, 11, 14, 15, and 17 above:

5. _____   11. _____

6. _____   14. _____

8. _____   15. _____

9. _____   17. _____

10. _____

Exercise 6δ

Put the number of the Greek sentence in column A in front of the corresponding translation of the verb in column B:

A

1. λούω τὸν κύνα.

2. λούομαι.

3. ἐγείρομαι.

4. ἐγείρω τὴν γυναῖκα.

5. φέρω τὴν ὑδρίᾱν.

6. φέρομαι τὸ ἀργύριον.

7. λύω τοὺς βοῦς.

8. λύομαι τὴν θυγατέρα.

B

____ I ransom X

____ I wake up X

____ I carry off X

____ I wash X

____ I wash

____ I carry X

____ I release X

____ I wake up

Exercise 6ε

Give an English equivalent of:

1. βασιλεύουσι(ν) _____

2. ὁ ἑταῖρος _____

3. δεχόμεθα _____

4. ἡ νύξ _____

5. δεινός _____

6. ἐκεῖ _____

7. ἀποκτείνει _____

8. βούλεσθε _____

9. ἡ νῆσος _____

10. ἐκφεύγεις _____

11. ἔρχομαι _____

12. μετὰ τῶν φίλων _____

Exercise 6ζ

Give the Greek equivalent of:

1. day   _____
2. I arrive   _____
3. I sail   _____
4. I save   _____
5. I obey   _____
6. maiden   _____
7. I am afraid   _____
8. after the dinner   _____
9. I come to the
    rescue   _____

10. I become   _____
11. king   _____
12. ship   _____
13. it happens   _____
14. I fear   _____
15. I send   _____
16. papa (voc.)   _____
17. I am
    frightened   _____

(β)

Exercise 6η

Put the number of the Greek sentence in column A in front of the corresponding translation of the verb in column B:

A	B
1. καθίζομαι.	____ I turn around
2. καθίζω τὴν παῖδα.	____ I set out
3. τρέπομαι.	____ I make X sit down
4. τρέπω τὸ ἄροτρον.	____ I seat myself
5. ὁρμῶ τὴν ναῦν.	____ I turn X
6. ὁρμῶμαι κατὰ τὴν ὁδόν.	____ I put X to flight
7. πείθω τὸν αὐτουργόν.	____ I fear X
8. πείθομαι τῷ αὐτουργῷ.	____ I set X in motion
9. φοβοῦμαι τὸν ἄνθρωπον.	____ I obey X
10. φοβῶ τὸν ἄνθρωπον.	____ I persuade X

Exercise 6θ

Complete the sentence with the correct form of the word(s) suggested:

____ 1. οἱ παῖδες _____ πείθονται. (ἐγώ)

____ 2. _____ (*to the girls*) σῖτον παρέχομεν. (αἱ κόραι)

____ 3. ἀπὸ _____ ὁ ἄνθρωπος ἀφικνεῖται. (ἡ νῆσος)

____ 4. ἔστιν _____ μεγάλη οἰκίᾱ. (ὑμεῖς)

____ 5. _____ (on the next day) αἱ φίλαι ἀφικνοῦνται. (ἡ ὑστεραίᾱ)

____ 6. _____ (with the stone) ὁ παῖς τὸν λύκον βάλλει (pelts). (ὁ λίθος)

____ 7. μετὰ _____ ἐξερχόμεθα. (οἱ φίλοι)

____ 8. _____ ἑπόμεθα. (ὁ φίλος)

____ 9. καθίζομεν ἐπὶ _____ . (ὁ λίθος)

____ 10. τρέπονται πρὸς (at)_____ αἱ παρθένοι. (ἡ ὁδός)

____ 11. οἱ παῖδες ἐκ _____ φεύγουσιν. (ὁ ἀγρός)

____ 12. μένετε ἐν _____ , ὦ παῖδες. (ὁ οἶκος)

____ 13. ἡγούμεθα _____ εἰς τὴν οἰκίᾱν. (ὁ ἄνθρωπος)

____ 14. πάρεχε τὸ ἄροτρον _____ . (ὁ δοῦλος)

____ 15. ὁ παῖς, Φίλιππος _____ (in name), πάρεστιν. (ὄνομα)

____ 16. βαίνομεν ἐκ _____ . (ἡ οἰκίᾱ)

____ 17. ὁ Ξανθίας ὑπὸ _____ καθεύδει. (τὸ δένδρον)

____ 18. ὁ Θησεὺς τὸν Μῑνώταυρον _____ (with his right hand) τύπτει. (ἡ δεξιά)

____ 19. ὁ Μῑνώταυρος ἐν _____ οἰκεῖ. (ὁ λαβύρινθος)

____ 20. ἡ παρθένος _____ βοηθεῖ. (ὁ νεᾱνίᾱς)

Exercise 6ι

In the blanks to the left of the items in the previous exercise, label each use of the genitive, dative, or accusative case with the letter next to the correct descriptor below:

A. Indirect object
B. Dative of the possessor
C. Dative of respect
D. Dative of means or instrument
E. Dative of time when

F. Dative with certain verbs
G. Dative with certain prepositions
H. Genitive with certain prepositions
I. Accusative with certain prepositions

Exercise 6κ

Give an English equivalent of:

1. ἡγέομαι _____   5. αἱ πύλαι _____
2. δή _____   6. ὡς _____
3. προχωρέω _____   7. παρέχω _____
4. φᾱσί(ν) _____   8. πολλάκις _____

Exercise 6λ

Give the Greek equivalent of:

1. at least _____   4. I fight _____
2. in no way _____   5. often _____
3. I go out of _____   6. I journey _____

Exercise 6μ

Translate into English on a separate sheet of paper:

Ο ΔΙΚΑΙΟΠΟΛΙΣ ΑΓΑΝΑΚΤΕΙ

[1] ἡ μὲν οὖν μήτηρ ὀλίγον χρόνον σῑγᾷ καὶ πρὸς τοὺς παῖδας βλέπει. ἡ δὲ Μέλιττα, "τί δέ, ὦ μῆτερ;" φησίν, "τί σῑγᾷς; τί ἔπειτα γίγνεται; ἀκούειν γὰρ βούλομαι τὸν μῦθον. ἆρ' οὐ βούλει καὶ σὺ τὸν μῦθον ἀκούειν, ὦ Φίλιππε;" "μάλιστά γε· βούλομαι γὰρ γιγνώσκειν τί ποιεῖ ὁ Θησεύς. ὦ μῆτερ, ὡς καλός ἐστιν ὁ μῦθος."

[ΑΓΑΝΑΚΤΕΙ, *Is Displeased / Vexed*   ὀλίγον, *short (small)*   σῑγᾷ, *is silent* μάλιστά γε, *certainly*]

[2] ἐν δὲ τούτῳ οἱ παῖδες τόν τε Ξανθίᾱν ὁρῶσι καὶ τὸν Δικαιόπολιν· ὁ μὲν γὰρ Ξανθίᾱς τρέχει πρὸς τὴν οἰκίᾱν καὶ τοῖς παισὶ προσχωρεῖ, ὁ δὲ Δικαιόπολις διώκει αὐτὸν καὶ μέγα βοᾷ καί, "ποῖ φεύγεις," φησίν, "ὦ κατάρᾱτε; τί οὐκ ἐν τῷ ἀγρῷ μένεις καὶ συλλαμβάνεις; ἆρα ἤδη καθεύδειν βούλει; τί οὐ πείθει μοι; ἰδού, δέχου τὸ σπέρμα καὶ ἕπου μοι πρὸς τοὺς ἀγροὺς καὶ ἐργάζου."

[ἐν ... τούτῳ, *meanwhile*   μέγα, *loudly*   ποῖ, *to where*   ὦ κατάρᾱτε, *you cursed creature*   τὸ σπέρμα, *the seed*   ἕπου, *follow!*   ἐργάζου, *work!*]

[3] ὁ δὲ Ξανθίᾱς· "ἤδη πολὺν χρόνον ἐν τῷ ἀγρῷ πονῶ. ἤδη μεσημβρίᾱ ἐστίν. φλέγει δὲ ὁ ἥλιος, καὶ ἐγὼ μάλα κάμνω· βούλομαι οὖν ὀλίγον χρόνον ἡσυχάζειν." ὁ δὲ Δικαιόπολις, "οὐ δυνατόν ἐστιν ἡσυχάζειν," φησίν· "μακρὸς γάρ ἐστιν ὁ πόνος. ἰδού, ἆρα ὁρᾷς ταύτην τὴν βακτηρίᾱν; ἆρα οὐ φοβεῖ;" ὁ δὲ Ξανθίᾱς· "μάλιστά γε· τὴν βακτηρίᾱν ὁρῶ καὶ μάλα φοβοῦμαι. ὁ δὲ ἥλιος κατατρίβει με καὶ οὐ δυνατόν ἐστι πρὸς τὸν ἀγρὸν ἕπεσθαί σοι."

[μεσημβρίᾱ, *noontime*   φλέγει, *is blazing*   κάμνω, *I am tired*   ὀλίγον, *short (small)*   **ἡσυχάζειν**, *to rest*   **ταύτην τὴν**, *this*   **βακτηρίᾱν**, *stick*   **μάλιστά γε**, *certainly*   **κατατρῑ́βει**, *wears X down*   **ἕπεσθαί**, *to follow*]

[4] ἡ δὲ Μυρρίνη πρὸς τὸν ἄνδρα· "μὴ οὕτω βόᾱ, ὦ ἄνερ· ὁ μὲν γὰρ πάππος μάλα κάμνει· καθεύδει οὖν καὶ οὐ βούλεται ἐγείρεσθαι. μὴ ἡγοῦ τῷ δούλῳ πρὸς τὸν ἀγρὸν ἐν μεσημβρίᾳ, ἀλλ᾽ ἔᾱ αὐτὸν ἡσυχάζειν ὀλίγον χρόνον." ὁ μὲν οὖν Δικαιόπολις σῑγᾷ καὶ καθίζει ἐν τῇ σκιᾷ, ὁ δὲ Ξανθίᾱς καὶ αὐτὸς καθίζει καὶ δι᾽ ὀλίγου καθεύδει· τὸν μὲν γὰρ Δικαιόπολιν φοβεῖται, μάλα δὲ κάμνει.

[**κάμνει**, *is tired*   **ἐγείρεσθαι**, *to wake up*   **μεσημβρίᾳ**, *noontime*   **ἔᾱ . . . ἡσυχάζειν**, *let X rest!*   **ὀλίγον**, *a little (small)*   **σῑγᾷ**, *is silent*   **τῇ σκιᾷ**, *the shade*]

[5] ὁ μὲν οὖν Φίλιππος, "ὦ μῆτερ," φησίν, "τί οὐ λέγεις τῷ πατρὶ περὶ τοῦ λύκου;" ἡ δὲ Μυρρίνη· "οὐδαμῶς, ὦ Φίλιππε· νῦν γὰρ μάλα κάμνει καὶ ἀγανακτεῖ· βούλομαι δὲ πάντα αὐτῷ λέγειν οἴκοι μετὰ τὰ ἔργα."

[**περὶ**, *about*   **κάμνει**, *is tired*   **ἀγανακτεῖ**, *is displeased, vexed*   **πάντα**, *all things, everything*   **οἴκοι**, adv., *at home*   **τὰ ἔργα**, *the works, work*]

7
Ο ΚΥΚΛΩΨ (α)

Exercise 7α

Translate the underlined word(s) into English:

1. οἱ ἀγαθοὶ desire ἀγαθά. *Good men* ___ *good women* ___
2. πολλαὶ go to the spring daily. *Many women*
3. They always suffer πολλὰ καὶ δεινά. *many terrible thing*
4. Why do οἱ κακοὶ always do κακά? *good men*
   bad thing
5. We expect πολλοὺς to want to do this. *many men (people)*

Exercise 7β

Complete the following phrases with the correct form of the word supplied:

1. οἱ __παίδες__ (παῖς)
2. τῷ __παιδί__ (παῖς)
3. τοὺς __παίδας__ (παῖς)
4. τοῦ __ὀνόματος__ (ὄνομα)
5. τὰ __ὀνόματα__ (ὄνομα)
6. τοῖς __ὀνόμασι(ν)__ (ὄνομα)
7. ὁ __φύλαξ__ (φύλαξ)
8. τὸν __φύλακα__ (φύλαξ)
9. τῶν __φυλάκων__ (φύλαξ)
10. τοῦ __αἰγός__ (αἴξ)
11. τῷ __αἰγί__ (αἴξ)
12. τοὺς __αἶγας__ (αἴξ)
13. αἱ __ἐλπίδες__ (ἐλπίς)
14. τὴν __ἐλπίδα__ (ἐλπίς)
15. ταῖς __ἐλπίσι__ (ἐλπίς)
16. τὰς __ἐλπίδας__ (ἐλπίς)

Exercise 7γ

Write the form of the reflexive pronoun that translates the underlined word:

1. I see myself in the mirror. __ἐμαυτόν__ or __ἐμαυτήν__
2. The girls lifted themselves onto the wagon. __ἡμᾶς αὐτάς__
3. Why don't we let ourselves into the house, guys? __ἡμᾶς αὐτούς__
4. Dicaeopolis, give yourself more time on this task. __σεαυτόν__
5. Get yourself up and go to work, Xanthias. __σεαυτόν__
6. The men did not want to show themselves. __ἑαυτούς__

7.   He instructed the fellow to follow (ἔπεσθαι + dat.) him(self) into the next
     room. _____

8.   Why don't you do something good for yourself, Myrrhine?

     _____

9.   She could hardly hear (ἀκούω + gen.) herself. _____

10. Show yourselves to be men and fight the monster bravely.

     _____

11. She saw herself in the mirror. _____

12. The boy wanted a chariot of his own. _____

13. We women wanted to give ourselves a good dinner. _____

14. You Athenians ought to hear (ἀκούω + gen.) yourselves.

     _____

15. You, the Queen, lifted yourself onto the throne. _____

Exercise 7δ

Give an English equivalent of:

1. ἐπαίρω   I get up   6. κελεύω   I command
2. οὐδείς   no one   7. τίς;   why?
3. ἡ θάλαττα   the sea   8. μέγιστος   AMAP
4. ἡ αἴξ   goat   9. παρασκευάζω   I prepare
5. τίς ἀνήρ;   which father   10. περί   around

Exercise 7ε

Give the Greek equivalent of:

1. I take   λαμβάνω   6. of myself   ἐμοῦ
2. name   ὄνομα   7. someone   τις
3. to go   βαίναιν   8. I find   _____
4. city   ἡ πόλις   9. some man   τις ἀνήρ
5. I get up   ἐπαίρω   10. about   περί

(β)

Exercise 7ζ

Complete each phrase with the correct form of the word supplied:

1. οἱ _____ (χειμών)
2. τῷ _____ (χειμών)
3. τοὺς _____ (χειμών)
4. τοῖς _____ (χειμών)
5. τοὺς _____ (κλώψ)
6. τοῖς _____ (κλώψ)
7. τὸν _____ (κλώψ)
8. τοῦ _____ (κλώψ)
9. ὦ _____ (κλώψ)
10. τῷ _____ (κύων)
11. ὁ _____ (κύων)
12. τοῖς _____ (κύων)
13. τῶν _____ (κύων)
14. τοῖς _____ (ῥήτωρ)
15. τῷ _____ (ῥήτωρ)
16. οἱ _____ (ῥήτωρ)
17. ἡ _____ γυνή
    (σώφρων)
18. τῷ _____ παιδί
    (σώφρων)
19. τὰς _____ παρθένους
    (σώφρων)
20. ταῖς _____ παρθένοις
    (σώφρων)

Exercise 7η

Write the form of the pronoun or adjective that translates the underlined word (do not put accent marks on forms that would be enclitic):

1. <u>Who</u> is at the door? _____
2. <u>Whose</u> house is this? _____
3. <u>Whom</u> do you see just up ahead? _____
4. Did you see <u>anyone</u> in the house? _____
5. <u>What</u> women (γυναῖκες) will be here? _____
6. <u>What</u> names (ὀνόματα) will we give them? _____
7. <u>What</u> did you do yesterday? _____
8. To <u>what</u> children (παισί) did you give the toys? _____
9. I saw <u>some</u> children (παῖδάς) at your house. _____
10. Does <u>anyone</u> know what time it is? _____
11. <u>A certain thing</u> is bothering me about this. _____
12. <u>To whom</u> (sing.) will you give this gift? _____

Exercise 7θ

Give an English equivalent of:

1. μέλλω	_____	6. σώφρων	_____
2. ὁ οἶνος	_____	7. πόθεν	_____
3. δύο	_____	8. παύω	_____
4. τὸ πῦρ	_____	9. πάντες	
5. ὁρμάω	_____	ἄνθρωποι	_____

Exercise 7ι

Give the Greek equivalent of:

1. Cyclops	_____	6. I throw	_____
2. how?	_____	7. one (thing)	_____
3. eye	_____	8. I answer	_____
4. stranger	_____	9. hither	_____
5. I pelt	_____	10. I set myself in motion	_____

Exercise 7κ

Translate into English on a separate sheet of paper:

ΤΟ ΤΟΥ ΜΥΘΟΥ ΤΕΛΟΣ

[1] ἐπεὶ δὲ ὁ Φίλιππος περαίνει τὸν μῦθον, ἡ Μέλιττα, "τί δὲ μετὰ ταῦτα γίγνεται," φησίν, "τῷ Ὀδυσσεῖ καὶ τοῖς ἑταίροις αὐτοῦ; εἰς τίνα νῆσον ἔπειτα πλέουσιν; ἆρα εἰς τὴν πατρίδα ἀφικνοῦνται; τίνες τῶν ἑταίρων σῴζονται ἐκ τῆς θαλάττης; μὴ παῦε, ὦ Φίλιππε, ἀλλ᾽ εἰπέ μοι πάντα τὸν μῦθον τὸν περὶ τοῦ Ὀδυσσέως."

[ΤΟ . . . ΤΕΛΟΣ, *The End*   περαίνει, *ends*   ταῦτα, *these things, this*   τὴν πατρίδα, *his fatherland*   σῴζονται, *are saved*]

[2] ὁ δὲ Φίλιππος· "οὐκ ἀφικνοῦνται εἰς τὴν ἑαυτῶν πατρίδα, ἐπεὶ ὁ τοῦ Κύκλωπος πατὴρ ἐχθρὸς αὐτοῖς γίγνεται καὶ οὐκ ἐᾷ αὐτοὺς οἴκαδε ἐπανιέναι κατὰ θάλατταν, οὐδὲ ὁ Ὀδυσσεὺς δυνατός ἐστιν αὐτοὺς σῴζειν ἐκ τῆς θαλάττης εἰς τὸν λιμένα."

[πατρίδα, *fatherland*   ἐπεί, *since*   ἐχθρός, *hostile*   ἐᾷ, *allows*   ἐπανιέναι, *to return*   κατὰ θάλατταν, *by sea*   δυνατός, *able*   τὸν λιμένα, *the harbor*]

[3] ἡ δὲ Μέλιττα· "τί λέγεις; τίνος ἐστὶν υἱὸς ὁ Κύκλωψ;" ὁ δὲ Φίλιππος· "τοῦ Ποσειδῶνος, τοῦ τῆς θαλάττης θεοῦ. ὁ γὰρ Ὀδυσσεὺς ἀπὸ τοῦ τῆς νήσου αἰγιαλοῦ

ἀποπλεῖ ἀλλ' ἐκ μέσης τῆς θαλάττης οὕτω βοᾷ· 'ὦ Κύκλωψ, δεινὸς μὲν εἶ σύ, ἐγὼ δὲ ἀνδρεῖος καὶ ἰσχῡρός εἰμι. τί οὐ καλῶς δέχει τοὺς ξένους εἰς τὴν οἰκίᾱν σου; ἆρ' ἀγνοεῖς ὅτι ὁ Ζεὺς τοὺς ξένους ἀεὶ σῴζει; νῦν δὲ οὐκέτι τὸν ὀφθαλμὸν ἐν μέσῳ τῷ μετώπῳ ἔχεις. ἐγὼ δὲ αἴτιός εἰμι, καὶ τὸ ὄνομά μου Ὀδυσσεύς ἐστιν. Ὀδυσσεύς εἰμι πολύμητις, υἱὸς τοῦ Λᾱέρτου, καὶ ἐν τῇ Ἰθάκῃ οἰκίᾱν ἔχω.' ὁ δὲ Κύκλωψ μέγαν λίθον ἐκ τοῦ ὄρους αἴρει καὶ βάλλει αὐτὸν εἰς τὴν τοῦ Ὀδυσσέως ναῦν. ὁ μὲν οὖν λίθος τῇ θαλάττῃ ἐμπίπτει, ὁ δὲ Ὀδυσσεὺς καὶ οἱ ἑταῖροι ἀποφεύγουσιν.

[υἱός, *son*   τοῦ Ποσειδῶνος, *Poseidon*   θεοῦ, *god*   αἰγιαλοῦ, *shore, beach* μέσης, *middle of*   καλῶς, *well*   ἀγνοεῖς, *do you not know?*   μέσῳ τῷ μετώπῳ, *the middle of your forehead*   πολύμητις, *of many counsels*   τοῦ Λᾱέρτου, *of Laertes* τῇ Ἰθάκῃ, *Ithaka*   ἐμπίπτει, *falls into*]

[4] "ἀλλ' ὁ Κύκλωψ τὸν Ποσειδῶνα τὸν ἑαυτοῦ πατέρα καλεῖ καὶ λέγει· 'ὦ Πόσειδον πάτερ, ὦ δέσποτα καὶ βασιλεῦ τῆς θαλάττης, ὅρᾱ τί πάσχω ὑπὸ τοῦ Ὀδυσσέως· βοήθει οὖν μοι καὶ μὴ ἔᾱ αὐτὸν οἴκαδε ἐπανιέναι. εἰ δὲ μὴ τοῦτο δυνατόν ἐστιν, ἀπόκτεινε πάντας τοὺς ἑταίρους αὐτοῦ.'" ἡ δὲ Μέλιττα· "τί δὴ γίγνεται; ἆρα ὁ Ποσειδῶν χειμῶνα ποιεῖ ἐν τῇ θαλάττῃ; ἆρα ὁ Ὀδυσσεὺς σῴζεται ἐκ τοῦ χειμῶνος; ἆρα ἐν τῷ χειμῶνι οἱ ἑταῖροι αὐτοῦ ἀποθνῄσκουσιν; ἆρα σῷοί εἰσι πάντες ἐπεὶ ὁ χειμὼν παύεται; εἰπέ μοι, ὦ Φίλιππε, εἰπέ μοι, καὶ μὴ παῦε."

[ὑπό, *by*, i.e., *at the hand of*   ἔᾱ, *allow!*   ἐπανιέναι, *to return*   τοῦτο, *this*   σῴ-ζεται, *is saved*   ἀποθνῄσκουσιν, *die*   σῷοί, *safe*]

[5] ὁ δὲ Φίλιππος· "ὦ Μέλιττα, μὴ θόρυβον ποίει ἀλλ' ἄκουε τὸ τοῦ μύθου τέλος· ἐγὼ μὲν γὰρ τὸν μῦθον λέγειν βούλομαι, σὺ δὲ σῑγᾶ καὶ ἄκουέ μου."

[θόρυβον, *commotion*   τέλος, *end*   σῑγᾶ, *be silent!*]

[6] ἡ μὲν οὖν Μέλιττα σῑγᾷ, ὁ δὲ Φίλιππος, "ὁ τ' Ὀδυσσεύς," φησίν, "καὶ οἱ ἑταῖροι αὐτοῦ πολλὰ καὶ δεινὰ πάσχουσιν, πολλάκις χειμῶνας ὑπέχουσιν, καὶ οἱ μὲν σῴζονται, οἱ δὲ ἐν τῇ θαλάττῃ ἀποθνῄσκουσιν. τέλος δὲ ἀφικνοῦνται εἰς τὴν τοῦ Αἰόλου νῆσον."

[σῑγᾷ, *is silent*   ὑπέχουσιν, *suffer*   οἱ μέν, *some*   σῴζονται, *are saved*   οἱ δέ, *others*   ἀποθνῄσκουσιν, *die*   τέλος, *finally*   τοῦ Αἰόλου, *of Aeolus*]

8
ΠΡΟΣ ΤΟ ΑΣΤΥ (α)

Exercise 8α

Complete the following sentences with a participle of the verb supplied; make it agree with the underlined phrase or complete the meaning of the underlined verb:

____ 1. αἱ παρθένοι _____ χαίρουσιν. (ἐργάζομαι)

____ 2. τῷ παιδὶ τῷ _____ τὸν κύνα προσχωρῶ. (θεάομαι)

____ 3. τοὺς αὐτουργοὺς τοὺς πρὸς τὸ ἄστυ _____ ὁρῶ.
(πορεύομαι)

____ 4. οἱ δοῦλοι παύονται _____ . (ἐργάζομαι).

____ 5. ἀκούομεν τῶν ποιητῶν _____ . (διαλέγομαι)

____ 6. ὁ αὐτρουργὸς τὴν παρθένον _____ χαίρει. (λύομαι)

____ 7. τοὺς παῖδας τοὺς ταῖς κόραισιν _____ ὁρῶμεν. (ἕπομαι)

____ 8. αἱ παρθένοι τὸν ξένον _____ φεύγουσιν. (φοβέομαι)

____ 9. οἱ δοῦλοι οἱ ἐν τῷ ἀγρῷ_____ ἰσχῡροί εἰσιν. (μάχομαι)

____ 10. αἱ γυναῖκες παύονται _____ . (ἐργάζεσθαι)

____ 11. ὁ δοῦλος ὁ εἰς τὸν ἀγρὸν τῷ δεσπότῃ _____ τὸ ἄροτρον φέρει.
(ἕπομαι)

____ 12. ἡ παρθένος ἡ ἐν τῇ οἰκίᾳ _____ κάμνει (*is tired*).
(ἐργάζομαι)

____ 13 οἱ αὐτουργοὶ τῶν πόνων _____ καθεύδουσιν. (παύομαι)

____ 14. ἡ γυνὴ οἴκαδε ἰέναι _____ τὰς φίλᾱς λείπει. (βούλομαι)

____ 15. οἱ παῖδες δι' ὀλίγου παύονται _____. (μάχομαι)

____ 16. ὁ ἀνὴρ ὁ τοῖς βουσὶν _____ δοῦλός ἐστιν. (ἡγέομαι)

____ 17. καλῶ τὸν δοῦλον τὸν ἐν τῷ ἀγρῷ_____. (ἐργάζομαι)

____ 18. ὁ γέρων Ἀθήνᾱζε _____ μάλα κάμνει. (πορεύομαι)

____ 19. οἱ παῖδες τὸν πατέρα _____ οἴκαδε ἔρχονται. (φοβέομαι)

____ 20. ὁ Φίλιππος τῷ πατρὶ _____ πρὸς τὸν ἀγρὸν ἔρχεται.
(πείθομαι)

Exercise 8β

In the blanks to the left of the items in the previous exercise, label each use of the participle with the letter next to the correct descriptor below:

A. Attributive
C. Circumstantial
S. Supplementary

Exercise 8γ

Give an English equivalent of:

1. θεάομαι _____
2. τὸ ἄστυ _____
3. διαλέγομαι _____
4. ὁ θεός _____
5. οἴκοι _____

6. εὖ γε _____
7. ὅμως _____
8. ἐκεῖσε _____
9. ἐν ᾧ _____
10. ὁ Διόνῡσος _____

Exercise 8δ

Give the Greek equivalent of:

1. I follow _____
2. well _____
3. just as _____
4. evening _____

5. work _____
6. I accomplish _____
7. door _____
8. poet _____

Exercise 8ε

Translate into English on a separate sheet of paper:

ΟΙ ΘΕΟΙ ΤΟΥΣ ΕΡΓΑΖΟΜΕΝΟΥΣ ΦΙΛΟΥΣΙΝ

[1] ὁ μὲν Φίλιππος εἰσέρχεται εἰς τὴν οἰκίᾱν καὶ τήν τε Μυρρίνην καὶ τὴν Μέλιτταν καὶ τὸν Δικαιόπολιν διαλεγομένους ἀλλήλοις ὁρᾷ. ὁ μὲν οὖν Δικαιόπολις παύεται διαλεγόμενος καὶ πρὸς τὸν παῖδα βλέπει· ἡ δὲ Μέλιττα παύεται ἐργαζομένη καὶ πρὸς τὸν Φίλιππον τρέχει. ἡ δὲ Μυρρίνη, "ἰδού, ὦ Δικαιόπολι," φησίν· "ὁ λυκοκτόνος εἰσέρχεται. ἆρα οὐ βούλει σὺ τὸν λυκοκτόνον τῑμᾶν;" ὁ δὲ Δικαιόπολις ἀποκρῑνόμενος λέγει· "ἀλλὰ βούλομαι δὴ τὸν λυκοκτόνον τῑμᾶν ἔγωγε. δεῦρο ἐλθέ, ὦ παῖ, καί μοι βουλομένῳ τῑμᾶν σε πάντα τὰ περὶ τοῦ λύκου λέγε." ὁ δὲ Φίλιππος, πειθόμενος τῷ πατρί, καθίζει καὶ αὖθις πάντα λέγει.

[**ΤΟΥΣ ΕΡΓΑΖΟΜΕΝΟΥΣ,** *Those Who Work* **ἀλλήλοις,** *one another* **ὁ λυκο-κτόνος,** *the wolf-slayer* **ἔγωγε,** *I indeed*]

[2] ἔπειτα δὲ ὁ Δικαιόπολις· "εὖ γε, ὦ παῖ· μάλα ἀνδρεῖος γὰρ εἶ καὶ ἰσχῡρός. βούλομαι οὖν σε τῑμᾶν, διότι τοσοῦτον λύκον, θηρίον δεινὸν καὶ ἄγριον, ἀπέκτονας.

μέλλομεν οὖν πρὸς τὸ ἄστυ πορεύεσθαι· ἐκεῖ γὰρ οἱ Ἀθηναῖοι ἑορτὴν ποιοῦνται τῷ
Διονύσῳ. ἆρ' οὐ βούλει σὺ τούς τε ἀγῶνας θεᾶσθαι καὶ τοὺς χοροὺς τοὺς ἐν τῇ
ἑορτῇ;"

[διότι, because   θηρίον, wild beast   ἀπέκτονας, you have killed   ἀγῶνας, contests]

[3] ὁ δὲ Φίλιππος· "βούλομαι, ὦ πάτερ· οὕτω σπανίως γὰρ πρὸς τὸ ἄστυ
πορευόμεθα ὥστ' ἀδύνατόν ἐστί μοι ἐν τοῖς ἀγροῖς ἐργαζομένῳ ἑορτὰς καὶ ἀγῶνας
θεᾶσθαι. ἡγοῦ οὖν ἡμῖν πρὸς τὰς Ἀθήνας, ὦ πάτερ." ὁ δὲ Δικαιόπολις, "ἔστω οὖν,"
φησίν. "καὶ ἐγὼ γὰρ βούλομαι τὸν Διόνῡσον τῑμᾶν. σὺ δέ, ὦ παῖ, μὴ κακῶς λέγε
τοὺς ἐργαζομένους ἐν τοῖς ἀγροῖς· ἡ γὰρ γεωργίᾱ ἰσχῡροὺς ποιεῖ τοὺς ἀνθρώπους. οἱ
δὲ θεοὶ τοὺς ἀργοὺς ἀνθρώπους καὶ μὴ ἐργαζομένους οὐ φιλοῦσιν· τῷ δὲ ἐργαζομένῳ
φίλοι εἰσὶν ἀεὶ οἱ θεοί."

[σπανίως, rarely   ἀδύνατόν, impossible   ἀγῶνας, contests   ἔστω, let it be so!
κακῶς λέγε, speak badly of, belittle   γεωργίᾱ, farming   μὴ ἐργαζομένους: μή
with the participle generalizes—men of the sort who don't work   φίλοι + dat., loving,
friendly (to)]

[4] ὁ δὲ Φίλιππος, "ἀλλ' ἐγώ," φησίν, "ἐθέλω μὲν ἐργάζεσθαι, βούλομαι δὲ καὶ
πρὸς τὸ ἄστυ πορεύεσθαι καὶ τοὺς ἀγῶνας θεᾶσθαι."

[τοὺς ἀγῶνας, the contests]

[5] ἐπεὶ δὲ νὺξ γίγνεται, ὁ Δικαιόπολις, "νῦν," φησίν, "καιρός ἐστι καθεύδειν·
αὔριον γὰρ ἅμα τῇ ἡμέρᾳ εἰς τὸ ἄστυ πορεύεσθαι μέλλομεν. καθεύδετε οὖν."

[αὔριον, tomorrow   ἅμα + dat., together with]

[6] μετ' οὐ πολὺν χρόνον οὖν ὕπνος τὸν Φίλιππον λαμβάνει. ἐν δὲ τοῖς ὕπνοις ὁ
παῖς ἑαυτὸν ὁρᾷ τοὺς ἐν Ἀθήναις ἀγῶνας θεώμενον. ἐν ᾧ δὲ θεᾶται τοὺς ἀγῶνας,
ἰδού, ὁ θεὸς αὐτὸς ἐν τῷ θεάτρῳ πάρεστιν. ὁ οὖν Διόνῡσος μέγα βοᾷ καὶ λέγει· "ὦ
παῖ, χαίρω ὁρῶν ὅτι τοὺς χοροὺς θεᾷ ἐν τῷ θεάτρῳ καὶ ὅτι ἐμὲ οὕτω τῑμᾷς. τῑμῶ δὲ
καὶ ἐγὼ σέ τε καὶ τὸν πατέρα σου· ἀεὶ γὰρ μάλα πονεῖ ἐν τοῖς ἀγροῖς καὶ τῶν
ἀμπέλων ἐπιμελεῖται καὶ πολὺν οἶνον ποιεῖ. ἐγὼ γὰρ ἀεὶ ῡ̔μᾶς ἐπισκοπῶ, καὶ εἰ
ῡ̔μεῖς με μὴ ὁρᾶτε· πανταχοῦ γὰρ πάρειμι καὶ τῑμῶ τοὺς ἀγαθοὺς καὶ τοὺς
ἐργαζομένους, τοὺς δὲ κακοὺς καὶ ἀργοὺς ἀτῑμάζω. καλός τε οὖν καὶ ἀγαθὸς ἀεὶ
ἴσθι, ὦ παῖ, ἐπεὶ ἐγὼ καὶ οἱ ἄλλοι θεοὶ πάντες ἀεί σε ἐπισκοπούμεθα."

[ὕπνος, sleep   τοῖς ὕπνοις, sleep; dreams   ἀγῶνας, contests   τῷ θεάτρῳ, the theater   μέγα, loudly   ὁρῶν, seeing   τῶν ἀμπέλων, the grape vines   ἐπιμελεῖται +
gen., he takes care of   ἐπισκοπῶ, look upon, watch   εἰ, if   πανταχοῦ, everywhere
τούς . . . κακούς, the bad   ἀτῑμάζω, I do not honor   ἐπεί, since]

[7] ὁ δὲ παῖς μάλα φοβεῖται καὶ ἀποκρίνεσθαι βούλεται ἀλλὰ τὸν θεὸν οὐκέτι
ὁρᾷ. σκότος δὲ γίγνεται πανταχοῦ, καὶ ὁ παῖς λέγει· "οἴμοι, τί γίγνεται; ὦ πάτερ,
ποῦ εἶ σύ; σῷζέ με."

[σκότος, *darkness*   πανταχοῦ, *everywhere*   οἴμοι, *alas!*]

[8] ἐν δὲ τούτῳ ὁ πατὴρ προσχωρεῖ τῷ παιδὶ καί, "τί σοι γίγνεται, ὦ παῖ;" φησίν. "ἔπαιρε σεαυτόν. τί βοᾷς; θάρρει."

[ἐν ... τούτῳ, *meanwhile*   θάρρει, *cheer up!*]

[9] ὁ δὲ Φίλιππος ἐξ ὕπνου ἐγείρεται μάλα φοβούμενος καί, "ὦ πάτερ," φησίν, "τὸ λοιπὸν ἀεὶ μετὰ σοῦ ἐν τοῖς ἀγροῖς ἐργάζεσθαι μέλλω· ὁ γὰρ θεὸς ἀτῑμάζει τοὺς ἀργούς."

[ὕπνου, *sleep*   τὸ λοιπὸν, *hereafter*   ἀτῑμάζει, *does not honor*]

[10] ὁ δὲ Δικαιόπολις· "ἀλλ' ἡσύχαζε νῦν, ὦ παῖ, καὶ ἡδὺν ὕπνον κάθευδε· ὁ γὰρ θεὸς ἵλεώς ἐστί σοι καὶ χαίρει εἰ οἱ ἄνθρωποι αὐτὸν τῑμῶσιν καὶ εἰς τὸ ἄστυ ἔρχονται τὴν ἑορτὴν αὐτοῦ θεωρεῖν βουλόμενοι."

[ἡσύχαζε, *rest!*   ἡδὺν, *sweet*   ὕπνον, *sleep*   ἵλεώς, *propitious*   εἰ, *if*]

(β)

Exercise 8ζ

Complete the following phrases with the correct form of the noun supplied:

1.	τοῦ _____ (ἀνήρ)		13.	τῶν _____ (γυνή)
2.	αἱ _____ (μήτηρ)		14.	τῇ _____ (χείρ)
3.	τὴν _____ (θυγάτηρ)		15.	τῷ _____ (πατήρ)
4.	τοῖς _____ (ἀνήρ)		16.	τὰς _____ (μήτηρ)
5.	ὦ (sing.) _____ (πατήρ)		17.	ταῖς _____ (θυγάτηρ)
6.	τῆς _____ (γυνή)		18.	τὴν _____ (γυνή)
7.	αἱ _____ (χείρ)		19.	οἱ _____ (ἀνήρ)
8.	τὴν _____ (μήτηρ)		20.	τῶν _____ (θυγάτηρ)
9.	τοὺς _____ (ἀνήρ)		21.	ὦ (pl.) _____ (μήτηρ)
10.	τῇ _____ (θυγάτηρ)		22.	τῆς _____ (χείρ)
11.	τοῖς _____ (πατήρ)		23.	τὸν _____ (πατήρ)
12.	τὰς _____ (χείρ)		24.	τῷ _____ (ἀνήρ)

Exercise 8η

Complete the following phrases with the correct form of πᾶς, πᾶσα, πᾶν, and then translate the phrase into English on the line below:

___ 1. _____ τὴν θάλατταν

___ 2. τοῦ _____ ἔργου

___ 3. _____ οἱ ἄνδρες

___ 4. _____ γυνή

___ 5. _____ τὰ ἄροτρα

___ 6. _____ τὰς γυναῖκας

___ 7. _____ ἔργον

___ 8. _____ τῶν ἀνδρῶν

___ 9. _____ ταῖς μητράσιν

___ 10. τῆς _____ γυναικὸς

___ 11. _____ τοὺς πατέρας

___ 12. _____ τῶν παρθένων

___ 13. τὸ _____ ἄστυ

___ 14. _____ αἱ μητέρες

___ 15. τὸν _____ οἶκον

___ 16. _____ τῷ ἔργῳ

___ 17. _____ ὁ πόνος

___ 18. _____ τοῖς ἀνδράσιν

___ 19. _____ θυγατρί

___ 20. _____ ἄνθρωπος

Exercise 8θ

In the blanks to the left of the items in the previous exercise, write an A if the adjective is being used in the attributive position and a P if the adjective is being used in the predicate position. If there is no definite article, do not write an A or a P.

Exercise 8ι

Select the English equivalent from the pool below this exercise and write it on the line in front of each Greek numerical adjective:

1.	_____ τέταρτος		12.	_____ πέντε
2.	_____ ἑπτά		13.	_____ ἕν
3.	_____ ἔνατος		14.	_____ τρίτος
4.	_____ ἕξ		15.	_____ πρῶτος
5.	_____ δέκατος		16.	_____ εἷς
6.	_____ ὀκτώ		17.	_____ δύο
7.	_____ δεύτερος		18.	_____ ἕβδομος
8.	_____ τρεῖς		19.	_____ ἕκτος
9.	_____ δέκα		20.	_____ τέτταρες
10.	_____ πέμπτος		21.	_____ ἐννέα
11.	_____ ὄγδοος		22.	_____ μία

```
3   8th   5th   4th   10   9   10th   8   2nd   9th
4   7   7th   5   6   1st   1   2   3rd   6th
```

Exercise 8κ

Give the correct form of the number supplied to agree with each noun; be sure to change acute accents on final syllables to grave accents:

1. _____ ἔργον (εἷς, μία, ἕν)
2. _____ ἄνθρωπος (εἷς, μία, ἕν)
3. _____ γυνή (εἷς, μία, ἕν)
4. _____ ἄνθρωπον (εἷς, μία, ἕν)
5. _____ γυναικός (εἷς, μία, ἕν)
6. _____ ἔργου (εἷς, μία, ἕν)
7. _____ ἀνθρώπῳ (οὐδείς, οὐδεμία, οὐδέν)
8. _____ ἔργον (οὐδείς, οὐδεμία, οὐδέν)
9. _____ γυναῖκα (οὐδείς, οὐδεμία, οὐδέν)
10. _____ γυναῖκες (δύο)
11. _____ γυναικῶν (δύο)
12. _____ ἀνθρώποις (δύο)
13. _____ ἔργα (δύο)

14. _____ ἄνδρες (δύο)

15. _____ γυναῖκες (τρεῖς, τρία)

16. _____ ἔργοις (τρεῖς, τρία)

17. _____ ἀνθρώπους (τρεῖς, τρία)

18. _____ ἀνθρώπων (τρεῖς, τρία)

19. _____ ἄνδρας (τρεῖς, τρία)

20. _____ κρῆναι (τέτταρες, τέτταρα)

21. _____ γυναῖκας (τέτταρες, τέτταρα)

22. _____ ἀνθρώπων (τέτταρες, τέτταρα)

23. _____ ἔργοις (τέτταρες, τέτταρα)

24. _____ ἔργα (τέτταρες, τέτταρα)

Exercise 8λ

Translate the underlined word or phrase and in the blank before each item,
indicate the type of time expression used, with A for time when, *B for* duration
of time *and C for* time within which:

___ 1.   We worked τρεῖς ἡμέρᾱς.   _____

___ 2.   It all took place τριῶν ἡμερῶν.   _____

___ 3.   She arrived τρίτῃ ἡμέρᾳ.   _____

___ 4.   They had the work finished
          πέντε ἡμερῶν.   _____

___ 5.   πᾶσαν τὴν ἡμέρᾱν the farmer
          was working.   _____

___ 6.   The athlete received a prize
          πέμπτῃ ἡμέρᾳ.   _____

___ 7.   τῇ ὑστεραίᾳ they left for the
          harbor.   _____

___ 8.   They traveled πολὺν χρόνον.   _____

Exercise 8μ

Give an English equivalent of:

1. ἐγείρω   _____   4. ὁ νεᾱνίᾱς   _____

2. ὑπὲρ τῆς μητρός _____   5. ἐν . . . τούτῳ   _____

3. ὁ βωμός   _____   6. ἀναβαίνω   _____

Exercise 8ν

Give the Greek equivalent of:

1. in the end   _____   5. citizen   _____
2. on the next day   _____   6. I pray   _____
3. city center   _____   7. I set   _____
4. hand   _____   8. I seat myself _____

Exercise 8ξ

Translate into English on a separate sheet of paper:

Ο ΠΟΛΕΜΑΡΧΟΣ ΚΑΙ ΟΙ ΠΑΙΔΕΣ

[1] ὁ μὲν οὖν πατὴρ ἡγεῖται αὐτοῖς εἰς τὸ ἄστυ· ὁ δὲ πάππος ἐπὶ τῇ βακτηρίᾳ ἐρειδόμενος μετ' αὐτοῦ βραδέως πορεύεται. ἡ δὲ μήτηρ, ὑπὲρ τῶν παίδων μάλα φοβουμένη, τὸν ὅμιλον περισκοπεῖ καὶ τῷ ἀνδρὶ ἕπεται· ἡγεῖται δὲ τῇ θυγατρὶ καὶ τῷ υἱῷ. ἡ δὲ θυγάτηρ, "ὦ μῆτερ," φησίν, "ποῖ βαίνουσι πάντες; τί οὕτω σπεύδουσιν;" ἡ δὲ Μυρρίνη ἀποκρίνεται· "πάντες σπεύδουσιν εἰς τὴν Ἀκρόπολιν, ὥσπερ ἡμεῖς, ὦ θύγατερ, βουλόμενοι τοὺς θεοὺς τῑμᾶν. καὶ ἡμεῖς γὰρ τοὺς θεοὺς τῑμᾶν βουλόμεθα πάντας, καὶ μάλιστα τὸν Δία, τῶν ἄλλων θεῶν πάντων πατέρα, καὶ τὴν Ἀθηνᾶν, τὴν θυγατέρα αὐτοῦ, καὶ τὸν Διόνῡσον· ἑορτὴν γὰρ τῷ Διονῡσῳ ποιοῦνται οἱ Ἀθηναῖοι, καὶ πάντες οἱ πολῖται τὴν ἑορτὴν θεωρεῖν βούλονται. ἰδού, οἱ πατέρες τοῖς θ' υἱοῖς καὶ ταῖς θυγατράσιν ἡγοῦνται εἰς τὴν ἑορτήν, ἐκ τῶν ἀγρῶν πορευόμενοι, ὥσπερ ἡμεῖς· πάντες δὲ οἱ παῖδες καὶ πᾶσαι αἱ κόραι τοῖς πατράσι καὶ ταῖς μητράσιν ἕπονται, ἐπεὶ πολὺς μέν ἐστιν ὁ ὅμῑλος, πολὺς δὲ ὁ θόρυβος, καὶ οὐ ῥᾴδιόν ἐστιν εἰς τὴν Ἀκρόπολιν βαδίζειν διὰ τοσούτων ἀνδρῶν καὶ γυναικῶν, πολῑτῶν τε καὶ ξένων. καὶ ὑμεῖς οὖν μὴ ἀπολείπετε ἡμᾶς ἀλλ' ἀεὶ ἕπεσθε ἅμ' ἡμῖν."

[τῇ **βακτηρίᾳ**, *his staff*   **ἐρειδόμενος**, *leaning upon*   τὸν **ὅμῑλον**, *the crowd*   **περισκοπεῖ**, *looks around at*   τῷ **υἱῷ**, *her son*   **ποῖ**, *to where?*   τὴν **Ἀθηνᾶν**, *Athena*   **κόραι**, *girls*   **ἐπεὶ**, *since*   ὁ **θόρυβος**, *the commotion*   **διὰ** + gen., *through*   **ἀπολείπετε**, *abandon!*   **ἅμ(α)** + dat., *together with*]

[2] ἐν δὲ τούτῳ ἀνήρ τις πρὸς τὸν Δικαιόπολιν διὰ τοῦ ὁμίλου τρέχει καὶ τῆς χειρὸς αὐτοῦ λαμβάνεται. "ὦ Δικαιόπολι," φησίν, "πῶς ἔχεις; τί ἐν Ἀθήναις ποιεῖς; ποῖ δὲ πορεύει καὶ πόθεν;" ὁ δὲ Δικαιόπολις πρὸς αὐτὸν ἀποκρῑνόμενος· "ἥκω, ὦ Πολέμαρχε, ἐκ τῶν ἀγρῶν εἰς τὸ ἄστυ βουλόμενος εὔχεσθαί τε τοῖς θεοῖς πᾶσι καὶ ἅμα τὴν ἑορτὴν θεωρεῖν. ἡγοῦμαι δὲ τῷ πατρὶ καὶ τῇ γυναικί, καὶ τῇ τε θυγατρὶ καὶ τῷ παιδί." ὁ δὲ Πολέμαρχος, "δεῦρο δή," φησίν, "καθιζόμενος λέγε μοι πάντα τά τε περὶ τοῦ οἴκου σου καὶ περὶ τῶν ἀγρῶν. καθίζεσθε δὲ καὶ ὑμεῖς. ἆρα

σὺ Φίλιππος εἶ; ὦ Ζεῦ, ὡς καλὸς παῖς εἶ· ὁ δὲ πατὴρ οὕτω σπανίως σοι εἰς τὸ ἄστυ ἡγεῖται ὥστε μόλις γνωρίζομαί σε."

[διὰ + gen., *through*   τοῦ ὁμίλου, *the crowd*   πῶς ἔχεις; *how are you?*   ποῖ, *to where?*   ἅμα, *at the same time*   σπανίως, *rarely*   γνωρίζομαι, *I recognize*]

[3] ἐν δὲ τούτῳ τρεῖς παῖδες ἐξ οἰκίας τινὸς ἐξέρχονται καὶ πρὸς τὸν Πολέμαρχον βοῶσιν· "ὦ πάτερ, τί οὐκ ἐρχόμεθα πρὸς τὴν ἑορτήν; ἡγοῦ ἡμῖν ἐκεῖ, ὥσπερ πάντες οἱ ἄλλοι πατέρες τοῖς ἑαυτῶν παισὶν ἡγοῦνται." ὁ δὲ Δικαιόπολις· "εἷς, δύο, τρεῖς· ὁ δὲ δὴ τέταρτος, ὦ φίλε Πολέμαρχε, ποῦ ἐστιν;"

[4] "τί λέγεις, ὦ Δικαιόπολι; ὦ Ζεῦ, ὡς σπανίως εἰς τὸ ἄστυ ἔρχει· οὐκέτι γὰρ τέτταρες, ἀλλ᾽ ἤδη πέντε μοι παῖδές εἰσιν· ὁ δὲ πέμπτος ἅμα τῇ μητρὶ ἐν τῇ οἰκίᾳ μένει. ὁ δὲ πρῶτος ἤδη μειράκιόν ἐστιν, καὶ μετὰ πάντων τῶν ἄλλων μειρακίων νῦν ἐν τῇ Ἀκροπόλει διατρίβει, τὴν ἑορτὴν θεωρεῖν βουλόμενος. πολλοὺς οὖν παῖδας ἔχω, ἀλλ᾽ οὐχ ὅσους ὁ σὸς φίλος Κτήσιππος. πόσους παῖδας νῦν ἔχει;"

[σπανίως, *rarely*   ἅμα + dat., *together with*   μειράκιόν, *a teenager*   διατρίβει, *he is spending time*   ὅσους, *as many as*   πόσους, *how many?*]

[5] ὁ δὲ Δικαιόπολις ἀποκρίνεται· "τίς εἰς ἀριθμὸν εἰπεῖν δύναται; ἕξ, ἑπτά, ὀκτώ, ἐννέα, δέκα—ἀεὶ γὰρ παῖδας ποιεῖ, ὥσπερ ταῦρός τις, ὥστε νῦν κώμη, οὐκ οἶκός ἐστιν αὐτῷ."

[εἰς ἀριθμὸν, lit., *to a number*, i.e., *exactly, precisely*   εἰπεῖν, *to say*   ταῦρός, *bull*   κώμη, *village*]

[6] ὁ δὲ Πολέμαρχος, "ἐγὼ δέ," φησίν, "μετὰ τὸν πέμπτον οὐκέτι παῖδας ἄλλους ποιεῖν βούλομαι· χαλεπὸς γάρ ἐστιν ὁ βίος, καὶ οὐ ῥᾴδιόν ἐστι σῖτον πᾶσι τοῖς υἱοῖς παρέχειν. ἔστι μοι δὲ καὶ μία θυγάτηρ."

[τοῖς υἱοῖς, *my sons*]

[7] ὁ δὲ Δικαιόπολις ἀποκρῑνόμενος, "ἐγὼ δέ," φησίν, "καὶ σὺ τὸ αὐτὸ ζυγὸν ἕλκομεν, ὦ Πολέμαρχε. ὁ γὰρ βίος πᾶσι χαλεπός ἐστιν, καὶ οὐ πολὺν σῖτον ὁ ἀγρὸς παρέχει. ἀλλὰ τίνα ἐστὶ τὰ τῶν παίδων ὀνόματα;"

[ζυγὸν, *yoke*   ἕλκομεν, *we drag*]

[8] "τῷ μὲν πρώτῳ Νῑκόβουλος ὄνομά ἐστιν, τῷ δὲ δευτέρῳ Ἱέρων, τῷ δὲ τρίτῳ Μελάνιππος, τῷ δὲ τετάρτῳ Φιλότῑμος, τῷ δὲ πέμπτῳ Διαγόρας· τῇ δὲ μιᾷ θυγατρὶ ὄνομά ἐστιν Ἥβη."

[Ἥβη, *Hebe = Youth*]

[9] "νὴ τὸν Δία, ὡς χαλεπός ἐστιν ὁ βίος, ὦ Πολέμαρχε. ἡμεῖς γὰρ πολὺν χρόνον ἀγαθὰς γυναῖκας ζητοῦμεν· οὐδεὶς γὰρ βούλεται τέκνα ποιεῖσθαι ἐκ κακῆς γυναικός. ἔπειτα δὲ τεκνοποιούμεθα. καὶ ὁ μὲν ἀνὴρ τῇ γυναικὶ σῖτον παρέχει· ἡ δὲ γυνὴ φέρει πολὺν χρόνον τὸ παιδίον ἐν ἑαυτῇ καὶ πολλάκις κινδύνους μεγάλους ὑπέχει περὶ τοῦ ἑαυτῆς βίου. ἐπεὶ δὲ τίκτει, οὐδεμία γυνὴ ἀπολείπει τὸ ἑαυτῆς

παιδίον ἀλλὰ τρέφει πολὺν χρόνον καὶ ἡμέρᾱς καὶ νυκτὸς ἀεὶ πονεῖ καὶ πόνον οὐδένα φεύγει. ἀλλὰ πολλάκις, ἐπεὶ οἱ παῖδες ἡβῶσιν καὶ μειράκια καὶ νεᾱνίαι γίγνονται, οὔτε τῷ πατρὶ οὔτε τῇ μητρὶ οὔτε ἄλλῳ οὐδενὶ πείθονται· οὐδενὸς γὰρ ὑπακούουσιν. εἰ γὰρ ὁ πατὴρ αὐτούς τι κελεύει, οὐδὲν ποιεῖν ἐθέλουσιν."

[νὴ τὸν Δία, yes, by Zeus   τέκνα, acc. pl., children   κακῆς, bad   τεκνοποιούμεθα: deduce from τέκνα and ποιέω   τὸ παιδίον, the little child   ὑπέχει,
suffers   βίου, life   τίκτει, she gives birth   ἀπολείπει, abandons   τρέφει,
nourishes   ἡβῶσιν, grow up   μειράκια, teenagers   ὑπακούουσιν + gen., they listen to, heed]

[10] "ὁ δὲ Ζεὺς ἵλεώς ἐστι καὶ ἐμοὶ καὶ σοί, ὦ Δικαιόπολι· οὐδεὶς γὰρ τῶν ἡμετέρων υἱῶν οὕτω ποιεῖ, ἀλλὰ καλοί τε καὶ ἀγαθοί εἰσι πάντες."

[ἵλεώς, propitious   υἱῶν, sons]

[11] πολὺν χρόνον οὕτω διαλέγονται ἀλλήλοις ὅ τε Δικαιόπολις καὶ ὁ Πολέμαρχος. τέλος δὲ ὁ Δικαιόπολις, "καιρός ἐστι νῦν ἡμῖν," φησίν, "πρὸς τὴν ἀγορὰν καὶ πρὸς τὴν Ἀκρόπολιν πορεύεσθαι. χαῖρε, ὦ φίλε Πολέμαρχε· εἰς αὖθις."

[ἀλλήλοις, one another   χαῖρε, farewell!]

9
Η ΠΑΝΗΓΥΡΙΣ (α)

Exercise 9α

Complete the following sentences with a participle of the verb supplied; make it agree with the underlined phrase or complete the meaning of the underlined verb:

____ 1.   ἡ γυνή τὴν θυγατέρα _____ οἴκαδε τρέχει. (φιλέω)

____ 2.   τοῖς παισὶ τοῖς _____ ἕπονται. (τρέχω)

____ 3.   οἱ πολῖται οἱ τὴν πόλιν _____ τῑμῶσιν αὐτήν. (φιλέω)

____ 4.   ὁ δεσπότης ἀκούει τῶν δούλων τῶν _____. (πονέω)

____ 5.   τῷ ποιητῇ τῷ τὸν βασιλέᾱ _____ σῖτον παρέχουσιν. (τῑμάω)

____ 6.   οἱ πατέρες τὰς θυγατέρας _____ καλοῦσιν. (ὁράω)

____ 7.   ὁ παῖς ὁ τὴν παρθένον _____ οὐ σώφρων ἐστίν. (καλέω)

____ 8.   ἡ παρθένος τοῦ πατρὸς _____ οἴκαδε ἔρχεται. (ἀκούω)

____ 9.   ὁ δοῦλος ἐν τῷ ἀγρῷ _____ οὐ πονεῖ. (καθεύδω)

____ 10. αἱ θυγατέρες οὐ παύονται τοὺς πατέρας _____. (τῑμάω)

____ 11. τὸν αὐτουργὸν τὸν πρὸς τὸν ἀγρὸν _____ καλοῦμεν. (σπεύδω)

____ 12. ὁ νεᾱνίᾱς πολὺν οἶνον _____ κάμνει. (πίνω)

____ 13. τοὺς πολίτᾱς τοὺς τὸν σῖτον _____ ὁρῶ. (ἐσθίω)

____ 14. ἔχω τὸν ἵππον τὸν τοῦ ξένου τοῦ _____. (καθεύδω)

____ 15. τῷ θεῷ τῷ τὴν εὐχὴν (*the prayer*) _____ τῑμὴν (*honor*) παρέχουσιν. (ἀκούω)

____ 16. οἱ δοῦλοι οὐ παύονται _____. (καθεύδω)

____ 17. ἀκούομεν τῶν γυναικῶν τῶν _____. (βοάω)

____ 18. οἱ ἄνδρες ἀνδρεῖοι _____ οὐ φοβοῦνται. (εἰμί)

____ 19. ἡ γυνὴ _____ τὸν ἄνδρα καλεῖ. (βοάω)

____ 20. τὸν ἄνδρα τὸν _____ ὁρῶμεν. (πονέω)

____ 21. οὐχ ὁρῶσι <u>τὸν ἄνδρα</u> τὸν θεὸν _____. (τῑμάω).

____ 22. <u>ὁ πολίτης ὁ</u> τὴν πόλιν _____ ἀγαθός ἐστιν. (τῑμάω)

Exercise 9β

In the blanks to the left of the items in the exercise above, label each use of the participle with the letter next to the correct descriptor below:

A. Attributive
C. Circumstantial
S. Supplementary

Exercise 9γ

Give an English equivalent of:

1. ἐσθίω   _____   4. κάλλιστος   _____

2. διά   _____   5. ἡ ἀριστερά   _____

3. ἐπανέρχομαι   _____   6. τὸ ἱερόν   _____

Exercise 9δ

Give the Greek equivalent of:

1. come on!   _____   5. right hand   _____

2. I am sick   _____   6. upon   _____

3. I drink   _____   7. danger   _____

4. goddess   _____   8. Nike   _____

(β)

Exercise 9ε

Complete the following phrases with the correct form of the word supplied:

1. οἱ _____ (βασιλεύς)
2. τῇ _____ (πόλις)
3. τὰς _____ (ναῦς)
4. τοῦ _____ (ἄστυ)
5. τοῖς _____ (βοῦς)
6. τὴν _____ (πόλις)
7. ὁ _____ (βασιλεύς)
8. τὸν _____ (γέρων)
9. τῶν _____ (ἄστυ)
10. τῆς _____ (ναῦς)
11. τὸν _____ (βοῦς)
12. τοῖς _____ (γέρων)
13. ἡ _____ (πόλις)
14. τοῦ _____ (βοῦς)
15. τῷ_____ (γέρων)
16. τὰ _____ (ἄστυ)
17. τοὺς _____ (βασιλεύς)
18. ταῖς _____ (πόλις)
19. τῶν _____ (βοῦς)
20. αἱ _____ (ναῦς)
21. τὸ _____ (ἄστυ)
22. ταῖς _____ (ναῦς)
23. τῶν _____ (γέρων)
24. τῷ _____ (βασιλεύς)

Exercise 9ζ

Translate the following Greek sentences into English:

____ 1. τὸ τοῦ ξένου ὄνομά ἐστιν Ἄδμητος.

_____

____ 2. ἀπὸ τοῦ ἀγροῦ ἥκομεν.

_____

____ 3. τὸ ἔργον διαπρᾱξομεν (*we will finish*) δυοῖν ἡμερῶν.

_____

____ 4. ἀκούομεν τοῦ μεγίστου ποιητοῦ.

_____

____ 5. ὁ νεᾱνίᾱς τῆς παρθένου ἐρᾷ.

_____

____ 6.   ἄριστός ἐστι τῶν ποιητῶν.

_____

____ 7.   ὑπὲρ τῆς πόλεως μαχόμεθα.

_____

____ 8.   λαμβάνομαι τοῦ μεγάλου λίθου.

_____

____ 9.   τοὺς τοῦ ἀγγέλου λόγους (*words*) ἀκούομεν.

_____

____ 10. πολλοὶ τῶν αὐτουργῶν ἄπεισιν.

_____

Exercise 9η

In the blanks to the left of the items in the exercise above, label each use of the genitive case with the letter next to the correct descriptor below:

A. Possessive   D. With certain verbs
B. Partitive   E. Time within which
C. With certain prepositions

Exercise 9θ

Translate the underlined phrases:

1.   <u>οἱ ἐν τῇ ἀγορᾷ</u> πολὺν χρόνον μένουσιν.   _____

2.   <u>οἱ μὲν</u> πονοῦσιν, <u>οἱ δὲ</u> καθεύδουσιν.   _____

3.   <u>αἱ φίλαι</u> ἀεὶ διαλέγονται.   _____

4.   ἡ γυνὴ <u>τὸν ἐν τῷ ἀγρῷ ἐργαζόμενον</u> καλεῖ.   _____

5.   <u>οἱ μένοντες</u> τὴν ἅμαξαν ἀκούουσιν.   _____

6.   <u>ἡ τοὺς χοροὺς θεωμένη</u> χαίρει.   _____

7.   <u>ὁ ἐν τῇ ὁδῷ</u> πρὸς τὸν οἶκον βαδίζει.   _____

8.   <u>αἱ πρὸς τὴν κρήνην τρέχουσαι</u> τὰς ὑδρίας ἔχουσιν. _____

9.   <u>οἱ πολέμιοι</u> τῷ ἄστει προσχωροῦσιν.   _____

10. ὁ ἄριστος <u>τὸ αἰσχρὸν</u> οὐ φιλεῖ.   _____

11. <u>τοὺς πάλαι</u> ὁ ποιητὴς ᾄδει (*sings of*).   _____

12. <u>τὰ εἴσω</u> ὁρᾶν βουλόμεθα.   _____

13. οἱ σοφοὶ (*the wise*) ἀεὶ ζητοῦσι <u>τὸ ἀληθές</u>.   _____

14. <u>ἡ μὲν</u> τὸν νεᾱνίᾱν φιλεῖ, <u>ἡ δὲ</u> οὔ.   _____

Exercise 9ι

Give an English equivalent of:

1. αὐξάνω   5. ὁ ἱερεύς

2. γέρων   6. σῑγάω

3. τὸ ἱερεῖον   7. ἡ πομπή

4. ἵλεως   8. μέσος

Exercise 9κ

Give the Greek equivalent of:

1. I burn   6. old man

2. ready   7. the people

3. I enjoy   8. best

4. herald   9. heaven

5. sky   10. The
                                 Thunderer

Exercise 9λ

Translate into English on a separate sheet of paper:

ΤΟ ΤΗΣ ΜΕΛΙΤΤΗΣ ΟΝΑΡ

[1] σῑγὴ πολλὴ νῦν πρὸς ταῖς πύλαις ἐστίν. ὁ δὲ Δικαιόπολις καὶ οἱ ἄλλοι χαμαὶ καθεύδουσιν· οὐ πολλοὶ δὲ ἔτι ἐν τῷ ἄστει κωμάζουσι μεθύοντες καὶ βοῶντες. τῇ δὲ Μελίττῃ ἡσυχάζειν οὐ δυνατόν ἐστιν. πολλὰ γὰρ καὶ δεινὰ ἐν τοῖς ὕπνοις ὁρῶσα μάλα φοβεῖται· δοκεῖ γὰρ ἑαυτῇ Χρῡσου εἶναι θυγάτηρ, τοῦ ἱερέως κώμης τινὸς πρὸς τῇ Τροίᾳ. πολλάκις γὰρ ὁ πάππος περὶ τοῦ τε Χρῡσου λέγει καὶ περὶ τῆς Τροίας. ἐν δὲ τῷ ὕπνῳ ἡ Μέλιττα πολλοὺς βασιλέας τῶν Ἑλλήνων ὁρᾷ διαλεγομένους ἀλλήλοις πρὸς πυρὶ καιομένῳ· ἐν δὲ τοῖς βασιλεῦσιν ὁ Ἀγαμέμνων ἐστίν, ἀνὴρ ἰσχῡρὸς μέν, χαλεπὸς δὲ καὶ μάλα δεινός. οἱ δὲ ἄλλοι βασιλῆς πάντες αὐτὸν φοβοῦνται οὕτω χαλεπὸν ὄντα· ὁ γὰρ Ἀγαμέμνων μέγιστός ἐστι τῶν βασιλέων, καὶ οἱ ἄλλοι πάντες αὐτὸν τῑμῶσιν. ἡ δὲ τοῦ Χρῡσου θυγάτηρ νῦν δούλη ἐστὶ τοῦ Ἀγαμέμνονος, τοῦ μεγίστου βασιλέως· ὁ δὲ πατὴρ αὐτῆς, ἱερεὺς ὢν τοῦ Ἀπόλλωνος, τῇ θυγατρὶ βοηθῶν, σῴζειν αὐτὴν βούλεται. οἱ δὲ τῶν Ἑλλήνων βασιλῆς τὸν ἱερέᾱ δέχονται καὶ αὐτοῦ λέγοντος ἀκούουσιν. ὁ δὲ ἱερεὺς τοῖς βασιλεῦσι πᾶσιν, μάλιστα δὲ τῷ Ἀγαμέμνονι, λέγει τάδε· "ὦ βασιλῆς τῶν Ἑλλήνων, ἐγὼ μὲν ἱερεὺς τοῦ Ἀπόλλωνός εἰμι. ἐὰν οὖν τὴν θυγατέρα μου ἀπολύῃτε, οἱ θεοὶ οἱ ἐν Ὀλύμπῳ τὰς οἰκίας ἔχοντες καὶ μάλιστα ὁ Ἀπόλλων

μέλλουσι βοηθεῖν ὑμῖν τὴν Τροίᾱν αἱρεῖν βουλομένοις καὶ σῴζειν ὑμᾶς εἰς τὴν
πατρίδα. ἐγὼ δὲ ὑμῖν χρῡσὸν πολὺν φέρω καὶ παρέχω· δέχεσθε οὖν αὐτὸν καὶ
λύετέ μοι τὴν φίλην θυγατέρα."

[ΤΟ . . . ΟΝΑΡ, *The Dream* σῑγὴ, *silence* χαμαὶ, *on the ground* κωμάζουσι,
are reveling μεθύοντες, *being drunk* ἡσυχάζειν, *to rest* τοῖς ὕπνοις, *her
sleep/dreams* δοκεῖ . . . ἑαυτῇ . . . εἶναι θυγάτηρ, *she seems to herself to be the
daughter* Χρῡσου, *of Chryses* κώμης, *village* τῶν Ἑλλήνων, *of the Greeks*
ἀλλήλοις, *one another* Ἀπόλλωνος, *of Apollo* τάδε, *these things* ἐὰν . . .
ἀπολύητε, *if you set free, release* Ὀλύμπῳ, *Mount Olympus* τὴν πατρίδα, *your
fatherland* χρῡσὸν, *gold*]

[2] πάντες μὲν οὖν οἱ ἄλλοι βασιλῆς τὸν ἱερέᾱ τῑμᾶν ἐθέλουσι καὶ βούλονται τῷ
ἱερεῖ πειθόμενοι τόν τε χρῡσὸν δέχεσθαι καὶ τὴν κόρην ἀπολύειν. ὁ δὲ Ἀγαμέμνων,
ὀργίλως ἔχων, τὸν γέροντα ἱερέᾱ κελεύει ἀποχωρεῖν καὶ αὖθις μὴ ἐπανιέναι.
λέγει δὲ τῷ ἱερεῖ τάδε· "ἐγὼ οὐκ ἔχω ἐν νῷ τὴν θυγατέρα σου λύειν· νῦν γὰρ
δούλη μού ἐστιν, καὶ ἐν Ἄργει μέλλει γηράσκειν ἐν τῇ ἐμῇ οἰκίᾳ μετὰ τῶν ἄλλων
δουλῶν. ἄπιθι οὖν, εἰ σῶος οἴκαδε ἐπανιέναι βούλει."

[χρῡσὸν, *gold* τὴν κόρην, *the girl* ἀπολύειν, *to set free, release* ὀργίλως ἔχων,
being angry ἀποχωρεῖν, *to go away* τάδε, *these things* Ἄργει, *Argos*
γηράσκειν, *to grow old* ἄπιθι: deduce from ἀπο- + ἴθι εἰ, *if* σῶος, *safe(ly)*]

[3] ὁ μὲν οὖν γέρων ἱερεὺς φοβεῖται καὶ ἀπέρχεται σῑγῇ, ἡ δὲ θυγάτηρ αὐτοῦ τὸν
πατέρα ἀπιόντα ὁρῶσα στενάζει καὶ δακρύει. οἱ μὲν ἄλλοι βασιλῆς οἰκτίρουσι τὸν
ἱερέᾱ, ἡ δὲ θυγάτηρ στενάζουσα λέγει· "ὦ πάτερ, ὦ ἱερεῦ τοῦ Ἀπόλλωνος τοῦ
μεγάλου, μὴ κατάλειπέ με ἐνταῦθα μετὰ τῶν ξένων δούλην οὖσαν· σῷζέ με, ὦ
πάτερ."

[σῑγῇ, adv., *in silence* ἀπιόντα, *going away* δακρύει, *cries* οἰκτίρουσι, *pity*
κατάλειπέ, *desert!*]

[4] "σῷζέ με, σῷζέ με," στενάζουσα δ' ἡ Μέλιττα βοᾷ καὶ ἐγείρεται. ἡ δὲ
Μυρρίνη, τῇ τῆς θυγατρὸς βοῇ ἐγειρομένη, "τί πάσχεις," φησίν, "ὦ θύγατερ; οὐδεὶς
κίνδῡνός ἐστι νῦν· ἡσυχάζουσα δὲ κάθευδε παρ' ἐμοί· δι' ὀλίγου γὰρ ὁ ἥλιος μέλλει
ἀνατέλλειν, ἡμεῖς δὲ μέλλομεν εἰς τὸ θέᾱτρον βαίνειν. ἆρα οὐ βούλει θεωρεῖν τούς
τε χοροὺς καὶ τοὺς ἀγῶνας; μὴ δάκρῡε οὖν ἀλλ' ἡσύχαζε παρ' ἐμοί."

[βοῇ, *shout* ἐγειρομένη, *awakened* ἡσυχάζουσα, *resting* παρ(ὰ) + dat., *beside*
ἀνατέλλειν, *to rise* τὸ θέᾱτρον, *the theater* τοὺς ἀγῶνας, *the contests*
δάκρῡε, *cry!*]

VOCABULARY
CHAPTERS 6–9

VERBS

-ω Verbs

ἀναβαίνω	*I go up, get up;* + ἐπί + acc., *I climb, go up onto*
ἀποκτείνω	*I kill*
αὐξάνω	*I increase*
βάλλω	*I throw; I put; I pelt; I hit, strike*
βασιλεύω	*I rule*
ἐγείρω	*active, transitive, I wake* X *up; middle, intransitive, I wake up*
ἐκφεύγω	*I flee out, escape*
ἐπαίρω	*I lift, raise*
ἐσθίω	*I eat*
εὑρίσκω	*I find*
καθίζω	*active, transitive, I make* X *sit down; I set; I place; active, intransitive, I sit; middle, intransitive, I seat myself, sit down*
καίω or κάω	*active, transitive, I kindle, burn; middle, intransitive, I burn, am on fire*
κάμνω	*I am sick; I am tired*
κελεύω	+ acc. and infin., *I order, tell (someone to do something)*
μέλλω	+ infin., *I am about (to); I am destined (to); I intend* (to)
παρασκευάζω	*I prepare*
παρέχω	*I hand over; I supply, provide*

παύω	*active, transitive, I stop* X; *middle, intransitive, I stop doing* X; + gen., *I cease from*
παῦε	*stop!*
πείθω	*I persuade*
πέμπω	*I send*
πίνω	*I drink*
σῴζω	*I save*
τέρπω	*I delight, gladden, cheer* X

Deponent or Middle -ω Verbs

ἀποκρίνομαι	*I answer*
βούλομαι	+ infin., *I want; I wish*
γίγνομαι	*I become*
γίγνεται	*he / she / it becomes; it happens*
δέχομαι	*I receive*
διαλέγομαι	+ dat., *I talk to, converse with*
ἕπομαι	+ dat., *I follow*
ἐργάζομαι	*I work; I accomplish*
ἔρχομαι	*I come; I go*
ἀπέρχομαι	*I go away*
ἐξέρχομαι	+ ἐκ + gen., *I come out of; I go out of*
ἐπανέρχομαι	*I come back, return;* + εἰς or πρός + acc., *I return to*
εὔχομαι	*I pray;* + dat., *I pray to;* + acc. and infin., *I pray (that)*
μάχομαι	*I fight*
πείθομαι	+ dat., *I obey*
πορεύομαι	*I go; I walk; I march; I journey*
τέρπομαι	*I enjoy myself;* + dat., *I enjoy* X; + participle, *I enjoy doing* X

-άω Contract Verbs

ὁρμάω	active, transitive, *I set X in motion;* active, intransitive, *I start; I rush;* middle, intransitive, *I set myself in motion; I start; I rush; I hasten*
σῑγάω	*I am silent*

Deponent -άω Contract Verbs

θεάομαι	*I see, watch, look at*

-έω Contract Verbs

αἱρέω	*I take*
βοηθέω	*I come to the rescue; + dat., I come to X's aid; I come to rescue / aid X*
πλέω	*I sail*
προχωρέω	*I go forward; I come forward, advance*
φοβέω	*I put X to flight; I terrify X*

Deponent or Middle -έω Contract Verbs

ἀφικνέομαι	*I arrive; + εἰς + acc., I arrive at*
ἡγέομαι	*+ dat., I lead*
φοβέομαι	intransitive, *I am frightened, am afraid;* transitive, *I fear, am afraid of* (something or someone)

Imperatives and Infinitives Listed Separately

ἄγε; pl., ἄγετε	*come on!*
ἰέναι	*to go*

-μι Verbs

φᾱσί(ν)	*they say*

NOUNS

1st Declension

ἀγορ ά, -ᾶς, ἡ	*agora, city center, market place*
ἀριστερά, -ᾶς, ἡ	*left hand*
δεξιά, -ᾶς, ἡ	*right hand*
ἑσπέρᾱ, -ᾱς, ἡ	*evening*
ἡμέρᾱ, -ᾱς, ἡ	*day*
θάλαττα, -ης, ἡ	*sea*
θύρᾱ, -ᾱς, ἡ	*door*
νεᾱνίᾱς, -ου, ὁ	*young man*
ποιητής, οῦ, ὁ	*poet*
πολίτης, -ου, ὁ	*citizen*
πομπή, -ῆς, ἡ	*procession*
πύλαι, -ῶν, αἱ	pl., *double gates*

2nd Declension

βωμός, -οῦ, ὁ	*altar*
δῆμος, -ου, ὁ	*the people*
ἔργον, -ου, τό	*work; deed*
ἑταῖρος, -ου, ὁ	*comrade, companion*
θεός, -οῦ, ἡ	*goddess*
θεός, οῦ, ὁ	*god*
ἱερεῖον, -ου, τό	*sacrificial victim*
ἱερόν, -οῦ, τό	*temple*
κίνδῡνος, -ου, ὁ	*danger*
νῆσος, -ου, ἡ	*island*
ξένος, -ου, ὁ	*foreigner; stranger*
οἶνος, -ου, ὁ	*wine*
οὐρανός, -οῦ, ὁ	*sky, heaven*
ὀφθαλμός, -οῦ, ὁ	*eye*
πάππας, -ου, ὁ	*papa*
παρθένος, -ου, ἡ	*maiden; girl*

3rd Declension

αἴξ, αἰγός, ὁ or ἡ	*goat*
ἄστυ, ἄστεως, τό	*city*
βασιλεύς, βασιλέως, ὁ	*king*
γέρων, γέροντος, ὁ	*old man*
ἱερεύς, ἱερέως, ὁ	*priest*
κῆρυξ, κήρῡκος, ὁ	*herald*
ναῦς, νεώς, ἡ	*ship*
νύξ, νυκτός, ἡ	*night*
ὄνομα, ὀνόματος, τό	*name*
πόλις, πόλεως, ἡ	*city*
πῦρ, πυρός, τό	*fire*
χειμών, χειμῶνος, ὁ	*storm; winter*
χείρ, χειρός, ἡ	*hand*

PRONOUNS

ἐμαυτοῦ,
σεαυτοῦ,
ἑαυτοῦ — *of myself, of yourself, of him-, her-, itself*

οὐδείς, οὐδεμία,
οὐδέν — *no one; nothing*

τις, τινός — *someone; something; anyone; anything*

τίς; τίνος; — *who?*

ADJECTIVES

1st/2nd Declension

ἄριστος, -η, -ον — *best; very good; noble*

δεινός, -ή, -όν — *terrible*

δύο — *two*

ἕτοιμος, -η, -ον — *ready*

κάλλιστος, -η, -ον — *most beautiful; very beautiful*

μέγιστος, -η, -ον — *very big, very large; very great; biggest, largest; greatest*

μέσος, -η, -ον — *middle (of)*

Attic Declension

ἵλεως, -ω — *propitious*

3rd Declension

γέρων, γέροντος — *old*

σώφρων, σῶφρον — *of sound mind; prudent; self-controlled*

τις, τινός — *a certain; some; a, an*

τίς; τίνος; — *which ... ? what ... ?*

3rd and 1st Declension

εἷς, μία, ἕν — *one*

οὐδείς, οὐδεμία, οὐδέν — *no*

πᾶς, πᾶσα, πᾶν — *all; every; whole*

PREPOSITIONS

διά — + gen., *through*

ἐπί — + dat., *upon, on;* + acc., *at; against; onto, upon*

μετά — + gen., *with;* + acc., *after*

περί — + gen., *about, concerning;* + acc., *around*

ὑπέρ — + gen., *on behalf of, for*

ADVERBS

ἐκεῖ — *there*

ἐκεῖσε — *to that place, thither*

ἐνθάδε — *here; hither; there; thither*

εὖ — *well*

οἴκοι — *at home*

οὐδαμῶς — *in no way, no*

πόθεν; — *from where? whence?*

πολλάκις — *many times, often*

πῶς; — *how?*

τέλος — *in the end, finally*

ὡς — in exclamations, *how ...!*

ὥσπερ — *just as*

CONJUNCTION

ὅμως — *nevertheless*

PARTICLES

γε — *at least; indeed*

δή — *indeed, in fact*

EXPRESSIONS

ἐν ... τούτῳ — *meanwhile*

ἐν ᾧ — *while*

ἐπαίρω ἐμαυτόν — *I get up*

εὖ γε — *good! well done!*

τῇ ὑστεραίᾳ — *on the next day*

PROPER NAMES

Ἀγαμέμνων, Ἀγαμέμνονος, ὁ — *Agamemnon*

Ἀθηνᾶ, -ᾶς, ἡ — *Athena (daughter of Zeus)*

Ἀθῆναι, -ῶν, αἱ — *Athens*

Αἰγεύς, Αἰγέως, ὁ — *Aegeus (king of Athens)*

Ἀκρόπολις,
  Ἀκροπό-
  λεως, ἡ   *the Acropolis* (the
                    citadel of Athens)
Ἀριάδνη, -ης, ἡ   *Ariadne* (daughter of
                    King Minos)
Ἀχαιοί, -ῶν, οἱ   *Achaeans; Greeks*
Βρόμιος, -ου, ὁ   *the Thunderer* (a
                    name of Dionysus)
Διόνῡσος, -ου, ὁ   *Dionysus*
Ζεύς, Διός, ὁ   *Zeus* (king of the
                    gods)
Θησεύς, Θη-
  σέως, ὁ   *Theseus* (son of King
                    Aegeus)
Κνωσός, -οῦ, ἡ   *Knossos*
Κρήτη, -ης, ἡ   *Crete*
Κύκλωψ, Κύ-
  κλωπος, ὁ   *Cyclops* (one-eyed
                    monster)

Μίνως, Μίνω, ὁ   *Minos* (king of Crete)
Μῑνώταυρος,
  -ου, ὁ   *Minotaur*
Νίκη, -ης, ἡ   *Nike* (the goddess of
                    victory)
Ὀδυσσεύς,
  Ὀδυσσέως, ὁ   *Odysseus*
Παρθένος, -ου, ἡ   *the Maiden* (= the
                    goddess Athena)
Παρθενών,
  Παρθε-
  νῶνος, ὁ   *the Parthenon* (the
                    temple of Athena
                    on the Acropolis in
                    Athens)
Τροίᾱ, -ᾱς, ἡ   *Troy*
ὁ Φειδίᾱς,
  -ου, ὁ   *Pheidias* (the great
                    Athenian sculptor)

10
Η ΣΥΜΦΟΡΑ (α)

Exercise 10α

Translate the English phrases with the correct form of the Greek verb supplied:

Active

1. λύω: they will loosen _____
2. λύω: we will loosen _____
3. ἐθέλω: you (pl.) will be willing _____

Middle

4. λύομαι: he/she will ransom _____
5. γίγνομαι: (αἱ γυναῖκες) being about to become _____

Consonant Stems

6. πέμπω: I will send _____
7. δέχομαι: you (sing.) will receive _____ or
   _____
8. λέγω: they will say _____
9. πείθω: he/she will persuade _____
10. παρασκευάζω: you (sing.) will prepare _____
11. γράφω: (ὁ ἀνὴρ) being about to write _____
12. γράφω: he/she will write _____
13. φυλάττω: he/she will guard _____
14. ἔχω: you (sing.) will have _____
15. ἔχω: you (sing.) will get _____
16. σπεύδω: they will hurry _____

Verbs in -ίζω

17. κομίζω: he/she will bring _____
18. κομίζω: they will bring _____
19. κομίζομαι: I will acquire _____

Contract Verbs

20. ἡγέομαι: you (pl.) will lead _____

21. τῑμάω: they will honor   _____

22. φιλέω: I will love   _____

23. νῑκάω: to be about to conquer   _____

Verbs with Deponent Futures

24. ὁράω: I will see   _____

25. βαίνω: to be about to walk   _____

26. βαίνω: we will walk   _____

27. ἀκούω: you (pl.) will hear   _____

28. πλέω: I will sail   _____

29. γιγνώσκω: you (pl.) will learn   _____

30. πίνω: we will drink   _____

31. τρέχω: we will run   _____

32. βαδίζω: they will go   _____

33. πίπτω: he/she will fall   _____

34. θαυμάζω: you (sing.) will admire _____ or

                                       _____

35. βλέπω: we will look   _____

36. πίπτω: (τὸ ἱερεῖον) being about to fall   _____

37. φεύγω: I will flee   _____

38. πάσχω: they will suffer   _____

39. διώκω: we will pursue   _____

The Verb εἰμί

40. εἰμί: he/she/it will be   _____

41. εἰμί: you (pl.) will be   _____

42. εἰμί: to be about to be   _____

43. πάρειμι: we will be present   _____

Exercise 10β

Give an English equivalent of:

1. νῑκάω   _____   5. φεῦ   _____

2. γίγνομαι   _____   6. καλῶς   _____

3. εὑρίσκω   _____   7. ἀφικνέομαι   _____

4. θεάομαι   _____   8. ἀφικνοῦμαι
                                         εἰς τὸ θέᾱτρον _____

Exercise 10γ

Give the future of:

1. θεάομαι _____
2. νῑκάω _____
3. ἀφικνέομαι _____

4. γίγνομαι _____
5. εὑρίσκω _____

Exercise 10δ

Translate into English on a separate sheet of paper:

ΟΙ ΑΓΑΘΟΙ ΠΟΛΙΤΑΙ

[1] ἔστι μὲν πολὺς θόρυβος ἐν τῷ ἄστει. οὐ γὰρ παύονται πολλοὶ ἄνθρωποι, ἄνδρες καὶ γυναῖκες, παῖδες, πολῖταί τε καὶ ξένοι, πορευόμενοι εἰς ἄστυ ἔκ τε τῶν ἀγρῶν καὶ ἐκ τοῦ Πειραιῶς. πολλοὶ δὲ γεωργοὶ ἤδη ἐξ ἄστεως ἀποχωροῦσιν, εἰς τοὺς κλήρους ἐπανιέναι βουλόμενοι. ὅτε γὰρ αἱ ἑορταὶ ἐν ταῖς Ἀθήναις καὶ ἐν ἄλλοις ἄστεσι γίγνονται, ἀεὶ οἱ ἄγροικοι σπεύδουσιν εἰς τὰ ἄστη ὡς τοὺς χοροὺς θεᾱσόμενοι καὶ κωμάσοντες. μετ' οὐ πολὺν δὲ χρόνον πόθος αὐτοὺς λαμβάνει τοῦ ἀγροίκου βίου, καὶ ἐκ τῶν ἄστεων ἐπανέρχονται εἰς τοὺς ἀγρούς. οὐδεὶς γὰρ ἄγροικος τὰ ἄστη φιλεῖ. ἡσυχίᾱν γὰρ οἱ ἐν τοῖς ἀγροῖς οἰκοῦντες μάλα φιλοῦσιν, ἐν δὲ τοῖς ἄστεσι πολὺς θόρυβός ἐστιν. "ὦ πόλι, πόλι," στενάζει ὁ Δικαιόπολις, "ἀποβλέπω εἰς τοὺς ἀγρούς, ἡσυχίᾱς ἐρῶν, μῑσῶν μὲν ἄστυ, τὸν δ' ἐμὸν κλῆρον ποθῶν. πάντες γὰρ οἱ ἐν τῷ ἄστει οἰκοῦντες φαίνονταί μοι κακοί. εἰ γὰρ θεός τις μέλλει πόλιν τινὰ εὐεργετήσειν, ἄνδρας ἀγαθοὺς ἐν αὐτῇ ποιεῖ· εἰ δὲ μέλλει κακὰ πείσεσθαι πόλις, ἐξαιρεῖ τοὺς ἄνδρας τοὺς ἀγαθοὺς ἐκ ταύτης τῆς πόλεως ὁ θεός. ἐν δὲ τῇ πόλει τῶν Ἀθηνῶν νῦν ποῦ εἰσιν οἱ ἀγαθοί; φεῦ, φεῦ τῆς πόλεως."

[θόρυβος, *commotion*   τοῦ Πειραιῶς, *the Piraeus* (*the port of Athens*)   γεωργοὶ, *farmers*   ἀποχωροῦσιν, *go away*   τοὺς κλήρους, *their farms*   ὅτε, *when*   οἱ ἄγροικοι, *the countrymen*   ὡς . . . θεᾱσόμενοι καὶ κωμάσοντες, *to watch . . . and to revel*   πόθος + gen., *longing for*   τοῦ ἀγροίκου βίου, *the country life*   ἡσυχίᾱν, *peace and quiet*   ἐρῶν + gen., *loving*   μῑσῶν, *hating*   κλῆρον, *farm*   ποθῶν, *longing for*   φαίνονταί, *appear*   κακοί, *bad, evil*   εἰ, *if*   εὐεργετήσειν, *to benefit*   ἐξαιρεῖ, *takes out*   ταύτης τῆς, *this*]

[2] ὁ δὲ πάππος, "σὺν θεοῖς, ὦ φίλον τέκνον," φησίν, "οἱ ἀγαθοὶ γενήσονται τῇ πόλει."

[σὺν θεοῖς, *by the will of the gods*   τέκνον, *child*]

[3] ἐν δὲ τούτῳ ὁ Δικαιόπολις φίλον τινὰ διὰ τοῦ ὁμίλου μόλις προχωροῦντα ὁρᾷ, καί, "χαῖρε, ὦ φίλε Ἱερώνυμε," φησίν, "ὡς σπανίως σ' ὁρῶ."

[τοῦ ὁμίλου, *the crowd*   σπανίως, *rarely*]

[4] ὁ δὲ Ἱερώνυμος, "οὐ γὰρ δυνατόν μοί ἐστιν, ὦ Δικαιόπολι," φησίν, "εἰς τοὺς ἀγροὺς πορεύεσθαι. οἱ γὰρ πολῖται, εἴ τι βούλονται διαπράττειν πρὸς ἄλλᾱς πόλεις, ἀεὶ πρός με πρῶτον ἔρχονται. φαίνομαι γὰρ αὐτοῖς ἱκανὸς ἄγγελος εἶναι· ἐν δὲ ταῖς ἄλλαις πόλεσι τοὺς τῶν πολῑτῶν λόγους ἀκούω, ἔπειτα δὲ ἐκ τῶν ἄλλων πόλεων εἰς τὰς Ἀθήνᾱς ἀγγελίᾱς φέρω. πολλάκις μὲν οὖν καὶ εἰς ἄλλᾱς πόλεις πορεύομαι, ἄγγελος ὢν τῶν Ἀθηνῶν. δι᾽ ὀλίγου δὴ εἰς τὴν Λακεδαίμονα πορεύσομαι· διὰ τοῦτο μὲν οὖν οὕτω σπανίως σχολή ἐστί μοι βαίνειν εἰς τοὺς ἀγρούς."

[εἴ, *if*   τι . . . διαπράττειν πρὸς + acc., *to accomplish anything with*   φαίνομαι, *I appear*   ἱκανὸς, *sufficient, competent*   λόγους, *words*   ἀγγελίᾱς, *messages*   τὴν Λακεδαίμονα, *Lacedaemon, Sparta*   διὰ τοῦτο, *for this reason*   σπανίως, *rarely*   σχολή ἐστί μοι, *I have leisure*]

[5] ὁ δὲ Δικαιόπολις, "ἀλλ᾽ ἀγαθὸς ἀνὴρ εἶ·" φησίν, "σὺ γὰρ ἱκανὸς εἶ τὴν σεαυτοῦ πόλιν εὐεργετεῖν."

[ἱκανὸς, *sufficient, competent*   εὐεργετεῖν, *to benefit*]

[6] ὁ δὲ Ἱερώνυμος ἀποκρῑνόμενος, "καλὸς δὲ καὶ ἀγαθὸς ἀνήρ," φησίν, "βουλήσεται γιγνώσκειν πῶς οἱ ἄνθρωποι τάς τε οἰκίᾱς καὶ τὰς πόλεις καλῶς διοικήσουσιν, καὶ τοὺς ἑαυτῶν γονέᾱς τῑμήσουσιν, καὶ πολίτᾱς τε καὶ ξένους καλῶς ὑποδέξονταί τε καὶ ἀποπέμψουσιν. ἀλλ᾽ ὡς σπανίως οἱ ἀγαθοὶ ἄνδρες ἐν ταῖς πόλεσι γίγνονται νῦν, ὦ φίλε Δικαιόπολι."

[καλὸς . . . καὶ ἀγαθὸς ἀνήρ, *a good citizen*   διοικήσουσιν, *will manage*   γονέᾱς, *parents*   ὑποδέξονται, *will welcome*   σπανίως, *rarely*]

[7] οὕτω διαλέγονται ἀλλήλοις οἱ ἄνδρες ὀλίγον χρόνον περὶ τῆς τε πόλεως καὶ τῶν ἀγαθῶν πολῑτῶν. τέλος δὲ ὁ Ἱερώνυμος· "χαῖρε, ὦ φίλε. τοὺς θεοὺς εὔξομαι σοι παρασχήσειν πολλὰ καὶ ἀγαθά. ἴθι δὴ χαίρων. καιρὸς γάρ ἐστί μοι ἀπιέναι. ἴσως δὲ δι᾽ ὀλίγου σε αὖθις ὄψομαι ἢ ἐν τῷ ἄστει ἢ ἄλλοθί που."

[ἀλλήλοις, *one another*   ὀλίγον, *short (small)*   παρασχήσειν: future of παρέχω   ἴσως, *perhaps*   ἢ . . . ἢ, *either . . . or*   ἄλλοθί που, *somewhere else*]

(β)

Exercise 10ε

Translate the English phrases with the correct form of the Greek verb supplied:

1. μένω: we will stay   _____

2. αἴρω: to be about to lift   _____

3. μάχομαι: you (sing.) will fight _____ or

_____

4. ἐγείρω: he/she will wake X up _____

5. ἐγείρω: to be about to wake X up. _____

6. αἴρω: he/she will lift _____

7. ἀποκτείνω: they will kill _____

8. μάχομαι: to be about to fight. _____

9. ἀποκρίνομαι: I will answer _____

10. κάμνω: you (pl.) will be tired _____

11. ἀποκτείνω: (ὁ ξένος) being about to kill. _____

12. βάλλω: they will throw _____

13. ἐλαύνω: we will drive _____

14. βάλλω: (τὸν νεᾱνίᾱν) being about to throw _____

15. μένω: they will stay _____

16. ἀποκρίνομαι: (ἡ παρθένος) being about to answer. _____

Grammar

ἔρχομαι and εἶμι

In the present tense, only the indicative forms of the verb ἔρχομαι are generally used in Attic Greek. For the imperative, infinitive, and participle, forms of the verb εἶμι are used instead, with present meanings. Thus:

ἔρχομαι	ἴθι	ἰέναι	ἰών, ἰοῦσα, ἰόν, etc.
	ἴτε		
I come; I go	*come! go!*	*to come; to go*	*coming / going*

For the future indicative of ἔρχομαι, Attic Greek uses the verb εἶμι, *I will come; I will go.* We accordingly regard εἶμι as the second principal part of ἔρχομαι. The imperatives of εἶμι (ἴθι and ἴτε) are used with the same sense as any present imperative. The infinitive (ἰέναι) and the participles (ἰών, ἰοῦσα, ἰόν, etc.) of εἶμι are usually used with present meanings in Attic Greek, but you will find later when you study indirect statement that these forms may be used with a future sense in that construction. For the time being we use them only with a present sense.

Exercise 10ζ

Translate the English phrases with the correct form of the Greek verb supplied:

1. ἔρχομαι: he/she comes   _____

2. ἔρχομαι: you (sing.) come   _____ or

                                                   _____

3. ἔρχομαι: we go   _____

4. ἔρχομαι: to come   _____

5. ἔρχομαι: go! (sing.)   _____

6. ἔρχομαι: (ἡ παρθένος) coming   _____

7. ἔρχομαι: I will come   _____

8. ἔρχομαι: they will go   _____

9   ἔρχομαι: we will go   _____

10. ἔρχομαι: you (pl.) will come   _____

11. ἔρχομαι: you (sing.) will go   _____

12. ἔρχομαι: I will go   _____

13. ἔρχομαι: he/she will come   _____

14. εἰσέρχομαι: we will go in   _____

15. εἰσέρχομαι: go in! (sing.)   _____

16. εἰσέρχομαι: to go in   _____

17. ἐπανέρχομαι: I will return   _____

18. ἐπανέρχομαι: to return   _____

19. ἐπανέρχομαι: (ὁ δοῦλος) returning   _____

20. ἐπανέρχομαι: they are returning   _____

21. ἐξέρχομαι: he/she will go out of   _____

22. ἐξέρχομαι: to go out of   _____

23. ἐξέρχομαι: come (sing.) out of!   _____

24. ἐξέρχομαι: we are coming out of   _____

25. ἐξέρχομαι: (ἡ γυνή) coming out of   _____

26. ἀπέρχομαι: they will go away   _____

27. ἀπέρχομαι: to go away   _____

28. ἀπέρχομαι: they are going away   _____

29. ἀπέρχομαι: go away! (sing.)   _____

30. προσέρχομαι: to approach   _____

31. προσέρχομαι: approach! (pl.)   _____

32. προσέρχομαι: I will approach   _____

33. προσέρχομαι: you (pl.) are approaching   _____

34. ἔρχομαι: go! (pl.)   _____

35. ἔρχομαι: we are coming   _____

Exercise 10η

Translate the following Greek sentences into English:

1. ὁ πάππος τῷ Δικαιοπόλιδι προσέρχεται ὡς αὐτὸν πείσων ἐν τῷ ἄστει μένειν.

   _____

2. ἆρ' ἔξεστιν ἡμῖν ἐν τῷ ἄστει μένειν;

   _____

3. δεῖ ἡμᾶς ἐν τοῖς ἀγροῖς πονεῖν.

   _____

4. δεῖ ἡμᾶς οἴκαδε ἐπανιέναι ὡς ἔργα πολλὰ ἐργασόμενοι.

   _____

5. οἴκαδε ἰέναι βούλομαι ὡς ἀκουσόμενος τί γίγνεται.

   _____

Exercise 10θ

Put the number of the Greek word in column A in front of the corresponding English word in column B:

	A		B
1.	ἆρα;	____	when?
2.	πόθεν;	____	how?
3.	τίς;	____	for whom?
4.	ποῦ;	____	where to?
5.	πότε;	____	introduces a question
6.	τί;	____	whose?
7.	πῶς;	____	where from?
8.	τίνι;	____	who?
9.	ποῖ;	____	where?
10.	τίνος;	____	what?
		____	why?

Exercise 10ι

Give an English equivalent of:

1. ἀποφεύγω   _____
2. πρό   _____
3. δεῖ   _____
4. εὐθύς   _____

5. ἡ βοή   _____
6. μένω   _____
7. οἱ τεκόντες   _____
8. τύπτω   _____

Exercise 10κ

Give the Greek equivalent of:

1. I kill   _____
2. head   _____
3. I leave behind   _____
4. water   _____
5. once   _____
6. immediately   _____
7. I turn X   _____

8. it is allowed   _____
9. at some time   _____
10. I lift   _____
11. I desert   _____
12. I wait for   _____
13. I escape   _____
14. ever   _____

Exercise 10λ

Give the future of:

1. ἀποφεύγω   _____
2. τρέπω   _____
3. αἴρω   _____

4. καταλείπω   _____
5. ἀποκτείνω   _____
6. μένω   _____

Exercise 10μ

Translate into English on a separate sheet of paper:

Ο ΦΙΛΙΠΠΟΣ ΤΥΦΛΟΣ ΕΣΤΙΝ

[1] ὁ μὲν οὖν Δικαιόπολις τῷ παιδὶ προσχωρεῖ καί, "μὴ φοβοῦ, ὦ φίλε παῖ," φησίν· "ἵλιγγος γάρ τίς σε καὶ σκοτοδῑνίᾱ ἔλαβεν ὅτε κατέπεσες καὶ τὴν κεφαλὴν παρὰ τὴν γῆν προσέκρουσας. νῦν δὲ ἡσύχαζε ὀλίγον χρόνον. ἀμέλει γὰρ δι' ὀλίγου ἀναβλέψει. οὕτω γὰρ πολλάκις καὶ ἄλλοις ταῦτα πάσχουσι γίγνεται."

[ΤΥΦΛΟΣ, *Blind* ἵλιγγος, *dizziness* σκοτοδῑνίᾱ (σκότος, -ου, ὁ, *darkness* + δίνη, -ης, ἡ, *whirlpool; whirlwind; rotation*), *dizziness, vertigo* ἔλαβεν (aorist of λαμβάνω), *took, seized* ὅτε, *when* κατέπεσες (aorist of καταπῑπτω), *you fell down* παρὰ + acc., *against* προσέκρουσας (aorist of προσκρούω), *you struck* ἡσύχαζε, *rest!* ὀλίγον, *a short (small)* ἀμέλει, adv., *doubtless* ἀναβλέψει, *you will regain your sight* ταῦτα, *these things*]

[2] ὁ δὲ Φίλιππος, οὐδὲν ὁρῶν, οὐχ οἷός τ᾽ ἐστὶν ἥσυχος ἔχειν ἀλλὰ στενάζων τε καὶ δακρύων τάδε λέγει· "οἴμοι τάλας. οἱ γὰρ θεοί, κολάζειν με βουλόμενοι, ταύτην τὴν συμφορὰν ἔπεμψάν μοι καὶ τυφλὸν πάντα τὸν λοιπὸν βίον ἐποίησαν." ὁ δὲ Δικαιόπολις ἀποκρινάμενος, "μὴ ταῦτα νόμιζε, ὦ Φίλιππε," φησίν, "ἀλλὰ θάρρει. νῦν γὰρ εἶμι εἰς τὴν ἀγορὰν ὡς ζητήσων ἰατρόν τινα· ἀμέλει γὰρ ἰατρὸς οἷός τ᾽ ἔσται ὠφελεῖν σε καὶ τοὺς ὀφθαλμούς σοι ἰᾶσθαι. μένε οὖν ἐνταῦθα. δι᾽ ὀλίγου γὰρ ἐπάνειμι." "ποῖ βαίνεις, ὦ πάτερ; ἆρα ἐνταῦθα μενῶ ἄνευ σοῦ; τίς δὲ ἅμα ἐμοὶ μενεῖ; φοβοῦμαι γάρ, οὐδὲν ὁρῶν· πανταχοῦ δέ μοι σκότος εἶναι δοκεῖ." ἡ δὲ Μυρρίνη, "μηδὲν φοβοῦ, ὦ παῖ," δακρύουσά φησιν, "ἐγὼ γὰρ μετὰ σοῦ μενῶ, καὶ οὐκ ἄπειμι. ἔσται δὲ παρὰ σοὶ καὶ ὁ πάππος καὶ ἡ Μέλιττα· ἀνδρεῖος ἴσθι· ἡμῶν γὰρ οὐδεὶς καταλείψει σε. ὁ μὲν οὖν πατὴρ ἐπάνεισι μετ᾽ οὐ πολὺν χρόνον καὶ ἰατρὸν ἄξει. ἡμεῖς δέ σε φυλάξομεν ἀπὸ τῶν κινδύνων καὶ πρὸς τὴν στοὰν ἡγησόμεθά σοι, ὅπου ἡσυχάζειν ἔξεσται ὀλίγον χρόνον. λαμβάνου οὖν τῆς χειρός μου." ὁ δὲ Φίλιππος, "ὦ φίλη μῆτερ," φησίν, "κάλει τὸν πατέρα, καὶ μὴ ἔα αὐτὸν ἀπιέναι."

[οἷός τ᾽ ἐστὶν, *is able*   ἥσυχος ἔχειν, *to keep quiet*   δακρύων, *crying*   τάδε, *these things*   οἴμοι τάλας, *alas, wretched me!*   κολάζειν, *to punish*   ταύτην τὴν, *this*   συμφορὰν, *misfortune; disaster*   ἔπεμψάν (aorist of πέμπω), *sent*   τὸν λοιπὸν, *the rest of*   βίον, *life*   ἐποίησαν (aorist of ποιέω), *made*   ἀποκρινάμενος (aorist participle of ἀποκρίνομαι), *answering*   ταῦτα, *these things*   νόμιζε, *think!*   θάρρει, *cheer up!*   ἰατρόν, *doctor*   ἀμέλει, adv., *doubtless*   ὠφελεῖν, *to help*   ἰᾶσθαι, *to heal*   ἄνευ + gen., *without*   ἅμα + dat., *together with*   πανταχοῦ, *everywhere*   σκότος, *darkness*   δοκεῖ, *seems*   παρὰ + dat., *with*   στοὰν, *colonnade*   ὅπου, *where*   ἡσυχάζειν, *to rest*   ὀλίγον, *a short (small)*   ἔα, *allow! let!*]

[3] ἡ μὲν οὖν μήτηρ τῆς τοῦ ἀνδρὸς χειρὸς λαβομένη ψιθυρίζει τάδε· "τί δὲ πάσχει ὁ παῖς; τί οἱ ὀφθαλμοὶ αὐτοῦ οὐδὲν ὁρῶσι πλὴν σκότου; ἆρα ἀληθῶς δι᾽ ὀλίγου ἀναβλέψεται;" ὁ δὲ Δικαιόπολις ἀποκρινάμενος, "πολλὴν συμφορὰν πάσχει ὁ Φίλιππος, ὦ φίλη γύναι, καὶ οὐκ οἶδα τί γενήσεται. νῦν γὰρ τυφλός ἐστιν. δεῖ οὖν ἡμᾶς τοῖς θεοῖς πᾶσιν εὔχεσθαι."

[λαβομένη (aorist participle of λαμβάνομαι) + gen., *taking hold of*   ψιθυρίζει, *whispers*   τάδε, *these things*   πλὴν + gen., *except*   σκότου, *darkness*   ἀληθῶς, *truly*   ἀναβλέψεται, *will he regain his sight?*   ἀποκρινάμενος (aorist participle of ἀποκρίνομαι), *answering*   συμφορὰν, *misfortune; disaster*   οἶδα, *I know*]

11
Ο ΙΑΤΡΟΣ (α)

Grammar

Some Common Verbs with Thematic 2nd Aorists

Present	Aorist Stem	Aorist Indicative
ἄγω	ἀγαγ-	ἤγαγον
ἀποθνῄσκω	θαν-	ἀπ-έθανον
ἀφ-ικνέομαι	ἱκ-	ἀφῑκόμην
βάλλω	βαλ-	ἔβαλον
γίγνομαι	γεν-	ἐγενόμην
εὑρίσκω	εὑρ-	ηὗρον or εὗρον
ἔχω	σχ-	ἔσχον
κάμνω	καμ-	ἔκαμον
λαμβάνω	λαβ-	ἔλαβον
λείπω	λιπ-	ἔλιπον
μανθάνω	μαθ-	ἔμαθον
πάσχω	παθ-	ἔπαθον
πῑνω	πι-	ἔπιον
πῑπτω	irregular	ἔπεσον
φεύγω	φυγ-	ἔφυγον

Exercise 11α

Translate the following English phrases and words with the correct aorist form of the Greek verb supplied:

1. ἀφικνέομαι: he/she arrived _____

2. ἔχω: they had _____

3. ἀποθνῄσκω: they died _____

4. ἀποθνῄσκω: to die _____

5. μανθάνω: learn! (pl.) _____

6. βάλλω: we threw _____

7. βάλλω: throw! (sing.) _____

8. λαμβάνω: to take _____

9. λείπω: to leave _____

10. γίγνομαι: I became _____

11. πῑπτω: I fell _____

12. πάσχω: you (pl.) suffered _____
13. φεύγω: flee! (pl.) _____
14. καταλείπω: to leave behind _____
15. λαμβάνω: you (pl.) took _____
16. φεύγω: he/she fled _____
17. γίγνομαι: to become _____
18. πίνω: we drank _____
19. πάσχω: he/she suffered _____
20. ἄγω: lead! (sing.) _____
21. ἄγω: you (sing.) led _____
22. εὑρίσκω: he/she found _____ or
    _____

23. ἀφικνέομαι: (ὁ δῆμος) having arrived _____
24. εὑρίσκω: (ὁ ἄνθρωπος) upon finding _____
25. μανθάνω: (ἡ γυνή) having learned _____
26. ἀφικνέομαι: you (sing.) arrived _____
27. γίγνομαι: we became _____
28. ἀφικνέομαι: you (pl.) arrived _____
29. γίγνομαι: become! (sing.) _____
30. γίγνομαι: become! (pl.) _____

Exercise 11β

Indicate whether you would use the present or aorist tense to translate each of the following italicized verb forms into Greek by putting a P for present or A for aorist in the blank after the verb:

1. Dicaeopolis *led* ____ Philip and the rest of his family to his brother's house.

2. *Standing* ____ outside the door, Dicaeopolis finally *decided* ____ to *knock* ____.

3. When he *did* ____ so, his brother, *opening* ____ the door, *greeted* ____ Dicaeopolis.

4. "Dicaeopolis, why *are* ____ you here again?" he *asked* ____.

5. Dicaeopolis *explains* ____ what *happened* ____ to Philip and *asks* ____ his brother to allow them *to stay* ____.

6. The brother, *hearing* ____ the story, immediately *led* ____ them into the house.

7. *"Come in ____,"* he said. *"*and *stay* ____ here as long as you *wish* ____.*"*

8. The family, *entering* ____ the house, *expressed* ____ their thanks to him for his hospitality.

Exercise 11γ

Using the verb provided, form an aorist participle that agrees with each noun:

1. ἡ γυνὴ (ἔπαθε)   _____

2. τὸν ἄνθρωπον (ἔλαβε)   _____

3. τοῦ νεανίου (ἔβαλε)   _____

4. τὰς παρθένους (ἔφυγον)   _____

5. οἱ ἄνδρες (ἤγαγον)   _____

6. τῇ γυναικὶ (ἔλιπε)   _____

7. τῶν ξένων (ἀφίκοντο)   _____

8. τοῖς πολίταις (ἔσχον)   _____

9. τῆς θυγατρὸς (ἐγένετο)   _____

10. τοὺς ἀδελφοὺς (ἔπιον)   _____

11. αἱ μητέρες (ἔμαθον)   _____

12. τῷ βασιλεῖ (ἀπέθανε)   _____

13. τῶν γυναικῶν (ηὗρον)   _____

14. τὸ ἱερεῖον (ἀπέθανε)   _____

15. ὁ θεὸς (ἔμαθε)   _____

16. ταῖς θυγατράσι (ἔλιπον) _____

17. τὸν κήρυκα (ἀφίκετο)   _____

18. τῷ ἀρότρῳ (ἐγένετο)   _____

19. τοῦ βοὸς (ἔπεσε)   _____

20. τὰς γυναῖκας (ἔλαβον)   _____

Exercise 11δ

Give an English equivalent of:

1. δακρύω _____
2. ὁ ἀδελφός _____
3. τυφλός _____
4. εἰσάγω _____
5. κόπτω _____
6. λείπω _____

7. δοκεῖ _____
8. ἔφη _____
9. ὁ λόγος _____
10. πῶς ἔχεις; _____
11. αὔριον _____
12. παρὰ τὸν ἰᾱτρόν _____

Exercise 11ε

Give the Greek equivalent of:

1. I ask for _____
2. doctor _____
3. wise _____
4. I bring _____
5. I learn _____
6. I suffer _____

7. I die _____
8. I take _____
9. I am well _____
10. if _____
11. I consider _____
12. it seems _____

Exercise 11ζ

Give the future and aorist of:

1. μανθάνω _____
   _____
2. δοκεῖ _____
   _____
3. κομίζω _____
   _____
4. σκοπέω _____
   _____
5. αἰτέω _____
   _____
6. εἰσάγω _____
   _____

7. λείπω _____
   _____
8. πάσχω _____
   _____
9. δακρύω _____
   _____
10. κόπτω _____
    _____
11. ἀποθνῄσκω _____
    _____
12. λαμβάνω _____
    _____

(β)

Grammar

Some Common Verbs with Thematic 2nd Aorists from Unrelated Stems

Present	Aorist Stem	Aorist Indicative
αἱρέω	ἑλ-	εἷλον
ἔρχομαι	ἐλθ-	ἦλθον
ἐσθίω*	φαγ-	ἔφαγον
λέγω	εἰπ-	εἶπον
ὁράω	ἰδ-	εἶδον
τρέχω	δραμ-	ἔδραμον
φέρω	ἐνεγκ-	ἤνεγκον

*Not included in list in textbook

Exercise 11η

Translate the following English phrases and words with the correct aorist form of the Greek verb supplied:

1. αἱρέω: he/she took   _____

2. ὁράω: you (pl.) saw   _____

3. ἔρχομαι: they came   _____

4. αἱρέω: to take   _____

5. λέγω: you (pl.) said   _____

6. ἔρχομαι: he/she came   _____

7. τρέχω: you (sing.) ran   _____

8. λέγω: to say   _____

9. φέρω: they carried   _____

10. ὁράω: to see   _____

11. τρέχω: to run   _____

12. αἱρέω: take! (pl.)   _____

13. λέγω: I said   _____

14. ὁράω: I saw   _____

15. ὁράω: (ἡ γυνή) seeing   _____

16. αἱρέω: (ὁ ἄνθρωπος) after taking   _____

17. φέρω: to carry   _____

18. φέρω: carry! (sing.)   _____

19.   ἐσθίω: he ate   _____

20   ἐσθίω: eat! (pl.)   _____

Exercise 11θ

Place the accent on the following 2nd aorist imperatives:

1.	λιπε	4.	ἰδε	7.	δραμε	10.	εὑρε	13.	βαλετε
2.	φυγε	5.	εἰπε	8.	εἰπετε	11.	εὑρετε	14.	ἐνεγκετε
3.	ἐλθετε	6.	λαβετε	9.	ἰδετε	12.	δραμετε	15.	ἐλθε

Exercise 11ι

Augment the following stems:

1. αὐξ- _____   3. εὐχ- _____   5. ἐγείρ- _____

2. ὁρμα- _____   4. ὠφελε- _____   6. ἀκου- _____

Exercise 11κ

Give an English equivalent of:

1. ἔρχομαι   _____   5. ὁ μισθός   _____
2. πρὸς τὴν γῆν   _____   6. νοσέω   _____
3. οἴμοι   _____   7. ἡ δραχμή   _____
4. ὠφελέω   _____   8. κατὰ
                                              θάλατταν   _____

Exercise 11λ

Give the Greek equivalent of:

1. I say   _____   4. obol   _____
2. I see   _____   5. silver   _____
3. I approach   _____   6. I take   _____

Exercise 11μ

Give the future and aorist of:

1. ὁράω _____   4. ἔρχομαι _____

   _____   _____

2. αἱρέω _____

   _____

3. λέγω _____ or _____

   _____ or _____

Exercise 11ν

Translate into English on a separate sheet of paper:

ΕΝ ΤΩΙ ΑΝΤΡΩΙ

[1] νύξ ἐστιν, ἀλλὰ ὁ Φίλιππος οὐ βούλεται καθεύδειν· δακρύων γὰρ λέγει· "οἴμοι τάλας, τίς αἴτιος ταύτης τῆς συμφορᾶς μοι ἐγένετο; ἀμέλει τῶν θεῶν τις· ὅτε γὰρ ἐν τῇ ὁδῷ ἐπῆρα ἐμαυτὸν τυφλὸς γενόμενος, ἐξαίφνης ἔμαθον ὅτι οἱ θεοί με μῖσοῦσιν. τί οὐκ ἀπέθανον τότε; οὐ γὰρ βούλομαι πάντα τὸν βίον τυφλὸς εἶναι. ὦ πάππα φίλε, ὦ μαμμίᾱ, βοηθεῖτέ μοι ταῦτα παθόντι."

[ΤΩΙ ΑΝΤΡΩΙ, *The Cave*   τάλας, *suffering, wretched; poor me!*   ταύτης τῆς, *this*   συμφορᾶς, *misfortune*   ἀμέλει, adv., *doubtless*   ὅτε, *when*   ἐπῆρα: aorist of ἐπαίρω   ἐξαίφνης, *immediately, suddenly*   μῖσοῦσιν, *hate*   τότε, *then*   μαμμίᾱ, *mother*   ταῦτα, *these things*]

[2] ἡ δὲ μήτηρ· "μὴ δάκρῡε, ὦ τέκνον, ἀλλ' ἄκουέ μου. ἆρα γιγνώσκεις σὺ τὸν Χαιρεφῶντα, τὸν τοῦ πατρός σου φίλον καὶ ἑταῖρον;"

[τέκνον, *child*   Χαιρεφῶντα, *Chaerephon*]

[3] ὁ δὲ παῖς, "ναὶ μὰ τὸν Δία," ἔφη, "ἔχει γὰρ ἀγρὸν οὐ μακρὰν ἀπὸ τῆς οἰκίᾱς ἡμῶν, καὶ πολλάκις ὁ πατήρ με ἐκεῖσε ἤγαγεν."

[ναὶ μὰ τὸν Δία, *yes, by Zeus*   μακρὰν, *far*]

[4] καὶ ἡ Μυρρίνη· "ἆρα γιγνώσκεις τί ἔπαθε πάθος ἔτι παῖς ὤν;"

[πάθος, *experience, misfortune*]

[5] ὁ δὲ Φίλιππος, "οὐκ ἔγωγε, ὦ μῆτερ," ἔφη, "ἀλλὰ εἰπέ μοι."

[ἔγωγε, *I indeed*]

[6] "ἄκουε δή. ὁ Χαιρεφῶν, ἔτι παῖς ὤν, προελθών ποτε ὀλίγον ἀπὸ τοῦ ἑαυτοῦ κλήρου, ηὗρεν ἄντρον τι τοιοῦτον οἷον Ὅμηρος εἶπεν."

[προελθών, *having gone forward*   ὀλίγον, adv., *a little*   κλήρου, *farm*   ἄντρον, *cave*   τοιοῦτον, *such*   οἷον, *as*   Ὅμηρος, *Homer*]

[7] ὁ δὲ Φίλιππος ὑπολαβών, "ἆρα τὸ τοῦ Κύκλωπος," ἔφη, "λέγεις;"

[ὑπολαβών, *taking up* (the conversation)]

[8] "ναί. λαβὼν οὖν δύο ἑταίρους εἰσῆλθεν εἰς τὸ ἄντρον, περισκοπεῖν τὰ πάντα βουλόμενος."

[ναί, yes   τὸ ἄντρον, the cave   περισκοπεῖν, to look around at]

[9] "τίνας δὲ ἔσχεν ἑταίρους;" ἔφη ὁ Φίλιππος.

[10] ὁ δὲ Δικαιόπολις ὑπολαβών, "ἡμᾶς ἔλαβεν ἑταίρους τὸ ἄντρον εὑρών," ἔφη, "ἐμὲ καὶ τὸν ἀδελφόν μου ἔτι παῖδας ὄντας."

[ὑπολαβών, taking up (the conversation)   τὸ ἄντρον, cave]

[11] "τί οὖν ἐγένετο; εἰπέ μοι, ὦ παππία."

[παππία, father]

[12] "λαβόντες μὲν οὖν λαμπάδας πάντες ἅμα ἤλθομεν ὡς τὸ ἄντρον ζητήσοντες. ἐγὼ δέ, τὴν ὁδὸν αὖθις εὑρεῖν βουλόμενος, λίθους βαδίζων ἔλιπον μετ᾽ ἐμέ. εὑρόντες δὲ τὸ ἄντρον εἰσήλθομεν, ὡς ἡ μήτηρ σοι εἶπεν. ἆρ᾽ ἀληθῆ λέγω, ὦ ἄδελφε;"

[λαμπάδας, torches   ἅμα, together   ὡς . . . εἶπεν, as . . . said   ἀληθῆ, the truth]

[13] ὁ δὲ ἀδελφός· "πῶς γὰρ οὔ; ἐγὼ μὲν ἔλαβον δύο λαμπάδας· σὺ γὰρ οὐκ ἔλαβες, μῑκροὺς λίθους ἐν ταῖς χερσὶν ἔχων. ὁ δὲ Χαιρεφῶν, οἰόμενος εἰς μάχην τινὰ ἐλθεῖν, ὥσπερ ὁ Ὀδυσσεὺς ἐπὶ τὸν Κύκλωπα, ξίφος τῇ δεξιᾷ ἔλαβεν, τῇ δὲ ἀριστερᾷ λαμπάδα εἶχεν. οὕτως εἰσήλθομεν εἰς τὸν σκότον τὸν τοῦ ἄντρου.

[λαμπάδας, torches   οἰόμενος, thinking   μάχην, fight, battle   ξίφος, sword
τὸν σκότον, the darkness]

[14] "ἐλάβομεν καὶ τὸν κύνα μεθ᾽ ἡμῶν, μέγα τε καὶ καλὸν ζῷον ὄντα, ὀνόματι Κέρβερον."

[ζῷον, animal   Κέρβερον, Cerberus]

[15] ἡ δὲ μήτηρ ὑπολαβοῦσα, "ἀλλ᾽ οὐκ ἐλάβετε σῖτόν τε καὶ ὕδωρ, ὥσπερ εἰς μακρὰν ὁδὸν πορευόμενοι," ἔφη, "καὶ διὰ τοῦτο κίνδῡνος μέγας ἐγένετο ῡμῖν ἀποθανεῖν ἐν τῷ σπηλαίῳ. οὐδὲν γάρ, ὦ παῖ, ἔλαβον πλὴν τοῦ ξίφους καὶ τῶν λαμπάδων."

[ὥσπερ, as if   ὑπολαβοῦσα, taking up (the conversation)   διὰ τοῦτο, because of
this   τῷ σπηλαίῳ, the cave   πλὴν + gen., except   τοῦ ξίφους, the sword   τῶν
λαμπάδων, the torches]

[16] "προελθόντες δέ," ἔφη ὁ τοῦ Δικαιοπόλιδος ἀδελφός, "μόλις ἐν τῷ τοῦ σπηλαίου σκότῳ εἴδομέν τι, καίπερ τὰς λαμπάδας ἔχοντες. ἔπειτα ὁ Χαιρεφῶν ὁ προβαίνων ἐξαίφνης ἔπταισεν· κατέπεσε δὲ εἰς χάσμα τι τῆς γῆς. ἐγὼ δέ, βοηθεῖν βουλόμενος αὐτῷ πεσόντι, τὰς λαμπάδας ἀπέβαλον. αἱ δὲ πεσοῦσαι ἔσβησαν.

[προελθόντες, having gone forward   τοῦ σπηλαίου, the cave   σκότῳ, darkness
καίπερ, although   τὰς λαμπάδας, the torches   ὁ προβαίνων, the one going ahead

ἐξαίφνης, *suddenly*   **ἔπταισεν**, *stumbled*   **χάσμα**, *chasm*   **ἔσβησαν** (from σβέννῡμι), *went out*]

[17] "πανταχοῦ σκότος ἐξαίφνης ἐγένετο περὶ ἡμῶν. φόβος δὲ ἔλαβεν ἡμᾶς τότε μέγας. κατήλθομεν δὲ βραδέως εἰς τὸ χάσμα, καίπερ οὐδὲν ἰδόντες, γιγνώσκειν βουλόμενοι τί ποτε ὁ Χαιρεφῶν πεσὼν ἔπαθεν.

[**πανταχοῦ**, *everywhere*   **σκότος**, *darkness*   **ἐξαίφνης**, *immediately, suddenly*   **φόβος**, *fear*   **τότε**, *then*   **τὸ χάσμα**, *the chasm*   **καίπερ**, *although*]

[18] "μόλις δὲ αὐτὸν ἐν τῷ τοῦ χάσματος μυχῷ ηὕρομεν κείμενον. δι' ὀλίγου δὲ κῑνεῖται καὶ ἀναπνεῖ. τέλος δὲ ἐπαίρει ἑαυτὸν καί, 'τί,' λέγει, 'πανταχοῦ σκότος ἐστίν; ἆρα τυφλός εἰμι;' ὁ δὲ πατήρ σου, 'οὐδαμῶς,' ἔφη, 'οὐ γὰρ σὺ τυφλὸς εἶ, ἀλλὰ πάντες ἐν τῷ τοῦ σπηλαίου σκότῳ ὥσπερ τυφλοί ἐσμεν. οὐκέτι γὰρ λαμπάδας ἔχομεν. δεῖ οὖν ἡμᾶς ἐν τῷ σκότῳ βαδίζειν, εἰ τὴν τοῦ ἄντρου εἴσοδον αὖθις εὑρεῖν βουλόμεθα.'

[**τοῦ χάσματος**, *the chasm*   **μυχῷ**, *far corner*   **κείμενον**, *lying*   **κῑνεῖται**, *he moves*   **ἀναπνεῖ**, *he breathes again, recovers*   **πανταχοῦ**, *everywhere*   **σκότος**, *darkness*   **τοῦ σπηλαίου**, *the cave*   **λαμπάδας**, *torches*   **τοῦ ἄντρου**, *the cave*   **εἴσοδον**, *entrance*]

[19] "ἐγὼ μὲν οὖν, πάντων πρεσβύτατος ὤν, ἡγεμὼν τῶν ἄλλων ἐν τῷ σκότῳ ἐγενόμην. σὺ δέ, ὦ Δικαιόπολι, αἴτιος ἐγένου τῆς ἡμῶν πάντων σωτηρίᾱς. ὁ γὰρ σὸς πατήρ, ὦ παῖ, τῷ κυνί, 'ἴθι δή, ὦ Κέρβερε,' ἔφη, 'εὑρὲ τὴν ὁδόν.' ὁ δὲ κύων ὀσφραινόμενος τῆς ὁδοῦ οἴκαδε ἐπανῆλθεν. ἐν δὲ τούτῳ ἡμεῖς μάλα φοβούμενοι μόλις ἐν τῷ σκότῳ προχωρεῖν οἷοί τ' ἐγενόμεθα. ὦ παῖ, οὐδενὶ πώποτε τοσαύτη συμφορὰ ἐγένετο ὅση ἡμῖν τότε, ὡς ἐμοὶ δοκεῖ."

[**πρεσβύτατος**, *oldest*   **ἡγεμών**, *leader*   **τῷ σκότῳ**, *the darkness*   **σωτηρίᾱς**, *salvation*   **ὀσφραινόμενος** + gen., *catching the scent of*   **οἷοί τ' ἐγενόμεθα**, *we were able*   **πώποτε**, *ever*   **συμφορά**, *misfortune*   **ὅση**, *as*   **τότε**, *then*   **ὡς ... δοκεῖ**, *as it seems*]

[20] ὁ δὲ Φίλιππος, "ἆρα καὶ ῡ̔μεῖς," ἔφη, "οἷοί τε ἐγένεσθε τὴν τοῦ ἄντρου εἴσοδον εὑρεῖν;"

[**οἷοί τε ἐγένεσθε**, *were you able?*   **τοῦ ἄντρου**, *the cave*   **εἴσοδον**, *the entrance*]

[21] "οὐδαμῶς," ἔφη ἡ μήτηρ, "οὐ γὰρ ἱκανοὶ ἐγένοντο διὰ τὸν σκότον πορεύεσθαι καὶ τὴν ὁδὸν εὑρεῖν."

[**ἱκανοί**, *sufficient, competent, capable*   **διά** + acc., *through*   **τὸν σκότον**, *the darkness*]

[22] "πᾶσαν τὴν νύκτα," ὑπολαβὼν ὁ Δικαιόπολις ἔφη, "περιήλθομεν ἐν κύκλῳ τὸ σπήλαιον, ἐξελθεῖν οὐ δυνάμενοι, ὥσπερ εἰς λαβύρινθον ἐμπεσόντες. τέλος δὲ τοῦ κυνὸς ὑλακτοῦντος ἀκούομεν· ὁ δὲ πατὴρ ἡμῶν καλεῖ ἡμᾶς βοῶν. εἴδομεν δὲ μετ' οὐ πολὺν χρόνον λαμπάδος φῶς καὶ τὸν πατέρα εἰσελθόντα. ἰδὼν γὰρ τοὺς

λίθους τοὺς ἐν τῇ ὁδῷ καὶ τῷ κυνὶ ἑπόμενος ηὗρε τὸ ἄντρον. ἀλλὰ τότε δὴ ἠσθόμεθα ὅτι ὁ Χαιρεφῶν τυφλός ἐστιν. οὐδὲν γὰρ εἶδεν, οὔτε τὸ φῶς οὔτε τὸν κύνα οὔτε τὸν πατέρα ἡμῶν.

[ὑπολαβών, *taking up* (the conversation) κύκλῳ, *a circle* τὸ σπήλαιον, *the cave* δυνάμενοι, *being able* λαβύρινθον, *labyrinth* ὑλακτοῦντος, *barking* λαμπάδος, *a torch* φῶς, *light* τὸ ἄντρον, *the cave* τότε, *then* ἠσθόμεθα, *we perceived*]

[23] "λαβόντες οὖν αὐτὸν ἡγησάμεθα αὐτῷ ἐκ τοῦ σπηλαίου δακρύοντι καὶ στενάζοντι καὶ ἠγάγομεν αὐτὸν πρὸς τὴν οἰκίαν αὐτοῦ.

[ἡγησάμεθα: aorist of ἡγέομαι τοῦ σπηλαίου, *the cave*]

[24] "ὁ δὲ πατὴρ αὐτοῦ, ὡς εἶδε τὸν υἱὸν τυφλὸν γενόμενον, πρῶτον μὲν ἐστέναξεν, ἔπειτα δὲ εἶπεν ὅτι δεῖ ἡμᾶς τὸν παῖδα εἰς τὸ τοῦ Ἀσκληπιοῦ ἱερὸν τὸ ἐν Ἐπιδαύρῳ ἀγαγεῖν. ἡμεῖς δὲ οὐκ ἐδυνάμεθα· αὐτὸς οὖν τὸν υἱὸν ἤγαγεν. ἐπεὶ δὲ ἀφίκετο πρὸς τὸν θεὸν ἄγων τὸν ἑαυτοῦ παῖδα, πρῶτον μὲν ἐπὶ θάλατταν αὐτὸν ἤγαγε καὶ ἔλουσεν αὐτόν. ἔπειτα πρὸς τὸ τέμενος ἦλθον τοῦ θεοῦ. ἐκεῖ τὸν παῖδα κατέκλῑνεν, ὁ δὲ τῇ ὑστεραίᾳ ἠγείρατο βλέπων. καὶ σὺ εἶδες αὐτὸν νῦν πάντα ὁρῶντα."

[τὸν υἱόν, *his son* ἐδυνάμεθα, *we were able* ἐπί, *to* ἔλουσεν, *he washed* τὸ τέμενος, *the sacred precinct* κατέκλῑνεν, *he laid X down* ἠγείρατο, *he woke up*]

[25] ἡ δὲ μήτηρ, "μὴ οὖν φοβοῦ, ὦ φίλε παῖ," ἔφη· "δι' ὀλίγου γὰρ καὶ σὺ ἀναβλέψει. νῦν δὲ κάθευδε ἥσυχος· ὀψὲ γάρ ἐστιν."

[ἀναβλέψει, *you will regain your sight* ἥσυχος, *quiet(ly)* ὀψέ, *late*]

12
ΠΡΟΣ ΤΟΝ ΠΕΙΡΑΙΑ (α)

Exercise 12α

Translate the following English phrases and words with the correct sigmatic 1st aorist form of the Greek verb supplied:

Active

1. λύω: he/she loosened _____

2. κελεύω: order! (sing.) _____

Middle

3. λύομαι: they ransomed _____

4. λύομαι: ransom! (pl.) _____

Consonant Stems and Verbs in -ίζω

5. πέμπω: we sent _____

6. φυλάττω: to guard _____

7. πείθω: to persuade _____

8. γράφω: write! (sing.) _____

9. πείθω: he/she persuaded _____

10. πέμπω: send! (sing.) _____

11. δέχομαι: to receive _____

12. λέγω: he/she said _____

13. σπεύδω: you (sing.) hurried _____

14. δέχομαι: (ἡ γυνὴ) after receiving _____

15. κομίζω: (ὁ δῆμος) having brought _____

Contract Verbs

16. τῑμάω: they honored _____

17. τῑμάω: honor! (pl.) _____

18. φιλέω: I loved _____

19. βοάω: to shout _____

20. φιλέω: to love _____

21. ἡγέομαι: we led _____

22. ἡγέομαι: he/she led _____

23. θεάομαι: (ὁ ἄνθρωπος) after looking _____

24. θεάομαι: I watched _____

Verbs with Deponent Futures

25. ἀκούω: I heard   _____

26. πλέω: you (pl.) sailed   _____

27. διώκω: you (sing.) pursued   _____

38. θαυμάζω: he/she was amazed   _____

29. βαδίζω: walk! (pl.)   _____

30. βαδίζω: they walked   _____

Irregular Augment

31. ἐργάζομαι: we accomplished   _____ or

                                       _____

32. ἐργάζομαι: you (sing.) accomplished _____ or

                                       _____

Exercise 12β

Using the verb supplied, write a sigmatic 1st aorist participle in the form that agrees with the noun given:

1.   ὁ ἀνὴρ (ἐλύσατο)   _____

2.   οἱ φίλοι (ἐδίωξαν)   _____

3.   τὴν γυναῖκα (ἔλῡσε)   _____

4.   ταῖς μητράσι (ἐφίλησαν)   _____

5.   αὐτουργοὺς (ἔσπευσαν)   _____

6.   τὸν ἰᾱτρὸν (παρέσκευσε)   _____

7.   τῆς παρθένου (ἔβλεψε)   _____

8.   τῶν ἀδελφῶν (ἤκουσαν)   _____

9.   τῷ παιδὶ (ἐδέξατο)   _____

10. ῡ̔μᾶς (m.) (ἐτῑμήσατε)   _____

11. ἐγὼ (f.) (ἔλεξα)   _____

12. ὁ ἱερεὺς (ηὔξατο)   _____

Exercise 12γ

Give an English equivalent of:

1. ὁ ἡμίονος   _____
2. ὡς τάχιστα   _____
3. ὁ ὅμῑλος   _____
4. τὸ τεῖχος   _____

5. φροντίζω   _____
6. χαίρειν κελεύω   _____
7. κακός   _____
8. ἤ . . . ἤ   _____

Exercise 12δ

Give the Greek equivalent of:

1. most quickly   _____
2. or   _____
3. harbor   _____
4. although   _____

5. I am at a loss   _____
6. straight   _____
7. old   _____
8. correct   _____

Exercise 12ε

Give the future and aorist of:

1. φροντίζω   _____
   _____
2. φυλάττω   _____
   _____
3. πέμπω   _____
   _____

4. ἀπορέω   _____
   _____
5. βοάω   _____
   _____
6. πείθω   _____
   _____

(β)

Exercise 12ζ

Translate the following English phrases and words with the correct aorist form of the Greek verb supplied:

1. αἴρω: I lifted   _____
2. ἐγείρω: wake X up! (pl.)   _____
3. μένω: he/she stayed   _____
4. μένω: wait! (sing.)   _____
5. ἀποκτείνω: to kill   _____

6. αἴρω: lift! (pl.)   _____

7. ἀποκρίνομαι: to answer   _____

8. αἴρομαι: you (sing.) carried off/won   _____

9. ἀποκρίνομαι: he/she answered   _____

10. αἴρομαι: we carried off/won   _____

11. ἀποκρίνομαι: we answered   _____

12. μένω: we waited   _____

13. αἴρομαι: I carried off/won   _____

14. ἐγείρω: you (sing.) woke X up   _____

15. αἴρω: they lifted   _____

16. ἀποκρίνομαι: you (pl.) answered   _____

17. ἀποκτείνω: you (pl.) killed   _____

18. ἀποκρίνομαι: answer! (pl.)   _____

19. μένω: (ἡ γυνή) having waited   _____

20. ἀποκρίνομαι: (ὁ ἄνθρωπος) after
    answering   _____

Grammar

Some Irregular Sigmatic 1st Aorists

Present	Aorist Stem	Aorist Indicative
δοκεῖ	δοκ-	ἔδοξε
ἐθέλω	ἐθελε-	ἠθέλησα
ἐλαύνω	ἐλα-	ἤλασα
καίω or κᾱ́ω	καυ-	ἔκαυσα
καλέω	καλε-	ἐκάλεσα
μάχομαι	μαχε-	ἐμαχεσάμην
πλέω	πλευ-	ἔπλευσα

Exercise 12η

Translate the following English phrases with the correct aorist forms of the Greek verbs supplied:

1. καίω: he/she burned X   _____

2. πλέω: they sailed   _____

3. ἐλαύνω: you (sing.) drove   _____

4. ἐθέλω: you (pl.) wished   _____

5. καλέω: you (sing.) called   _____

6.   μάχομαι: to fight   _____

7.   ἐλαύνω: (ἡ γυνή) after driving X   _____

Exercise 12θ

Give the aorist indicative, 1st person singular of the following compound verbs:

1. ἐκβάλλω   _____   5. ἀπολείπω   _____

2. εἰσπέμπω   _____   6. προσπῑ́πτω   _____

3. ἀποχωρέω   _____   7. ἐκκομίζω   _____

4. καταφεύγω   _____   8. συμπέμπω

                                              (συν-)   _____

Exercise 12ι

Give an English equivalent of:

1. ἐρωτάω   _____   4. ὁ ναύκληρος   _____

2. πλείων   _____   5. μάλιστά γε   _____

3. τότε   _____   6. ἐξηγέομαι   _____

Exercise 12κ

Give the Greek equivalent of:

1. I appear   _____   4. sailor   _____

2. most   _____   5. greatly   _____

3. merchant   _____   6. to Athens   _____

Exercise 12λ

Give the future and aorist of:

1. ἐρωτάω   future   _____

                aorist   _____   or   _____

2. ἐξηγέομαι   future   _____

                aorist   _____

3. φαίνομαι   future   _____

Exercise 12μ

Ο ΘΕΟΣ ΜΕΓΑΣ ΕΣΤΙΝ

Translate into English on a separate sheet of paper:

[1] ἐν ᾧ δὲ ἐπανῇσαν ὁ τοῦ Δικαιοπόλιδος ἀδελφός τε καὶ ἡ Μυρρίνη πρὸς τὸ ἄστυ, ἀνήρ τις πρὸς τὸν Πειραιᾶ βαδίζων κατεῖδε πόρρωθεν αὐτοὺς καὶ ἐκέλευσε τὸν δοῦλον προδραμεῖν καὶ περιμεῖναι αὐτοὺς κελεῦσαι. καὶ ὁ δοῦλος προδραμὼν καὶ καλέσᾱς, "κελεύει ὑμᾶς," ἔφη, "Κέφαλος περιμεῖναι." ὁ δὲ ἀδελφός, "ποῦ δ' ἐστὶν αὐτός;" ἔφη. "προσέρχεται," ἀπεκρίνατο ὁ δοῦλος, "ἀλλὰ περιμένετε." περιέμειναν οὖν ὁ τοῦ Δικαιοπόλιδος ἀδελφός τε καὶ ἡ γυνή. ἡ δὲ γυνὴ οὐκ ἐπαύετο δακρῡουσα. καὶ ὀλίγῳ ὕστερον ὅ τε Κέφαλος ἀφίκετο καὶ Ἀδείμαντος ὁ τοῦ Κεφάλου ἀδελφὸς καὶ Νῑκήρατος καὶ ἄλλοι τινές.

[ἐπανῇσαν, *were returning* κατεῖδε, *observed* πόρρωθεν, *from afar* προδραμεῖν, *to run ahead* περιμεῖναι, *to wait* ὀλίγῳ, *a little* ὕστερον, *later*]

[2] ἰδὼν δὲ τὴν γυναῖκα δακρῡουσαν καὶ τὸν ἄνδρα λῡπούμενον, ὁ Κέφαλος ἔφη· "ὦ φίλε, τί ποτε πάσχεις; ἡμεῖς μὲν προσευξάμενοι τῷ θεῷ καὶ ἅμα τὴν ἑορτὴν θεᾱσάμενοι χαίροντες νῦν οἴκαδε ἐπανερχόμεθα. καλὴ μὲν γὰρ ἡμῖν ἡ τῶν Ἀθηναίων πομπὴ ἔδοξεν εἶναι, καλοὶ δὲ οἱ χοροὶ καὶ οἱ ἀγῶνες. ἆρα οὐκ ἐθεᾱσασθε ὑμεῖς τὴν ἑορτήν; σὲ γὰρ ἐζήτησα κατ' ἀγορὰν καὶ ἐθαύμασα ὅτι οὐχ οἷός τ' ἦν εὑρεῖν. πῶς δαὶ δὲ ἐκ τοῦ Πειραιῶς πρὸς ἄστυ βαδίζετε; λῡπούμενοι δέ μοι δοκεῖτε. τί πάσχετε σύ τε καὶ ἡ γυνὴ ἡ μετὰ σοῦ; τί δ' ἐστίν;"

[λῡπούμενον, *distressed* προσευξάμενοι: deduce from πρόσ- + εὔχομαι ἅμα, *at the same time* οἱ ἀγῶνες, *the contests* κατ(ὰ), *throughout* οἷός τ' ἦν, *I was able* δαὶ: colloquial for δή δοκεῖτε, *you seem*]

[3] "ὦ φίλε Κέφαλε," ἀπεκρίνατο ὁ τοῦ Δικαιοπόλιδος ἀδελφός, "δεινόν τι ἔπαθεν αὕτη, τοῦ ἐμοῦ ἀδελφοῦ γυνὴ οὖσα. σὺ μὲν ἐζήτησάς με, ἐγὼ δὲ οὐκ ἦν κατὰ πόλιν· εἰς λιμένα γὰρ κατῆλθον μετὰ τοῦ ἀδελφοῦ καὶ τῆς γυναικὸς καὶ τοῦ υἱοῦ αὐτοῦ. ὁ γὰρ υἱός, παῖς καλός τε καὶ ἀγαθὸς ὤν, συμφορᾷ τινι ἐν ἄστει τυφλὸς γενόμενος, πρὸς Ἐπίδαυρον ἔπλευσεν ἅμα τῷ πατρί. βούλεται γὰρ ὁ πατὴρ εὔχεσθαι τῷ Ἀσκληπιῷ, εἴ πως ἐθέλει αὐτὸν ἰᾶσθαι."

[αὕτη, *this (woman)* ἦν, *I was* κατὰ + acc., *anywhere in* κατῆλθον, *I went down* τοῦ υἱοῦ, *the son* συμφορᾷ, *misfortune* ἅμα + dat., *together with* πως, *somehow* ἰᾶσθαι, *to heal*]

[4] "ἀλλὰ θάρρει, ὦ γύναι," ἔφη ὁ Κέφαλος, "ὁ γὰρ θεὸς ὁ ἐν Ἐπιδαύρῳ μέγας ἐστίν, καὶ πάντας τοὺς νοσοῦντας ἰᾶσθαι δύναται, εἰ βούλεται. ἆρα σὺ Ἀμβροσίᾱς μέμνησαι, τῆς τυφλῆς;"

[θάρρει, *cheer up!* ἰᾶσθαι, *to heal* δύναται, *he is able* μέμνησαι + gen., *do you remember?*]

[5] ἡ δὲ Μυρρίνη· "πῶς γὰρ οὔ;"

[6] ὁ δὲ Κέφαλος· "ἡ οὖν Ἀμβροσίᾱ, τυφλὴ οὖσα, ἦλθέ ποτε πρὸς τὸν θεὸν τὸν ἐν Ἐπιδαύρῳ. βαδίζουσα δὲ κατὰ τὸ τέμενος, ἤκουσε πολλῶν λεγόντων ὅτι ὁ θεὸς αὐτοὺς ὑγιεῖς ἐποίησεν. τῇ Ἀμβροσίᾳ δὲ ἀδύνατον ἔδοξεν ὅτι χωλοὶ καὶ τυφλοὶ ὑγιεῖς ἐγένοντο ἐνύπνιον ἰδόντες μόνον. καθεύδουσα δὲ ὄψιν εἶδεν· ἔδοξε γὰρ τῇ γυναικὶ ὁ θεὸς εἰπεῖν ὅτι ὑγιῆ αὐτὴν ποιήσει. 'δεῖ δέ,' ἔφη ὁ Ἀσκληπιός, 'μισθόν σε παρασχεῖν εἰς τὸ ἱερὸν ὗν ἀργυροῦν.' ἔπειτα δὲ τοὺς ὀφθαλμοὺς τοὺς νοσοῦντας ἰᾱτρευσεν αὐτῇ ὁ θεός. τῇ ὑστεραίᾳ ὑγιὴς ἠγείρατο καὶ ἐκ τοῦ ἱεροῦ χαίρουσα ἐξῆλθεν. μὴ φοβοῦ οὖν, ὦ γύναι, ὑπὲρ τοῦ παιδός· ἀμέλει γὰρ ὁ θεὸς αὐτὸν ἰᾱτρεύσει."

[τέμενος, *sacred precinct*   ὑγιεῖς, *healthy, well*   ἀδύνατον, *impossible*   χωλοὶ, *lame*   ἐνύπνιον, *a dream*   ὄψιν, *a vision*   ὗν, *pig*   ἀργυροῦν, *silver*   ἰᾱτρευσεν, *healed*   ἀμέλει, adv., *doubtless*]

[7] χαίρειν οὖν κελεύσᾱς ὁ μὲν Κέφαλος καὶ οἱ ἄλλοι μετ' αὐτοῦ πρὸς τὸν λιμένα ἀπῆλθον, ὁ δὲ Δικαιοπόλιδος ἀδελφὸς τῇ γυναικὶ αὐτοῦ Ἀθήνᾱζε ἡγήσατο.

13
ΠΡΟΣ ΤΗΝ ΣΑΛΑΜΙΝΑ (α)

Exercise 13α

Translate the following English phrases and words with the correct imperfect form of the Greek verb supplied:

Active

1. λύω: he/she was loosening _____
2. μένω: they used to stay _____
3. λέγω: I was saying _____
4. πέμπω: we were sending _____
5. ἀκούω: you (pl.) were listening _____
6. πείθω: you (sing.) were persuading _____

Middle

7. λύομαι: they were ransoming _____
8. γίγνομαι: you (pl.) were becoming _____

Contract Verbs

9. φιλέω: I used to love _____
10. θεάομαι: you (sing.) were watching _____
11. θεάομαι: you (pl.) were watching _____
12. ἡγέομαι: he/she was leading _____
13. φοβέομαι: you (sing.) were afraid _____
14. αἱρέω: he/she was taking _____
15. θεάομαι: he/she was watching _____
16. φοβέομαι: we were afraid _____
17. θεάομαι: I was watching _____
18. θεάομαι: we were watching _____
19. θεάομαι: they were watching _____
20. φιλέω: we were loving _____

Irregular Verbs

21. εἰμί: they were _____
22. εἰμί: you (pl.) were _____
23. εἶμι: he/she/it was going _____ or

_____

24. εἶμι : they were going   _____ or

                                      _____

25. εἰμί: he/she/it was   _____

26. εἰμί: I was   _____ or

                                      _____

27. εἶμι: you (sing.) were going   _____ or

                                      _____

28. εἶμι: I was going   _____ or

                                      _____

29. εἶμι: we were going   _____

30. εἶμι: you (pl.) were going   _____

31. εἰμί: we were   _____

32. εἰμί: you (sing.) were   _____

Irregular Augment

33. ὁράω: he/she was seeing   _____

34. ἕπομαι: I was following   _____

35. ὁράω: they used to see   _____

36. ἐργάζομαι: I was working   _____ or

                                      _____

37. ἐργάζομαι: they were working   _____ or

                                      _____

38. ἔχω: I used to have   _____

39. ἕλκω: he/she was dragging   _____

40. ὁράω: I was seeing   _____

41. ὁράω: you (sing.) were seeing   _____

42. ὁράω: we were seeing   _____

43. ὁράω: you (pl.) were seeing   _____

Exercise 13β

Indicate whether an imperfect (I) or aorist (A) verb form would be used to translate the underlined verb or verbal phrase. Sometimes either could be used. If so, write both I and A:

1. The soldiers <u>were approaching</u> the gate.   ____ ____

2. They <u>attempted to storm</u> it by force.   ____ ____

3. Fortunately, the defenders <u>locked</u> the gate first. ____ ____

4. But the attackers <u>began to look</u> for another way in. ____ ____

5.   They quickly <u>ran</u> around to the other side of the fortress.   ____ ____

6.   The defenders <u>kept throwing</u> things down on them.   ____ ____

7.   Finally, the attackers <u>decided</u> to try using fire.   ____ ____

8.   They lit a fire and <u>began putting</u> torches in it.   ____ ____

9.   The defenders <u>saw</u> what they <u>were doing</u>.   ____ ____

10. They <u>tried to carry</u> buckets of water to the wall.   ____ ____

Exercise 13γ

Give an English equivalent of:

1. τὰ ἱστία   _____   3. βέβαιος   _____

2. ἐρέσσω   _____   4. ταχύς   _____

Exercise 13δ

Give the Greek equivalent of:

1. wind   _____   3. of one another _____

2. I keep quiet   _____   4. bright   _____

Exercise 13ε

Give the imperfect, future, and aorist of the following (forms you have not had are supplied):

1. ἡσυχάζω   _____   5. ἐργάζομαι   _____ or
                _____   _____
                _____
2. ἐρέσσω   _____   _____ or
                <u>no future</u>   _____
                _____   6. ἕπομαι   _____
3. ἕλκω   _____   <u>ἑσπόμην</u> _____
                _____
                <u>εἵλκυσα</u>   7. ὁράω   _____
4. ἔχω   _____   _____
                _____ or   _____
                _____   8. ἔρχομαι   _____ or
                                                    _____
                                                    _____
                                                    _____

(β)

Exercise 13ζ

Supply the correct forms of the Greek relative pronoun to match the English clues:

1. We saw τὸν ἄνδρα, _____ (who) went to Athens.
2. αἱ γυναῖκες, _____ (whom) we saw, were working every day.
3. Zanthias, bring τὸ ἄροτρον, _____ (with which; *use dative without a preposition*) you were plowing the field.
4. ἡ ναῦς, _____ (which) brought you home, is mine.
5. Where are οἱ παῖδες, _____ (whose) dog I see?
6. ὁ οἶκος ἐν _____ (which) you live is beautiful.
7. πάντα _____ (that) the men brought are no longer here.
8. ὁ νεᾱνίᾱς _____ (whom) you saw is the brother of Melissa.
9. The city honored τοὺς ἄνδρας _____ (who) conquered the enemy.
10. ἡ οἰκίᾱ, _____ (of which/whose) roof we are fixing, belongs to my brother.
11. αἱ παρθένοι σὺν (+ dat., *with*) _____ (whom) you were talking, are my friends.
12. ὁ παῖς, _____ (to whom) you gave the gift, seems ungrateful.
13. οἱ παῖδες, _____ (to whom) you gave the gift, seem ungrateful.
14. τὸ ἄροτρον _____ (that) you are carrying is broken.
15. ὁ ἄγγελος _____ (who) approaches is a Spartan.
16. ἡ μήτηρ _____ (whom) you saw did not attend the festival.
17. We saw τοὺς φύλακας _____ (who) were guarding the gate.
18. This slave did τὸ ἔργον _____ (that) the master ordered.
19. ἡ παῖς, _____ (for whom) you made the dinner, was hungry.
20. οἱ αὐτουργοί, _____ (whose) farms are ruined, are very unhappy.

Exercise 13η

Complete the following phrases with the correct form of the noun or adjective supplied:

1. τοῦ _____ (τεῖχος)
2. αἱ _____ (τριήρης)
3. τοὺς _____ (ἀληθής) λόγους
4. τῶν _____ (ψευδής) μύθων
5. τὰ _____ (ὄρος)
6. τῷ_____ (τεῖχος)
7. τὰς _____ (τριήρης)
8. τῶν _____ (ὄρος)
9. ταῖς _____ (τριήρης)
10. τὰ _____ (τεῖχος)
11. αἱ _____ (ἀληθής) ἀρεταί
12. τοῦ _____ (ψευδής) ὀνόματος

13. τὴν _____ (τριήρης)
14. τοῖς _____ (τεῖχος)
15. τὰ _____ (ψευδής)
16. τῷ _____ (ἀληθής) λόγῳ
17. τῷ_____ (ὄρος)
18. τὸν _____ (ψευδής) λόγον
19. τῶν _____ (τριήρης)
20. τοῖς _____ (ὄρος)
21. τῇ _____ (τριήρης)
22. τοῦ _____ (ὄρος)
23. τῆς _____ (ἀληθής) ἐλευθερίᾱς
24. τὸ _____ (τεῖχος)

Exercise 13θ

Complete the phrase with the correct form of the adjective supplied:

1. τοῖς _____ (ταχύς) παῖσιν
2. τὴν _____ (βραδύς) κύνα
3. τὸν _____ (ταχύς) νεᾱνίᾱν
4. τὰς _____ (βραδύς) τριήρεις
5. τὰ _____ (ταχύς) ζῷα

6. τὴν _____ (ταχύς) παρθένον
7. τοῦ _____ (βραδύς) κύματος
8. τοὺς _____ (ταχύς) κύνας
9. τῶν _____ (βραδύς) ζῴων
10. ταῖς _____ (ταχύς) παρθένοις

Exercise 13ι

Give an English equivalent of:

1. ἡ ἐλευθερίᾱ   _____
2. τὰ ἀληθῆ   _____
3. ἡ μάχη   _____
4. τὸ κῦμα   _____
5. ὅτε   _____
6. ἀμύνομαι   _____
7. ἡ τριήρης   _____
8. ὅσπερ   _____

9. μηδείς   _____
10. ἀμύνω   _____
11. ἐγγὺς τοῦ οἴκου   _____
12. ψευδής   _____
13. τῷ ὄντι   _____
14. ἤ   _____
15. ὡς δοκεῖ   _____

Exercise 13κ

Give the Greek equivalent of:

1. lies   _____
2. as   _____
3. fight   _____
4. who (m. sing.)   _____
5. fleet   _____
6. who (f. pl.)   _____
7. Greece   _____

8. that (neuter)   _____
9. I am angry   _____
10. beginning   _____
11. true   _____
12. barbarian   _____
13. straits   _____
14. together   _____

Exercise 13λ

Give the imperfect, future, and aorist of:

1. ὀργίζομαι   _____
    _____
    no aorist middle

2. ἀμύνω   _____
    _____
    _____

3. ἀμύνομαι   _____
    _____
    _____

Exercise 13μ

Translate into English on a separate sheet of paper:

Η ΑΡΕΤΗ ΑΕΙ ΤΗΝ ΥΒΡΙΝ ΝΙΚΑΙ

[1] ὁ δὲ ναύτης ὁ γεραιός, "πρῶτον μὲν," ἔφη, "βούλομαι ὑμῖν περὶ τῆς τῶν Ἀθηναίων ἀρετῆς τε καὶ τόλμης εἰπεῖν. ἐγὼ δέ, ὃς παρῆν, τὴν ἀληθῆ αἰτίαν ὑμῖν σαφῶς ἀποκαλύψω ἣ τὴν ἐλευθερίαν πᾶσι τοῖς Ἕλλησι παρέσχεν. ἡμεῖς γάρ, οἳ ἐν πάσῃ ἐλευθερίᾳ τὸν βίον διηγάγομεν, ἐνομίσαμεν ὅτι δεῖ ἡμᾶς μάχεσθαι βαρβάροις ὑπὲρ τῆς πάντων τῶν Ἑλλήνων ἐλευθερίας.

[Η ΑΡΕΤΗ, *Virtue*   ΤΗΝ ΥΒΡΙΝ, *Insolence, Pride*   τόλμης, *courage*   αἰτίαν, *cause*   σαφῶς, *clearly*   ἀποκαλύψω, *I will reveal*   τὸν βίον, *our life*   διηγάγομεν, *we had led / had lived*   ἐνομίσαμεν, *we thought*]

[2] "οἱ μὲν γὰρ ἡμέτεροι πρόγονοι κατεσκεύασαν καλὴν πολιτείαν. τῶν δὲ ἄλλων ἐθνῶν αἱ πολιτεῖαι τυραννίδες τε καὶ ὀλιγαρχίαι ἦσαν. ἡμεῖς δὲ οὐκ ἠξιοῦμεν δοῦλοι οὐδὲ δεσπόται ἀλλήλων εἶναι, ἀλλ' ἰσονομίαν ἐζητοῦμεν κατὰ νόμον. φίλοι γὰρ ἦμεν ἀλλήλοις καὶ ἐλεύθεροι πάντες, καὶ οὐδενὶ ἄλλῳ ὑπείκομεν εἰ μὴ τῇ ἀληθεῖ ἀρετῆς δόξῃ.

[πρόγονοι, *ancestors*   κατεσκεύασαν, *established*   πολιτείαν, *government*   ἐθνῶν, *nations, peoples*   τυραννίδες, *tyrannies*   ὀλιγαρχίαι, *oligarchies*   ἠξιοῦμεν, *we were thinking it fitting*   ἰσονομίαν, *equality of political rights*   κατὰ νόμον, *according to law*   ἐλεύθεροι, *free*   ὑπείκομεν + dat., *we were yielding (to) / submitting (to)*   εἰ μὴ, *except*   ἀρετῆς, *virtue*   δόξῃ, *notion*]

[3] "οἱ δὲ τύραννοι καὶ οἱ ἐν τυραννίδι τεθραμμένοι ἐλευθερίας καὶ φιλίας ἀληθοῦς ἀεὶ ἄγευστοί εἰσιν. ὕβρις γὰρ τὰς τῶν τυράννων ψυχὰς ἀεὶ λαμβάνει· ὕβρις δὲ ἐξανθοῦσα ἐκφέρει καρπὸν ἄτης, καὶ ἐξ αὐτοῦ οὐδὲν ἄλλο δρέπουσιν οἱ ἄνθρωποι ἢ δάκρυά τε καὶ πένθος. ὁ γὰρ Ζεύς, ὃς πάντα ὁρᾷ, κολάζει τὴν ὕβριν τὴν τῶν τυράννων, οἵ, θνητοὶ ὄντες, πρὸς τοὺς θεοὺς ἀγωνίζεσθαι τολμῶσιν.

[τύραννοι, *tyrants*   τυραννίδι, *tyranny*   τεθραμμένοι, *having been reared*   φιλίας, *friendship*   ἄγευστοί + gen., *not having tasted, without a taste of*   ὕβρις, *insolence*   ψυχὰς, *souls; minds*   ἐξανθοῦσα, *bursting into bloom*   ἐκφέρει, *produces*   καρπὸν, *fruit*   ἄτης, *recklessness; sin; ruin*   δρέπουσιν, *pluck*   δάκρυά, *tears*   (τὸ) πένθος, *grief, sorrow*   κολάζει, *punishes*   θνητοὶ, *mortal*   ἀγωνίζεσθαι, *to contend*   τολμῶσιν, *dare*]

[4] "ἡμεῖς δέ, ὥσπερ οἱ ἡμέτεροι πρόγονοι οἳ τοὺς βαρβάρους ἐνίκησαν ἐν Μαραθῶνι, νομίζοντες τὸν καλὸν θάνατον ἀθάνατον περὶ τῶν ἀγαθῶν ἀνδρῶν λόγον καταλείπειν, οὐκ ἐφοβούμεθα τὸ πλῆθος τῶν πολεμίων ἀλλὰ τῇ ἡμῶν αὐτῶν ἀρετῇ ἐπιστεύομεν. ἐν οὖν τοῖς τοῦ πολέμου κινδύνοις ἐκλιπόντες μὲν τὴν πόλιν, ἐμβάντες δ' εἰς τὰς τριήρεις, τὰς ἡμῶν ψυχάς, ὀλίγας οὔσας, ἀντετάξαμεν τῷ πλήθει τῷ τῆς Ἀσίας. ἐπεδείξαμεν μὲν οὖν πᾶσιν ἀνθρώποις, νικήσαντες τῇ ναυμαχίᾳ, ὅτι κρεῖττόν ἐστι μετ' ὀλίγων ὑπὲρ τῆς ἐλευθερίας κινδυνεύειν ἢ μετὰ

πολλῶν δούλων μάχεσθαι ὑπὲρ τῆς ἑαυτῶν δουλείᾱς. ἐπεδείξαμεν δὲ ὅτι καὶ ἐν τοῖς ναυτικοῖς κινδύνοις, ὥσπερ ἐν τοῖς πεζοῖς, ἡ ἀρετὴ ἀεὶ τοῦ πλήθους περιγίγνεται, νομίσαντες ἄνδρας εἶναι τῷ ὄντι πόλιν, καὶ οὐ τείχη οὐδὲ τριήρεις ἀνδρῶν κενᾱς. τὰ γὰρ τείχη καὶ αἱ οἰκίαι καὶ τὰ ἱερὰ ἄνευ τῆς τῶν ἀνδρῶν ἀρετῆς ὥσπερ σῶμα ἀκίνητόν εἰσιν.

[πρόγονοι, *ancestors*　νομίζοντες, *thinking*　θάνατον, *death*　ἀθάνατον, *immortal*　λόγον, *account, reckoning*　τὸ πλῆθος, *the multitude*　τῶν πολεμίων, *the enemy*　ἀρετῇ, *virtue*　ἐπιστεύομεν + *dat., we were trusting (in)*　τοῦ πολέμου, *war*　ἐκλιπόντες, *having left behind*　ἐμβάντες, *having gotten into*　ψῡχάς, *souls*　ὀλίγᾱς, *few*　ἀντετάξαμεν, *we set X (acc.) in battle against Y (dat.)*　ἐπεδείξαμεν, *we showed*　τῇ ναυμαχίᾳ, *in the naval battle*　κρεῖττόν, *better*　κινδῡνεύειν, *to run risks*　ἤ, *than*　δουλείᾱς, *slavery*　ναυτικοῖς, *naval*　πεζοῖς, *on foot, of the infantry*　ἀρετὴ, *virtue*　τοῦ πλήθους, *the multitude*　περιγίγνεται + *gen., is superior to, prevails over, overcomes*　νομίσαντες, *thinking*　κενᾱς + *gen., empty (of), without*　ἄνευ + *gen., without*　σῶμα, *body*　ἀκίνητόν, *motionless*]

[5] "ἡμεῖς δὲ πρῶτον μὲν τοὺς βαρβάρους ἀπὸ τῆς χώρᾱς καὶ ἀπὸ πάσης τῆς Ἑλλάδος ἠμῡνάμεν, ἔπειτα δὲ τὴν πόλιν ἀνοικοδομεῖν παρεσκευασάμεθα καὶ τὰ τείχη. οὕτω δὲ ἡ πόλις ἡμῶν ἔπαυσε δύναμιν ὕβρει πορευομένην ἐπὶ Εὐρώπην. δεῖ δὲ πάντα τὰ πράγματα ἀπ' ἀρχῆς διέρχεσθαι· ἀκούετε οὖν."

[τῆς χώρᾱς, *the land*　ἀνοικοδομεῖν, *to rebuild*　δύναμιν, *power; military forces*　ὕβρει, *with insolence, insolently*　τὰ πράγματα, *the deeds*　διέρχεσθαι, *to go through, recount*]

VOCABULARY
CHAPTERS 10–13

VERBS

-ω Verbs

αἴρω, ἀρῶ,
  ἦρα — *I lift;* with reflexive
pronoun, *I get up*

ἀμΰνω, ἀμυνῶ,
  ἤμῡνα — active, transitive, *I
ward off* X (acc.)
from Y (dat.);
middle, transitive,
I ward off X (acc.);
*I defend myself
against* X (acc.)

ἀποθνῄσκω,
  ἀποθανοῦμαι,
  ἀπέθανον — *I die*

ἀποκτείνω,
  ἀποκτενῶ,
  ἀπέκτεινα — *I kill*

ἀποφεύγω,
  ἀποφεύξομαι,
  ἀπέφυγον — *I flee away, escape*

δακρΰω,
  δακρΰσω,
  ἐδάκρῡσα — *I cry, weep*

εἰσάγω,
  εἰσάξω,
  εἰσήγαγον — *I lead in; I take in*

ἐρέσσω,
  no future,
  ἤρεσα — *I row*

εὑρίσκω,
  εὑρήσω,
  ηὗρον or
  εὗρον — *I find*

ἡσυχάζω,
  ἡσυχάσω,
  ἡσύχασα — *I keep quiet; I rest*

καταλείπω,
  καταλείψω,
  κατέλιπον — *I leave behind, desert*

κομίζω, κομιῶ,
  ἐκόμισα — *I bring; I take*

κόπτω, κόψω,
  ἔκοψα — *I strike; I knock on* (a
door)

λαμβάνω,
  λήψομαι,
  ἔλαβον — *I take;* middle + gen.,
I seize, take hold of

λέγω, λέξω or
  ἐρῶ, ἔλεξα or
  εἶπον — *I say; I tell; I speak*

λείπω, λείψω,
  ἔλιπον — *I leave*

μανθάνω,
  μαθήσομαι,
  ἔμαθον — *I learn; I understand*

μένω, μενῶ,
  ἔμεινα — intransitive, *I stay* (in
one place); *I wait;*
transitive, *I wait
for*

πάσχω,
  πείσομαι,
  ἔπαθον — *I suffer; I experience*

τρέπω, τρέψω,
  ἔτρεψα — active, transitive, *I
turn* X; middle,
intransitive, *I turn
myself, turn*

τΰπτω,
  τυπτήσω — *I strike, hit*

φροντίζω,
  φροντιῶ,
  ἐφρόντισα — *I worry; I care*

Deponent or Middle -ω Verbs

γίγνομαι,
  γενήσομαι,
  ἐγενόμην — *I become*

ἔρχομαι, εἶμι,
  ἦλθον — *I come; I go*

ὀργίζομαι,
  ὀργιοῦμαι, no
  aorist middle — *I grow angry; I am
angry;* + dat., *I
grow angry at; I
am angry at*

προσέρχομαι,
  πρόσειμι,
  προσῆλθον — + dat. or πρός + acc., *I
approach*

φαίνομαι,
  φανοῦμαι   *I appear*

-άω Contract Verbs

ἐρωτάω,
  ἐρωτήσω,
  ἠρώτησα or
  ἠρόμην   *I ask*
νῑκάω,
  νῑκήσω,
  ἐνίκησα   *I defeat; I win*
ὁράω, ὄψομαι,
  εἶδον   *I see*

Deponent -άω Contract Verbs

θεάομαι,
  θεᾱσομαι,
  ἐθεᾱσάμην   *I see, watch, look at*

-έω Contract Verbs

αἱρέω, αἱρήσω,
  εἷλον   *I take*
αἰτέω, αἰτήσω,
  ᾔτησα   *I ask; I ask for*
ἀπορέω,
  ἀπορήσω,
  ἠπόρησα   *I am at a loss*
δεῖ   impersonal + acc.
     and infin., *it is*
     necessary

δοκεῖ, δόξει,
  ἔδοξε(ν)   impersonal, *it seems*
     (good); + dat., e.g.,
     δοκεῖ μοι, *it seems*
     good to me; I think
     it best; + dat. and
     infin., e.g., δοκεῖ
     αὐτοῖς σπεύδειν, *it*
     seems good to
     them to hurry,
     they decide to
     hurry
νοσέω, νοσήσω,
  ἐνόσησα   *I am sick, ill*
σκοπέω,
  σκέψομαι,
  ἐσκεψάμην   *I look at, examine; I*
     consider
ὠφελέω,
  ὠφελήσω,
  ὠφέλησα   *I help; I benefit*

Deponent -έω Contract Verbs

ἀφικνέομαι,
  ἀφίξομαι,
  ἀφῑκόμην   *I arrive;* + εἰς + acc., *I*
     arrive at

ἐξηγέομαι,
  ἐξηγήσομαι,
  ἐξηγησάμην   *I relate*

-μι Verbs

ἔξεστι(ν)   impersonal + dat.
     and infin., *it is*
     allowed / possible

ἔφη   *he / she said*

NOUNS

1st Declension

ἀρχή, -ῆς, ἡ   *beginning*
βοή, -ῆς, ἡ   *shout*
δραχμή, -ῆς, ἡ   *drachma (a silver*
     coin worth six
     obols)
ἐλευθερίᾱ, -ᾱς, ἡ   *freedom*
κεφαλή, -ῆς, ἡ   *head*
μάχη, -ης, ἡ   *fight; battle*
ναύτης, -ου, ὁ   *sailor*

2nd Declension

ἀδελφός, -οῦ, ὁ
  ὦ ἄδελφε   *brother*
ἄνεμος, -ου, ὁ   *wind*
ἀργύριον, -ου, τό   *silver; money*
βάρβαρος,
  -ου, ὁ   *barbarian*
ἔμπορος, -ου, ὁ   *merchant*
ἡμίονος, -ου, ὁ   *mule*
ῑᾱτρός, -οῦ, ὁ   *doctor*
ἱστία, -ων, τά   *sails*
λόγος, -ου, ὁ   *word; story*
μισθός, -οῦ, ὁ   *reward; pay*
ναύκληρος,
  -ου, ὁ   *ship's captain*
ναυτικόν, -οῦ, τό   *fleet*
ὀβολός, -οῦ, ὁ   *obol (a silver coin of*
     slight worth)
ὅμῑλος, -ου, ὁ   *crowd*
στενά,
  στενῶν, τά   pl., *narrows, straits;*
     mountain pass

3rd Declension

ἀληθῆ,	
ἀληθῶν, τά	*the truth*
κῦμα,	
κύματος, τό	*wave*
λιμήν,	
λιμένος, ὁ	*harbor*
τεῖχος,	
τείχους, τό	*wall*
τεκόντες,	
τεκόντων, οἱ	pl., *parents*
τριήρης,	
τριήρους, ἡ	*trireme* (a warship)
ὕδωρ, ὕδατος, τό	*water*
ψευδῆ,	
ψευδῶν, τά	*lies*

PRONOUNS

ἀλλήλων	*of one another*
ὅς, ἥ, ὅ	*who, whose, whom, which, that*

ADJECTIVES

1st/2nd Declension

βέβαιος,	
-ᾱ, -ον	*firm, steady*
γεραιός,	
-ᾱ́, -όν	*old*
ἐκεῖνος, -η, -ο	*that;* pl., *those*
κακός, -ή, -όν	*bad; evil*
λαμπρός,	
-ᾱ́, -όν	*bright; brilliant*
ὀρθός, -ή, -όν	*straight; right, correct*
πλεῖστος,	
-η, -ον	*most; very great;* pl., *very many*
σοφός, -ή, -όν	*skilled; wise; clever*
τυφλός,	
-ή, -όν	*blind*

3rd Declension

ἀληθής,	
ἀληθές	*true*
πλείων/	
πλέων,	
πλέον	*more*
ψευδής, -ές	*false*

3rd and 1st Declension

μηδείς,	
μηδεμία,	
μηδέν	*used instead of* οὐδείς *with imperatives and infinitives, no one, nothing; no*
ταχύς, ταχεῖα,	
ταχύ	*quick, swift*

PREPOSITIONS

ἐγγύς	+ gen., *near*
παρά	+ acc., of persons only, *to*
πρό	+ gen., of time or place, *before*
πρός	+ dat., *at, near, by;* + acc., *to, toward; against*

ADVERBS

Ἀθήνᾱζε	*to Athens*
ἅμα	*together, at the same time*
αὔριον	*tomorrow*
εὐθύς	*straightway, immediately, at once*
καλῶς	*well*
μέγα	*greatly; loudly*
ὅτε	*when*
ποτέ	enclitic, *at some time, at one time, once, ever*
τάχιστα	*most quickly; most swiftly*
τότε	*then*
ὡς	*as*

CONJUNCTIONS

εἰ	*if;* in indirect questions, *whether*
ἤ	*or*
ἤ . . . ἤ	*either . . . or*
καίπερ	+ participle, *although*

INTERJECTIONS

οἴμοι	*alas!*
φεῦ	*alas!*

EXPRESSIONS

καλῶς ἔχω	*I am well*
κατὰ θά- λατταν	*by sea*
μάλιστά γε	*certainly, indeed*
πῶς ἔχεις;	*How are you?*
τῷ ὄντι,	*in truth*
χαίρειν κελεύω	+ acc., *I bid* X *farewell, I bid* *farewell to* X
ὡς δοκεῖ	*as it seems*
ὡς τάχιστα	*as quickly as possible*

PROPER NAMES

Ἀσκληπιός, -οῦ, ὁ	*Asclepius* (the god of healing)
Ἑλλάς, Ἑλλάδος, ἡ	*Hellas, Greece*
Ἐπίδαυρος, -ου, ἡ	*Epidaurus*
Πειραιεύς, -ῶς, ὁ, τῷ Πειραιεῖ, τὸν Πειραιᾶ	*the Piraeus* (the port of Athens)
Ποσειδῶν, Πο- σειδῶνος, ὁ	*Poseidon*
Σαλαμίς, Σαλα- μῖνος, ἡ	*Salamis*

14
Η ΕΝ ΤΑΙΣ ΘΕΡΜΟΠΥΛΑΙΣ ΜΑΧΗ (α)

Exercise 14α

Fill in the blanks with the correct form of the Greek word to match the English translation:

1. ὁ _____ ἄνθρωπος (prudent: σώφρων)

2. _____ φίλοι (many: πολύς)

3. ὁ _____ λόγος (true: ἀληθής)

4. ἡ _____ ἡμέρᾱ (worse: κακός)

5. ἡ _____ γυνή (more beautiful: καλός)

6. ἡ _____ γυνή (more prudent: σώφρων)

7. ὁ _____ ἄνθρωπος (most difficult: χαλεπός)

8. ὁ _____ παῖς (braver: ἀνδρεῖος)

9. ὁ _____ ποιητής (better: ἀγαθός)

10. ὁ _____ λόγος (most truthful: ἀληθής)

11. ὁ _____ στόλος (worst: κακός)

12. ἡ _____ οἰκίᾱ (bigger: μέγας)

13. ὁ _____ ἄνθρωπος (best: ἀγαθός)

14. ἡ _____ κόρη (beautiful: καλός)

15. ὁ _____ στρατιώτης (bravest: ἀνδρεῖος)

16. ὁ _____ χρόνος (smaller/shorter: ὀλίγος)

17. ὁ _____ ἔμπορος (worse: κακός)

18. οἱ _____ στρατιῶται (more difficult: χαλεπός)

19. ὁ _____ στρατός (larger: μέγας)

20. ὁ _____ πόνος (difficult: χαλεπός)

21. ἡ _____ κόρη (small: μῑκρός)

22. ὁ _____ στόλος (very great: πολύς)

23. ὁ _____ λύκος (biggest: μέγας)

24. ἡ _____ κόρη (smallest: μῑκρός)

25. ἡ _____ γυνή (most beautiful: καλός)

26. _____ σῖτος (more: πολύς)

Exercise 14β

Give English equivalents for the following Greek adverbs:

1.	ἀληθῶς	_____	10.	εὖ	_____
2.	ἀνδρειότερον	_____	11.	ἀληθέστερον	_____
3.	ἄριστα	_____	12.	κάκῑον	_____
4.	κακῶς	_____	13.	μάλιστα	_____
5.	μᾶλλον	_____	14.	πολύ	_____
6.	πλεῖστα	_____	15.	ἄμεινον	_____
7.	κάκιστα	_____	16.	μάλα	_____
8.	ἀνδρειότατα	_____	17.	πλέον	_____
9.	ἀνδρείως	_____	18.	ἀληθέστατα	_____

Exercise 14γ

Give a Greek equivalent for the underlined word or phrase:

1. He was <u>bigger than his brother</u>.   _____ or

   _____

2. The women were <u>much more prudent</u>.   _____

3. He acted <u>as bravely as possible</u>.   _____

4. The woman was <u>rather beautiful</u>.   _____

5. This ship was <u>biggest of all</u>.   _____

6. He was <u>smaller than his father</u>.   _____ or

   _____

7. The men were <u>very bad</u>.   _____

Exercise 14δ

Give an English equivalent of:

1.	ὁ ὁπλίτης	_____	6.	πρᾱ́ττω	_____
2.	ἤ	_____	7.	συμβάλλω	_____
3.	ὁ στρατιώτης	_____	8.	οὗτος	_____
4.	τὸ πλῆθος	_____	9.	συνέρχομαι	_____
5.	ἐν μέσῳ	_____			

Exercise 14ε

Give the Greek equivalent of:

1.	expedition	_____	8.	I send against	_____
2.	mountain pass	_____	9.	I hope	_____
3.	army	_____	10.	small	_____
4.	narrow	_____	11.	I attack	_____
5.	I use	_____	12.	I expect	_____
6.	I enjoy	_____	13.	fleet	_____
7.	straits	_____	14.	by land	_____

Exercise 14ζ

Give the imperfect, future, and aorist of:

1. προσβάλλω _____
   _____
   _____

2. ἐπιπέμπω _____
   _____
   _____

3. ἐλπίζω _____
   _____
   _____

4. χράομαι _____
   _____
   _____

5. συνέρχομαι _____ or
   _____
   _____

6. συμβάλλω _____
   _____
   _____

7. πράττω _____
   _____
   _____

Grammar

Review of Uses of the Cases (the page references are to the textbook)

Nominative
  1. Subject of a finite verb (see page 5), e.g.:
       ὁ ἄνθρωπος γεωργεῖ τὸν κλῆρον.
       The man *cultivates the farm.*
  2. Complement with the linking verb εἰμί and verbs of becoming such as γίγνομαι
     (see page 5), e.g.:
       ὁ κλῆρός ἐστι **μῑκρός**.
       *The farm is **small**.*
       οἱ δὲ εὐθὺς **σύες** γίγνονται.
       *And immediately they become **pigs**.*

Genitive
1. Genitive of possession (see page 147), e.g.:
    ὁ τοῦ παιδὸς κύων
    *the **boy's** dog* or *the dog **of the boy***
    Note that the word in the genitive case is here in the attributive position between the article and the noun. It may also be placed after the repeated article, e.g.:
    ὁ κύων ὁ τοῦ παιδός
    The genitive often simply links one noun to another without any notion of possession, e.g.:
    ὕβρις . . . ἐκφέρει καρπὸν ἄτης.
    *Insolence produces fruit **of ruin**.*
2. Genitive with certain adjectives, such as αἴτιος, *responsible (for)*, and ἄξιος, *worthy (of)*, e.g.:
    δεῖ γάρ σε ἄξιον γίγνεσθαι τῶν πατέρων.
    *You must become worthy **of your fathers**.*
3. Genitive of the whole or partitive genitive, (see pages 147 and 237) e.g.:
    τῶν παρόντων πολλοί, *many **of those present***
    ὁ Λεωνίδης πάντων τῶν στρατιωτῶν ἄριστος ἦν.
    *Leonidas was the best **of all the soldiers.***
4. Genitive of time within which (see page 129), e.g.:
    πέντε ἡμερῶν, ***within five days***
    νυκτός, ***at/by night***
5. Genitive of comparison (see page 237), e.g.:
    ὁ ἀνὴρ μείζων ἐστὶ τοῦ παιδός.
    *The man is bigger **than the boy**.*
6. Genitive with certain prepositions, often expressing ideas of place from which (see pages 20, 147, 267, and 269), e.g.:
    ἀπὸ τοῦ ἄστεως
    *from **the city***
7. Genitive with certain verbs (see page 147), e.g.:
    ὁ Θησεὺς τῇ ἀριστερᾷ λαμβάνεται τῆς τοῦ θηρίου κεφαλῆς.
    *Theseus **takes hold of the head** of the beast with his left hand.*
    The following verbs in the vocabulary lists of Book I are used with the genitive case:
    ἀκούω, *I hear* (a person talking; the accusative is used for the thing heard)
    ἔχομαι, *I hold onto*
    λαμβάνομαι, *I seize, take hold of*
    παύομαι, *I cease from*

Dative
1. Indirect object with verbs of giving, showing, and telling (see page 88), e.g.:
    οὕτω τῷ Μῑνωταύρῳ σῖτον παρέχουσιν.
    *In this way they supply food **to the Minotaur**.*
    *In this way they supply **the Minotaur** with food.*
2. Dative of the possessor (see page 88), e.g.:
    ἔστιν αὐτῷ παῖς τις ὀνόματι Θησεύς.
    literally: *There is **for him** a child, Theseus by name.*
    He has a child named Theseus.
3. Dative of respect (see page 88), e.g.:
    ὀνόματι Θησεύς
    *Theseus **by name***

4. Dative of means or instrument (see pages 88 and 269), e.g.:

τῇ **ἀριστερᾷ** λαμβάνεται τῆς τοῦ θηρίου κεφαλῆς.

*He takes hold of the head of the beast **with his left hand**.*

5. Dative of time when (see pages 88 and 128–129), e.g.:

τῇ **τρίτῃ ἡμέρᾳ** ἀφῑκόμεθα.

*We arrived **on the third day**.*

6. Dative of degree of difference with comparatives and superlatives (see page 237), e.g.:

ὁ ἀνὴρ **πολλῷ** μείζων ἐστὶ τοῦ παιδός.

*The man is **much** bigger (bigger **by much**) than the boy.*

7. Dative with certain prepositions, especially those that indicate the place where someone or something is or something happens (see page 88), e.g.:

παρὰ **τῇ κρήνῃ**

*by **the spring***

8. Dative with certain verbs (see page 88), e.g.:

ἕπεσθέ **μοι** ἀνδρείως.

*Follow **me** bravely.*

The following verbs in the vocabulary lists of Book I are used with the dative case:

ἀντέχω, *I resist*

βοηθέω, *I come to X's aid; I come to rescue / aid X*

διαλέγομαι, *I talk to, converse with*

δοκεῖ, impersonal, *it seems (good)*, e.g., δοκεῖ μοι, *it seems good to me; I think it best*; + dat. and infin., e.g., δοκεῖ αὐτοῖς σπεύδειν, *it seems good to them to hurry, they decide to hurry*

εἴκω, *I yield*

ἐμπίπτω, *I fall into; I fall upon; I attack*

ἔξεστι(ν), impersonal + dat. and infin., *it is allowed / possible*

ἐπιπλέω, *I sail against*

ἕπομαι, *I follow*

εὔχομαι, *I pray to*

ἡγέομαι, *I lead*

μάχομαι, *I fight against*

ὀργίζομαι *I grow angry at; I am angry at*

πείθομαι, *I obey*

πιστεύω, *I trust, am confident (in); I believe*

προσβάλλω, *I attack*

προσέρχομαι, *I approach*

προσχωρέω, *I go toward, approach*

συλλαμβάνω, *I help*

συμβάλλω, *I join battle with*

συμπίπτω, *I clash with*

τέρπομαι, *I enjoy*

χράομαι, *I use; I enjoy*

Accusative

1. Direct object of many verbs (see pages 5 and 20), e.g.:

ὁ ἄνθρωπος γεωργεῖ **τὸν κλῆρον**.

*The man cultivates **the/his farm**.*

You have also seen the accusative used as the *subject* of an infnitive, e.g.:

δεῖ ἡμᾶς <u>παρεῖναι</u>.
literally, *(For) us <u>to be there</u> is necessary.*
We must be there.

2. Duration of time (see pages 128–129), e.g.:

τρεῖς ἡμέρᾱς ἐμείναμεν.
*We stayed **for three days**.*

3. Accusative with certain prepositions, especially with those expressing motion toward someone or something (see page 20), e.g.:

πρὸς τὸν οἶκον βαδίζει.
*He/she walks toward **his/her house**.*

4. Adverbial, e.g.:

μέγα βοᾷ.
*He/She shouts **loudly**.*

Exercise 14η

Choose any paragraph from the readings in this workbook and identify the use of the case of each noun, pronoun, and adjective.

(β)

Exercise 14θ

Supply the correct form of the demonstrative provided to complete each phrase:

1. _____ ὁ ἄνθρωπος (οὗτος)

2. _____ τὸν γέροντα (οὗτος)

3. _____ τὴν γυναῖκα (ἐκεῖνος)

4. _____ τοὺς νεᾱνίᾱς (ἐκεῖνος)

5. _____ τῷ ὀνόματι (οὗτος)

6. _____ τὸ ἔργον (ὅδε)

7. _____ αἱ παρθένοι (ὅδε)

8. _____ τῆς παρθένου (οὗτος)

9. _____ τὸ δένδρον (ἐκεῖνος)

10. _____ τῇ πόλει (ὅδε)

11. _____ τῇ παρθένῳ (ὅδε)

12. _____ οἱ αὐτουργοί (οὗτος)

13. _____ τῶν γυναικῶν (ἐκεῖνος)

14. _____ τοῦ δένδρου (οὗτος)

15. _____ τῷ ἀνδρί (ἐκεῖνος)

16. _____ τὰς πόλεις (ὅδε)

17. _____ τοῖς ἀνθρώποις (οὗτος)

18. _____ τοῦ γέροντος (ὅδε)

19. _____ ταῖς μητράσι(ν) (ἐκεῖνος)

20. _____ ἡ πόλις (οὗτος)

Exercise 14ι

Give a Greek equivalent for the underlined English word or phrase:

1. To where ὁ ἀνὴρ ἔρχεται; _____

2. From where ἦλθεν οὗτος ὁ ξένος; _____

3. ἐκεῖναι αἱ γυναῖκες somewhere ἐν τῷ ἄστει οἰκοῦσιν. _____

4. βούλομαι Ἀθήναζε πορεύεσθαί (at) some time. _____

5. How τοῦτο τὸ ἔργον ἐποίησας; _____

6. ἆρά (to) somewhere ἐν τῇ Ἑλλάδι ἔρχεται ὁ ἀνήρ; _____

7. τοῦτο τὸ ἔργον somehow ἐποίησα. _____

8. Where οἰκοῦσιν ἐκεῖναι αἱ γυναῖκες; _____

9. When βούλει καθεύδειν; _____

10. ὁ ἀνήρ from somewhere ἐκ τῆς Ἑλλάδος ἔρχεται. _____

Exercise 14κ

Give an English equivalent of:

1. ἅπᾱς   _____   5. φράζω   _____

2. διέρχομαι   _____   6. ὁ πόλεμος   _____

3. ὡς   _____   7. ἀγγέλλω   _____

4. αἱ πύλαι   _____   8. οἱ πολέμιοι _____

Exercise 14λ

Give the Greek equivalent of:

1. until   _____   6. I write   _____

2. on the day before _____   7. I retreat   _____

3. this here   _____   8. I resist   _____

4. where   _____   9. I arrive   _____

5. hostile   _____   10. I withdraw _____

Exercise 14μ

Give the imperfect, future, and aorist of:

1. διέρχομαι _____ or 5. ἀναχωρέω _____
   _____   _____
   _____   _____

   _____ 6. γράφω _____

2. ἀντέχω _____   _____
   _____   _____

   _____ 7. παραγίγνομαι _____

3. φράζω _____   _____
   _____   _____
   _____

4. ἀγγέλλω _____
   _____
   _____

Exercise 14ν

Translate into English on a separate sheet of paper:

ΔΥΟ ΑΝΘΡΩΠΟΙ ΕΡΙΖΟΥΣΙΝ

[1] ἐν ᾧ δὲ ἔλεγε περὶ τῶν βαρβάρων πλεόντων εἰς τὸ Φάληρον ὁ ναύτης ὁ γεραιός, ἐξαίφνης πάντες οἱ ἐν τῇ νηὶ ἀνθρώπων μέγα βοώντων ἤκουσαν. δύο γὰρ ἄνθρωποι ἐρίζοντες ἀλλήλοις μέγα τὰς ἑαυτῶν φωνὰς ἐπῆραν.

[**ΕΡΙΖΟΥΣΙΝ**, *quarrel* **ἐξαίφνης**, *suddenly* **φωνὰς**, *voices*]

[2] ὁ μὲν ἕτερος, "οὐ μὰ Δία," ἔφη, "οὐ καταπροίξει τοῦτο λέγων." ὁ δὲ ἕτερος ἀποκρῑνόμενος, "βάλλ᾽ ἐς κόρακας," ἔφη. πάντες δὲ οἱ ἐν τῇ νηί, ταύτᾱς τὰς βοάς τε καὶ τοῦτον τὸν θόρυβον ἀκούσαντες, τοῖς ἐρίζουσιν ἐπλησίασαν, τὴν ταύτης τῆς ἔριδος αἰτίᾱν γιγνώσκειν βουλόμενοι. οἱ μὲν ἄνδρες, "παῖε, παῖε τὸν πανοῦργον," γελάσαντες ἔλεγον, αἱ δὲ γυναῖκες κλάζουσαι, "παύετε, παύετε τοὺς ἀνθρώπους ἐρίζοντας."

[**ὁ . . . ἕτερος**, *the one* **μὰ Δία**, *by Zeus* **καταπροίξει**: from **καταπροίξομαι**, *future only + participle, I will escape unpunished for doing* X (2nd person sing. here) **ὁ . . . ἕτερος**, *the other* **βάλλ᾽ ἐς κόρακας**, lit., *throw to the crows; go and be hanged!* **θόρυβον**, *commotion* **τοῖς ἐρίζουσιν**, *the men who were quarreling* **ἐπλησίασαν** + dat., *came close to* **ἔριδος**, *quarrel* **αἰτίᾱν**, *cause* **παῖε**, *strike!* **τὸν πανοῦργον**, lit., *the one who would do anything; the rogue* **γελάσαντες**, *breaking into laughter* **κλάζουσαι**, *screaming*]

[3] ὁ δὲ Δικαιόπολις· "τί ἐστιν; τίς οὗτος ὁ θόρυβος; τί τοῦτο τὸ πρᾶγμα; τίνες δὲ οἱ βοῶντες;"

[θόρυβος, commotion   πρᾶγμα, matter]

[4] ὁ δὲ ναύτης ὁ γεραιός, "ἐγὼ μέν," ἔφη, "ἀγνοῶ· δεῖ δ᾽ ἡμᾶς γιγνώσκειν τί γίγνεται. ἄγετε δή, ἔλθετε μετ᾽ ἐμοῦ." καὶ ταῦτα εἰπὼν ἐπῆρεν ἑαυτὸν καὶ ἐβάδισε πρὸς τοὺς ἐρίζοντας.

[ἀγνοῶ, I do not know   τοὺς ἐρίζοντας, the men who were quarreling]

[5] ὁ δὲ κυβερνήτης προσδραμών, "Ἡράκλεις, τί τοῦτο;" ἔφη, "τί τοῦτο τὸ κακὸν ποτέ ἐστιν; νὴ τὸν Ποσειδῶ, μαίνεσθε, ὡς ἐμοὶ δοκεῖ. παύσασθε, παύσασθε ἐρίζοντες πρὸς ἀλλήλους καὶ λέγετέ μοι ἐξ ἀρχῆς πόθεν ὑμῖν αὕτη ἡ ἔρις ἐγένετο."

[κυβερνήτης, steersman   Ἡράκλεις, voc., Hercules!   νὴ τὸν Ποσειδῶ, by Poseidon   μαίνεσθε, you are insane, out of your minds   ἐρίζοντες, quarreling   ἔρις, quarrel]

[6] ὁ μὲν οὖν ἄνθρωπος ἕτερος, "οὗτος," ἔφη, "τὸ μὲν πρῶτον πολλὰ καὶ μεγάλῃ τῇ φωνῇ κακῶς ἔλεγεν, ἔπειτα δὲ καὶ ἔπαισέ με, καὶ τοσαύτην κραυγὴν καὶ θόρυβον ἐποίησεν ὥστε καὶ σὺ καὶ οὗτοι οἱ ἄλλοι πάντες ἤλθετε. μαίνεται, ὡς ἐμοὶ δοκεῖ, οὗτος ὁ ἄνθρωπος."

[ὁ . . . ἄνθρωπος ἕτερος, the one man   φωνῇ, voice   ἔπαισέ, he struck   κραυγὴν, shouting   θόρυβον, commotion   μαίνεται, he's insane]

[7] ὁ δὲ ἕτερος ὑπολαβών, "εἰπέ μοι," ἔφη, "ὦ κάκιστε ἀνδρῶν πάντων· ἆρα τοῦτο τολμᾷς καὶ ἐμβλέπων ἐμοὶ λέγειν;"

[ὁ . . . ἕτερος, the other (man)   ὑπολαβών, taking up (the conversation)   τολμᾷς, do you dare   ἐμβλέπων, looking at]

[8] ὁ δὲ ἀποκρινόμενος, "σῖγα," ἔφη, "ὦ πανοῦργε· σὺ γὰρ ἐπ᾽ ἐμέ, ἐλεύθερον ἄνδρα ὄντα, ἔλαβες βακτηρίᾱν καὶ ἐμὲ ἔπαισες. ἆρ᾽ οὐχ ὕβρις αὕτη ἐστὶ πολλή;"

[πανοῦργε, rogue   ἐλεύθερον, free   βακτηρίᾱν, stick   ἔπαισες, you struck   ὕβρις, insolence]

[9] ὁ δὲ ἕτερος· "νὴ Δία, καὶ καλῶς ἐποίησα τύπτων σὲ ὄντα οὐ μόνον κλέπτην ἀλλὰ καὶ κατάσκοπον τῶν Λακεδαιμονίων καὶ οὐ τῷ ὄντι ἔμπορον Ἀθηναῖον."

[νὴ Δία, by Zeus   κλέπτην, thief   κατάσκοπον, spy]

[10] ὁ δέ· "τί λέγετε, ὦ ἄνθρωποι; ἆρ᾽ οὐχ ὑβρίζει με οὗτος ὁ πανοῦργος;"

[ὑβρίζει, is . . . insulting   πανοῦργος, rogue]

[11] ὁ δὲ ἕτερος· "βούλει σιωπᾶν; ἄκουε δέ, ὦ κυβερνῆτα· αὕτη γὰρ ἡ τῆς ἔριδος ἀρχὴ ἐγένετο. ἔπρᾱξε γὰρ οὗτος τοιαῦτα δι᾽ ἃ ὑπ᾽ ἐμοῦ νῦν εἰκότως μῑσεῖται. δεῖ δὲ καὶ ὑμᾶς πάντας, ὦ Ἀθηναῖοι, ταῦτα τὰ πράγματα ἅπαντα ἀκοῦσαι. οὗτος γὰρ ὁ ἄνθρωπος οὐκ ἔστιν ἔμπορος Ἀθηναῖος, ὡς φαίνεσθαι βούλεται, ἀλλά, κατάσκοπος τῶν Λακεδαιμονίων ὤν, ἐν τῷ ἡμετέρῳ ἄστει οἰκεῖ ἡμῖν ἐπιβουλεύων. ὁ γὰρ τούτῳ πατὴρ ἐξένιζεν καὶ οὐχ οἷός τ᾽ ἦν καλῶς ἀττικίζειν· ἐγὼ δὲ αὐτὸν τοῦτόν τε καὶ ξένον τινὰ ἐν τῇ ἀγορᾷ Δωριστὶ διαλεγομένους εἶδον.

νῦν δὴ δὲ τούτου ἤκουσα ὑπὲρ τῶν Λακεδαιμονίων λέγοντος· ἔλεγε γὰρ ὅτι ἡ τῶν
Σπαρτιᾱτῶν πόλις ἰσχῡροτέρᾱ ἢ ἡ ἡμετέρᾱ ἐστίν καὶ ὅτι οἱ Λακεδαιμόνιοι
ἀνδρειότεροι ἢ οἱ Ἀθηναῖοι ἀεὶ ἐγένοντο ἐν ταῖς μάχαις καὶ ὅτι οἱ Λακεδαιμόνιοι
σωφρονέστατοί εἰσι πάντων τῶν Ἑλλήνων καὶ πολλῷ σωφρονέστεροι τῶν
Ἀθηναίων καὶ ἄλλα τοιαῦτα πολλά."

[ὁ . . . ἕτερος, the other (man)   σιωπᾶν, to be quiet   κυβερνῆτα, steersman   τῆς
ἔριδος, the quarrel   τοιαῦτα, such things   δι(ὰ) ἃ, because of which   ὑπ(ὸ), by
εἰκότως, fairly, with reason   μῑσεῖται, he is hated   πρᾱ́γματα, matters
κατάσκοπος, spy   ἐπιβουλεύων + dat., plotting against   τούτῳ, for this man, his
ἐξένιζεν, spoke with a foreign accent   οὐχ οἷός τ' ἦν, was not able   ἀττικίζειν,
to speak Attic Greek   Δωριστὶ, in the Doric dialect]

[12] ὁ δὲ κυβερνήτης, "ὦ κάκιστε καὶ πονηρότατε ἀνθρώπων," ἔφη, "ταῦτα δὴ
τολμᾷς λέγειν πρὸς ἡμᾶς;"

[κυβερνήτης, steersman   πονηρότατε, most wicked   τολμᾷς, do you dare?]

[13] ὁ δ' ἔμπορος μάλα φοβούμενος, "οὐδαμῶς, ὦ κυβερνῆτα," ἔφη· "ἐγὼ δὲ μῑσῶ
μὲν τοὺς Λακεδαιμκονίους σφόδρα καὶ οὐκ ἀγνοῶ ὅτι ἄριστοι τῶν Ἑλλήνων οἱ
Ἀθηναῖοί εἰσιν, τὴν ἀρχὴν τὴν κατὰ θάλατταν ἔχοντες καὶ πλέονας τριήρεις ἢ οἱ
Λακεδαιμόνιοι. ἐκεῖνοι γὰρ μείζονα μὲν στρατὸν ἔχουσιν ἢ ἡμεῖς κατὰ γῆν, πολλῷ
δὲ ἐλάττονας ναῦς τε καὶ ναύτᾱς. οὐδεὶς γὰρ ἀγνοεῖ ὅτι τῇ ναυτικῇ τέχνῃ
ἀμείνονές εἰσιν οἱ Ἀθηναῖοι ἢ πάντες οἱ ἄλλοι Ἕλληνες. τοῦτο μόνον ἔλεγον, ὅτι οἱ
Λακεδαιμόνιοι, οἷς ἀεὶ ἀγανακτούμεθα, οὐκ εἰσὶν αἴτιοι ἀπάντων κακῶν.

[κυβερνῆτα, steersman   μῑσῶ, I hate   σφόδρα, very much, exceedingly   ἀγνοῶ, I
do not know   τὴν ἀρχὴν, the empire   ναυτικῇ, naval   τέχνῃ, skill   ἀγανακτούμεθα + dat., we are displeased (with), vexed (at)]

[14] "πῶς δ' οὐκ εἰμὶ ἀληθέστατα Ἀθηναῖος; ὑμέτερος γάρ εἰμι πολίτης, ὦ
φίλοι, Ἀθηναῖος ὢν καὶ τὰ πρὸς πατρὸς καὶ τὰ πρὸς μητρός. διαβάλλει γὰρ ὅδε ὁ
ἀνὴρ τὸν πατέρα μου, ἐπεὶ ἐξένιζεν. ἐκεῖνος δέ, ἐν πολέμῳ ὑπὸ τῶν πολεμίων
ληφθείς, δοῦλος ἐγένετο καὶ πολὺν χρόνον ἐν ἀλλοτρίᾳ χώρᾳ ἔμεινεν καὶ διὰ τοῦτο
οὐκέτι οἷός τ' ἦν καλῶς ἀττικίζειν. ἦν δὲ τῷ ὄντι ἀστός, καὶ οὐ ξένος, ὡς ὅδε ὁ
ἀνὴρ φλυᾱρεῖ, Ἀθηναῖοι δὲ ἦσαν καὶ ὁ ἐκείνου πατὴρ Χαρίσιος καὶ ἡ μήτηρ. περὶ δὲ
τῆς μητρὸς πρὸς ῡ̔μᾶς λέγειν βούλομαι τάδε· ἐμοὶ ἦν πάππος, ὦ ἄνδρες Ἀθηναῖοι,
τῆς μητρὸς πατήρ, ὃς ἦν εἷς τῶν ἐν Μαραθῶνι στρατευσαμένων καὶ
τελευτησάντων, καὶ ὁ ἐκείνου ἀδελφὸς ἐτελεύτησε πρὸς τῇ Σαλαμῖνι μετὰ
Θεμιστοκλέους στρατευόμενος.

[ἀληθέστατα, most truly   τὰ πρὸς, on the side of   διαβάλλει, slanders   ἐπεὶ,
since   ἐξένιζεν, he spoke (was speaking) with a foreign accent   ὑπὸ, by   ληφθείς
(aorist passive participle of λαμβάνω), taken, captured   ἀλλοτρίᾳ, foreign   χώρᾳ,
land   διὰ, because of   οἷός τ' ἦν, he was able   ἀττικίζειν, to speak Attic Greek
ἀστός, citizen   φλυᾱρεῖ, talks nonsense   στρατευσαμένων, having campaigned,

who campaigned τελευτησάντων, *having died, who died* Θεμιστοκλέους, *Themistocles*]

[15] "ἠκούσατε δὲ τοῦδε τοῦ ἀνδρὸς λέγοντος ὅτι ἐμὲ εἶδεν ἐν τῇ ἀγορᾷ ξένῳ τινὶ Δωριστὶ διαλεγόμενον. τί δέ; ἔμπορος γὰρ ὢν ἐκ τῆσδε τῆς πόλεως πολλάκις ὡρμησάμην καὶ ἐκ τῆσδε τῆς θαλάττης ἔπλευσα μὲν εἰς πολλὰς ἄλλας χώρᾱς, 'πολλῶν δ' ἀνθρώπων ἴδον ἄστεα καὶ νόον ἔγνων,' ὥσπερ ὁ Ὅμηρος λέγει περὶ τοῦ Ὀδυσσέως. οὐδὲν οὖν ἄτοπόν ἐστιν ὅτι πλείστων ἀνθρώπων καὶ τὰς διαλέκτους ἔμαθον. μὴ οὖν πίστευε τῷδε τῷ ἀνθρώπῳ ψευδῆ λέγοντι καὶ διαβολὰς, ὦ κυβερνῆτα.

[Δωριστὶ, *in the Doric dialect* χώρᾱς, *lands* ἴδον = εἶδον ἄστεα = ἄστη ἔγνων, *I came to know* ὁ Ὅμηρος, *Homer* ἄτοπόν, *out of place, strange* διαλέκτους, *dialects* πίστευε + dat., *believe!* διαβολάς, *slanders* κυβερνῆτα, *steersman*]

[16] "πρὸς ὑμᾶς δέ, ὦ ἄνδρες, τί δεῖ με πλείονα λέγειν; οἶμαι γὰρ ὅτι νῦν ὑμεῖς οὐδὲν ἀγνοεῖτε, ἐπεὶ τὰ ἀληθῆ ἠκούσατε."

[οἶμαι, *I think* ἀγνοεῖτε, *you do not know* ἐπεὶ, *since*]

[17] ὁ δὲ κυβερνήτης, "νῦν δέ," ἔφη, "ἡσυχάζετε καὶ μὴ θορυβεῖτε μηδὲ μάχεσθε πρὸς ἀλλήλους· δεῖ γὰρ ἡμᾶς ἡσύχως πλεῖν καὶ εἰς τὴν Ἐπίδαυρον ἀφικνεῖσθαι. σὺ μὲν οὖν, ὦ ἔμπορε, μὴ λέγε ὑπὲρ τῶν Λακεδαιμονίων, σὺ δέ, ὦ ναῦτα, μὴ ἀγανάκτει ἀλλὰ ἥσυχος ἔχε." τάδε εἰπὼν ἀπῆλθεν, καὶ δι' ὀλίγου καὶ πάντες οἱ ἄλλοι ἐκάθισαν.

[κυβερνήτης, *steersman* θορυβεῖτε, *cause a commotion!* ἡσύχως, *quietly, calmly* ἀγανάκτει, *be displeased, vexed!* ἥσυχος ἔχε, *be quiet!*]

[18] ὁ δὲ Δικαιόπολις· "ἰδού, ὦ γέρον, ὅση ἐστὶν ἡ τῶν πρᾱγμάτων μεταβολὴ ἐν τῇδε τῇ ἡμετέρᾳ χώρᾳ· σὺ μὲν γὰρ ἡμῖν διηγοῦ ὡς πάντες οἱ Ἕλληνες, οἵ τε Λακεδαιμόνιοι καὶ οἱ Ἀθηναῖοι, ἅμα ἐμαχέσαντο πρὸς τοὺς βαρβάρους ὑπὲρ τῆς ἐλευθερίας· νῦν δὲ οἱ ἄνθρωποι ἐν τῇ αὐτῇ πόλει οἰκοῦντες μῑσοῦσιν ἀλλήλους καὶ αἰτίᾱν τινὰ ἔχθρᾱς τε καὶ μάχης ζητοῦσιν. τότε μὲν γὰρ οἱ Ἕλληνες πᾶσαν τὴν Ἑλλάδα εἶναι κοινὴν πατρίδα ἐνόμιζον, νῦν δὲ μόνον τῶν ἑαυτῶν οἴκων ἐπιμελοῦνται. οἱ μὲν οὖν ἡμέτεροι πρόγονοι διεφύλαξαν τήν τε πρὸς τοὺς Ἕλληνας ὁμόνοιαν καὶ τὴν πρὸς τοὺς βαρβάρους ἔχθρᾱν· ὁμόνοια γὰρ μέγιστον ἀγαθὸν ἐδόκει ταῖς πόλεσιν εἶναι. νῦν δὲ οὐ μόνον οἱ Ἀθηναῖοι μῑσοῦσι τοὺς Λακεδαιμονίους καὶ οἱ Λακεδαιμόνιοι μῑσοῦσι τοὺς Ἀθηναίους, ἀλλὰ καὶ αὐτοὶ οἱ Ἀθηναῖοι ἔχθρᾱν ἔχουσι πρὸς ἀλλήλους. φεῦ, φεῦ τῆσδε τῆς πόλεως."

[ὅση, *how great* πρᾱγμάτων, *affairs* μεταβολή, *change* χώρᾳ, *land* διηγοῦ, *you were describing* ὡς, *how* μῑσοῦσιν, *hate* αἰτίᾱν, *cause* ἔχθρᾱς, *hatred* κοινὴν, *common* πατρίδα, *fatherland* ἐνόμιζον, *were thinking* ἐπιμελοῦνται + gen., *they care for* πρόγονοι, *ancestors* διεφύλαξαν, *carefully* guarded   **ὁμόνοιαν**, *oneness of mind, concord*   **οὐ μόνον**, *not only*   **ἀλλὰ καὶ**, *but also*]

[19] ὁ δὲ Φίλιππος ὑπολαβών, "ἐγὼ δέ," ἔφη, "βούλομαι ἀκούειν ὅπως οἱ Ἀθηναῖοι ἐμαχέσαντο πρὸς τοὺς βαρβάρους ἐν τῇ Σαλαμῖνι. μὴ οὖν παῦε διηγούμενος, ὦ ναῦτα, ἀλλ᾽ εἰπὲ ἡμῖν τί ἐγένετο ἐπεὶ οἱ βάρβαροι ἐν τῷ λιμένι ὥρμουν."

[**ὑπολαβών**, *taking up* (the conversation)   **ὅπως**, *how*   **διηγούμενος**, *describing* **ὥρμουν** (from ὁρμέω), *were lying at anchor*]

[20] ὁ δὲ ναύτης, "ἡσυχάζετε οὖν," ἔφη, "καὶ ἀκούετε."

15
Η ΕΝ ΤΗΙ ΣΑΛΑΜΙΝΙ
ΜΑΧΗ (α)

Exercise 15α

Translate the following English phrases and words with the correct aorist form of the Greek verb supplied (the verbs supplied are in the aorist, 1st person singular, indicative):

1. ἔβην: he/she stepped _____
2. ἔβην: (ἡ γυνὴ) having gone _____
3. ἔστην: stand! (sing.) _____
4. ἔβην: to walk _____
5. ἔγνων: you (sing.) learned _____
6. ἔγνων: I learned _____
7. ἔστην: they stood _____
8. ἔστην: stand! (pl.) _____
9. ἔγνων: to learn _____
10. ἔγνων: (ὁ ἄνθρωπος) after learning _____
11. ἔβην: you (pl.) went _____
12. ἔβην: they went _____
13. ἔστην: I stood _____
14. ἔστην: you (pl.) stood _____
15. ἔγνων: learn! (pl.) _____
16. ἔβην: you (sing.) went _____
17. ἔγνων: he/she learned _____
18. ἔστην: you (sing.) stood _____
19. ἔβην: we went _____
20. ἔγνων: (ἡ γυνὴ) having learned _____
21. ἔστην: (ὁ ἄνθρωπος) standing _____
22. ἔστην: he/she stood _____
23. ἔγνων: they learned _____
24. ἔστην: (ἡ γυνὴ) standing _____
25. ἔβην: I went _____

26. ἔστην: to stand   _____

27. ἔβην: go! (sing.)   _____

28. ἔγνων: know! (sing.)   _____

29. ἔβην: (ὁ ἄνθρωπος) having gone   _____

30. ἔγνων: you (pl.) learned   _____

31. ἔβην: go! (pl.)   _____

32. ἔστην: we stood   _____

Exercise 15β

Complete the following phrases with the correct form of the noun supplied:

1. τὸν _____ (Περικλῆς)

2. τῷ _____ ('Ηρακλῆς)

3. ὦ _____ (Σοφοκλῆς)

4. τοῦ _____ (Περικλῆς)

5. τῷ _____ (Θεμιστοκλῆς)

6. τὸν _____ (Θεμιστοκλῆς)

7. ὦ _____ (Περικλῆς)

8. τοῦ _____ ('Ηρακλῆς)

Exercise 15γ

Give an English equivalent of:

1. ἡ ἀπορίᾱ   _____   4. μόνον   _____

2. εἴκω   _____   5. ὁ νοῦς   _____

3. ἀναγκάζω   _____   6. ἡ φυγή   _____

Exercise 15δ

Give the Greek equivalent of:

1. admiral   _____   4. no longer   _____

2. general   _____   5. I destroy   _____

3. alone   _____   6. not only . . .
                                                       but also   _____

Exercise 15ε

Give the imperfect, future, and aorist of:

1. διαφθείρω   _____   3. εἴκω   _____
                  _____   _____
                  _____   _____

2. ἀναγκάζω   _____
                  _____
                  _____

(β)

Exercise 15ζ

Translate the following English phrases and words with the correct form (present or imperfect) of the Greek verb supplied:

1. δηλόω: they show   _____
2. δηλόω: show yourself! (sing.)   _____
3. ἐλευθερόω: we set free   _____
4. ἐλευθερόω: to set yourself free   _____
5. δουλόω: I enslave   _____
6. δουλόω: he/she enslaves   _____
7. δηλόω: he/she was showing   _____
8. ἐλευθερόω: they are setting
        themselves free   _____
9. δουλόω: to enslave   _____
10. δουλόω: enslave! (sing.)   _____
11. δηλόω: (ἡ κόρη) showing   _____
12. ἀρόω: you (pl.) were plowing   _____
13. δουλόω: they were enslaving   _____
14. ἀρόω: to plow   _____
15. ἐλευθερόω: you (sing.) were setting
        X free   _____
16. ἐλευθερόω: set yourselves free!   _____
17. ἀρόω: you (sing.) are plowing   _____

18. ἀρόω: we were plowing _____

19. πληρόω: you (pl.) are filling _____

20. πληρόω: fill! (pl.) _____

21. πληρόω: I was filling _____

22. ἐλευθερόω: he/she sets

himself/herself free _____

23. δουλόω: we are enslaving ourselves _____

24. δηλόω: I was showing myself _____

25. ἐλευθερόω: we were setting

ourselves free _____

26. δηλόω: (ὁ ἄνθρωπος) showing himself _____

27. ἐλευθερόω: they were freeing themselves _____

28. δηλόω: you show yourself _____

29. ἐλευθερόω: she was freeing herself _____

30. δουλόω: you (pl.) were enslaving

yourselves _____

Exercise 15η

Complete the phrase with the correct form of the noun ὁ νοῦς:

1. οἱ _____ 5. τῶν _____

2. τοῖς _____ 6. τῷ _____

3. τοῦ _____ 7. τοὺς _____

4. ὦ (sing.) _____ 8. τὸν _____

Exercise 15θ

Select the English equivalent from the pool below this exercise and write it on the line in front of each Greek numerical adjective:

1. _____ ἑκατόν 7. _____ ἕνδεκα

2. _____ δωδέκατος 8. _____ πεντακόσιοι

3. _____ τεττᾰράκοντα 9. _____ ἑκατοστός

4. _____ εἴκοσι(ν) 10. _____ ὀγδοήκοντα

5. _____ μύριοι 11. _____ δώδεκα

6. _____ χῑλιοστός 12. _____ ἑνδέκατος

| 11 | 40 | 1000th | 12 | 100 | 80 | 11th | 12th | 10,000 | 100th | 20 | 500 |

Exercise 15ι

Translate the Greek words or phrases in the following sentences:

1.   The slave did the work ὡς τάχιστα.

   _____

2.   The farmer lies down under the tree ὡς καθευδήσων.

   _____

3.   ὡς the woman went to the spring, her friends joined her there.

   _____

4.   ὡς δοκεῖ, the gods are smiling on our undertaking.

   _____

5.   I have often heard ὡς the Spartans are courageous in war.

   _____

6.   I now realize ὡς courageous they really are.

   _____

7.   They charge so menacingly ὥστε we are hardly able to withstand them.

   _____

Exercise 15κ

Give an English equivalent of:

1.	ὁ πρόγονος	_____	7.	πειράω	_____
2.	δεξιός	_____	8.	τὸ μέρος	_____
3.	πιστεύω	_____	9.	ἡ σπουδή	_____
4.	ὁ νεκρός	_____	10.	ναυμαχέω	_____
5.	πανταχοῦ	_____	11.	ὁ θόρυβος	_____
6.	συμπίπτω	_____	12.	ἐλευθερόω	_____

Exercise 15λ

Give the Greek equivalent of:

1. robe　　　　　　_____
2. on foot　　　　　_____
3. contest　　　　　_____
4. fatherland　　　_____
5. victory　　　　　_____
6. excellence　　　_____
7. I fall upon　　　_____
8. that (conj.)　　 _____

9. good order　　　_____
10. I show　　　　　_____
11. luck　　　　　　_____
12. I sail against　_____
13. I harm　　　　　_____
14. I stood up　　　_____
15. in order　　　　_____

Exercise 15μ

Give the imperfect, future, and aorist of:

1. συμπῑ́πτω　　　_____
　　　　　　　　　_____
　　　　　　　　　_____

2. ναυμαχέω　　　_____
　　　　　　　　　_____
　　　　　　　　　_____

3. ἐλευθερόω　　　_____
　　　　　　　　　_____
　　　　　　　　　_____

4. βλάπτω　　　　_____
　　　　　　　　　_____
　　　　　　　　　_____

5. ἐμπῑ́πτω　　　　_____
　　　　　　　　　_____
　　　　　　　　　_____

6. πειράω　　　　_____
　　　　　　　　　_____

7. πιστεύω　　　　_____
　　　　　　　　　_____

8. ἐπιπλέω　　　　_____
　　　　　　　　　_____

9. δηλόω　　　　　_____
　　　　　　　　　_____

Exercise 15ν

Translate the following into English on a separate sheet of paper:

ΟΙ ΘΕΟΙ ΤΟΝ ΞΕΡΞΗΝ ΕΚΟΛΑΣΑΝ

[1] ὁ δὲ ναύτης ὁ γεραιός, "ἡμεῖς γάρ," ἔφη, "ἐκινδῡνεύσαμεν ὑπὲρ τῆς πατρίδος καὶ ὑπὲρ τῆς τῶν πάντων Ἑλλήνων ἐλευθερίᾱς· καὶ διὰ τοῦτο ἀθανάτῳ εὐλογίᾳ τῷ ὄντι χρώμεθα, οὐκ ἐπεὶ ἐνῑκήσαμεν ἀλλὰ πολλῷ μᾶλλον ἐπεὶ δικαίᾱ ἦν ἡμῖν ἡ

τῆς μάχης αἰτία. μαχόμενοι γὰρ καὶ τὴν ἡμετέραν πατρίδα ἐλευθεροῦντες οὐ μόνον πᾶσι τοῖς τότε ἀνθρώποις ἐδηλοῦμεν τί ἐστιν ἡ ἀρετή, ἀλλὰ καὶ ἐπαύομεν εἰς ἅπαντα τὸν ἔπειτα χρόνον τοὺς Ἕλληνας φοβουμένους πλῆθος νεῶν τε καὶ ἀνδρῶν. οἱ γὰρ θεοὶ ἀεὶ τὴν μὲν ὕβριν κολάζουσιν, τὴν δ' ἀρετὴν τῑμῶσιν, καὶ μεγάλην δόξαν παρέχουσι τοῖς ὑπὲρ τῆς ἐλευθερίας μαχομένοις.

[ΕΚΟΛΑΣΑΝ (from κολάζω), *Punished* **ἐκινδῡνεύσαμεν**, *we ran risks* **διὰ** + acc., *because of* **ἀθανάτῳ**, *immortal* **εὐλογίᾳ**, *praise* **ἐπεὶ**, *since, because* **δικαίᾱ**, *just* **αἰτίᾱ**, *cause* **ὕβριν**, *insolence* **δόξαν**, *glory*]

[2] "ἐν ἐκείνῳ γὰρ τῷ χρόνῳ πᾶσα μὲν ἡ Ἀσίᾱ ἐδούλευε τῷ Ξέρξει, τετάρτῳ ἤδη βασιλεῖ τῶν Περσῶν. ὁ μὲν γὰρ πρῶτος, Κῦρος ὀνόματι, ἐλευθερώσᾱς Πέρσᾱς, τοὺς ἑαυτοῦ πολίτᾱς, ἅμα καὶ τοὺς δεσπότᾱς Μήδους ἐδουλώσατο καὶ ἦρξε τῆς ἄλλης Ἀσίᾱς μέχρι Αἰγύπτου. ὁ δὲ υἱὸς αὐτοῦ Καμβύσης ἐνέπεσεν ἄλλαις πολλαῖς χώραις Αἰγύπτου τε καὶ Λιβύης αὐτᾱς δουλούμενος. τρίτος δὲ Δαρεῖος πεζῷ στρατῷ μὲν εἰσέβη εἰς τὰς τῶν Σκυθῶν χώρᾱς, ναυσὶ δὲ τὴν ἀρχὴν τὴν τῆς θαλάττης ἔλαβε καὶ τῶν νήσων. ἐνέπεσεν οὖν τοῖς Ἀθηναίοις ἐν Μαραθῶνι ἀλλ' οὐκ ἐνίκησεν. ὁ οὖν Ξέρξης, τέταρτος τῶν Περσῶν βασιλεύς, πολλὰ καὶ ἄλλα ἔθνη ἐδουλοῦτο, εἶχε δὲ οὐ πιστούς τε καὶ ἐλευθέρους ἀνθρώπους ἀλλὰ μόνον δούλων μέγα πλῆθος. τῶν δὲ ἀλλοτρίων ἀεὶ ἐπιθῡμῶν, ὁ Ξέρξης διέγνω πολεμεῖν τοῖς Ἕλλησιν, καὶ εἰς τὴν Εὐρώπην διέβη. ποίῳ δὲ δικαίῳ χρώμενος ἐπὶ τὴν Ἑλλάδα ἐστράτευσεν; ὥσπερ ἐν παντὶ τῷ βίῳ, οὕτω καὶ τότε τὴν ἑαυτοῦ ὕβριν ἐδήλου, νομίζων ἀθάνατος εἶναι καὶ τῶν θεῶν καταφρονήσᾱς, οἳ αὐτῷ τοσαύτην ἀρχὴν παρέσχον. ὕβρις γὰρ κακὸν μέγιστον ἀνθρώποις ἐστὶν καὶ τυράννους φυτεύει. τί δὲ ἄλλο ἐστὶν ὕβρις εἰ μὴ ἀμείνων θεῶν εἶναι νομίζειν καὶ πάντας τοὺς ἀνθρώπους καταδουλοῦσθαι βούλεσθαι; διὰ τοῦτο ὁ Ζεὺς τὸν Ξέρξην ἐκόλασεν· οὐ γὰρ δυνατόν ἐστι θνητοῖς πρὸς ἀθανάτους μαχέσασθαι.

[**ἐδούλευε**, *was subject to* **Κῦρος**, *Cyrus* **Μήδους**, *the Medes* **ἐδουλώσατο**, *he enslaved* **ἦρξε** (from ἄρχω) + gen., *he ruled* **τῆς ἄλλης**, *the rest of* **μέχρι** + gen., *as far as* **Αἰγύπτου**, *Egypt* **υἱὸς**, *son* **Καμβύσης**, *Cambyses* **χώραις**, *lands* **Λιβύης**, *Lybia* **δουλούμενος**, *enslaving* **Δαρεῖος**, *Darius* **πεζῷ στρατῷ**, *with his infantry* **Σκυθῶν**, *Scythians* **τὴν ἀρχὴν τὴν** + gen., *control of* **Μαραθῶνι**, *Marathon* **ἔθνη**, *nations, peoples* **πιστούς**, *loyal* **ἐλευθέρους**, *free* **τῶν** ... **ἀλλοτρίων**, *things belonging to others* **ἐπιθῡμῶν** + gen., *desiring* **διέγνω**, *decided* **πολεμεῖν** + dat., *to make war upon* **τὴν Εὐρώπην**, *Europe* **διέβη**, *crossed* **ποίῳ** ... **δικαίῳ**, *what lawful (claim)* **ἐστράτευσεν**, *did he wage war?* **τῷ βίῳ**, *his life* **ὕβριν**, *insolence* **νομίζων**, *thinking* **ἀθάνατος**, *immortal* **καταφρονήσᾱς** + gen., *despising* **ἀρχὴν**, *empire* **τυράννους**, *tyrants* **φυτεύει**, *begets* **καταδουλοῦσθαι**, *to enslave* **διὰ** + acc., *because of* **ἐκόλασεν**, *punished* **θνητοῖς**, *for mortals*]

[3] "οἱ δὲ ἡμέτεροι πατέρες καὶ ἡμεῖς αὐτοὶ ἐκ παίδων διηγάγομεν τὸν βίον ἐν πάσῃ ἐλευθερίᾳ τὴν δουλείᾱν ἐχθαίροντες. καὶ διὰ τοῦτο πολλὰ καὶ καλὰ ἔργα

ἐποιοῦμεν ἐν παντὶ τῷ βίῳ καὶ ἰδίᾳ καὶ δημοσίᾳ. καὶ δὴ καὶ μαχόμενοι καὶ καταπολεμοῦντες τὴν ἐξ ἁπάσης τῆς Ἀσίᾱς δύναμιν ἐδηλοῦμεν πᾶσι τοῖς ἀνθρώποις ὅτι ἡ ἀρετὴ καὶ ἡ τόλμα ἀεὶ τὴν ὕβριν νῑκῶσιν. ὅτε δὲ ἐνεπέσομεν τοῖς πολεμίοις, οὐ προσέσχομεν τὸν νοῦν τοῖς τοῦ πολέμου κινδύνοις ἀλλ' ἐν νῷ ἔσχομεν τὴν πατρίδα σῴζειν καὶ τοὺς παῖδας καὶ τὰς γυναῖκας.

[διηγάγομεν, *we spent, lived*   **τὴν δουλείᾱν**, *slavery*   **ἐχθαίροντες**, *hating*   **διὰ** + acc., *because of*   **ἰδίᾳ**, *in private*   **δημοσίᾳ**, *in public*   **καὶ δὴ καὶ**, *and in particular*   **καταπολεμοῦντες**, *subduing*   **τὴν . . . δύναμιν**, *the military force, power*   **ἡ τόλμα**, *daring*   **τὴν ὕβριν**, *insolence*   **οὐ προσέσχομεν τὸν νοῦν** + dat., *we did not turn our attention (to)*]

[4] "ἀνδρείᾱν οὖν τε καὶ ἀρετὴν ἐδηλώσαμεν μετὰ νοῦ—ὅτε μὲν γάρ τι ποιεῖ ἄνευ νοῦ ἄνθρωπος, ἀεὶ πάσχει κακόν τι. ὁ νοῦς γὰρ ἡμῶν ἐστιν ἐν ἑκάστῳ θεός—καὶ διὰ τοῦτο οἱ θεοὶ πάντες ἐβοήθησαν μὲν ἡμῖν, ἐκόλασαν δὲ τοὺς βαρβάρους. οἱ γὰρ θεοί, εἰ τὰ ἀληθῆ λέγειν δεῖ, διέγνωσαν τὴν μὲν ἡμῶν νίκην, τὴν δὲ τῶν βαρβάρων ἧτταν.

[**ἀνδρείᾱν**, *manliness, courage*   **ἄνευ** + gen., *without*   **ἑκάστῳ**, *each*   **ἐκόλασαν**, *they punished*   **διέγνωσαν**, *decided, determined, ordained*   **ἧτταν**, *defeat*]

[5] "γνῶθι οὖν, ὦ παῖ, τὰ τῶν πατέρων ἔργα καὶ τὴν τόλμαν, καὶ δήλου καὶ σὺ ἀεὶ ἐν παντὶ τῷ βίῳ τὴν αὐτὴν ἀρετήν, εἰ τοῖς θεοῖς φίλος εἶναι βούλει καὶ τῆς πατρίδος ἄξιος ἐθέλεις γίγνεσθαι."

[**τὴν τόλμαν**, *daring*]

16
ΜΕΤΑ ΤΗΝ ΕΝ ΤΗΙ ΣΑΛΑΜΙΝΙ ΜΑΧΗΝ (α)

Exercise 16α

Translate the underlined verbs or verb phrases according to whether the verb is passive or middle voice:

1. ὁ ἀνὴρ <u>ἐγείρεται</u> ὑπὸ τῆς γυναικός. _____
2. ὁ πατὴρ <u>λύεται</u> τὴν θυγατέρα. _____
3. οἱ ὁπλῖται <u>παύονται</u> μαχόμενοι. _____
4. ὁ κύων ὑπὸ τοῦ παιδὸς <u>ἐλούετο</u>. _____
5. ὁ γέρων <u>ἐγείρεται</u>. _____
6. εἴδομεν τὴν γῆν <u>διαφθειρομένην</u>. _____
7. ὁ βοῦς <u>ἐλύετο</u> ὑπὸ τοῦ δούλου. _____
8. τὸ μάθημα (*the lesson*) ὑπὸ τοῦ παιδὸς <u>οὐ μανθάνεται</u>. _____
9. ἡ παῖς <u>λούεται</u>. _____
10. οἱ βόες ὑπὸ τῶν δούλων <u>λύονται</u>. _____
11. ὁ παῖς λίθοις <u>τύπτεται</u>. _____
12. ὁ αὐτουργὸς <u>παύεται</u> ἀρῶν. _____
13. οἱ παῖδες <u>ἐγείρονται</u> ὑπὸ τῆς μητρός. _____
14. ὁ κύων ἐν τῷ ποταμῷ (*river*) <u>ἐλούετο</u>. _____
15. οἱ πολέμιοι πρὸς τὴν πόλιν τρέχοντες <u>οὐκ ἐπαύοντο</u>. _____

Exercise 16β

Give an English equivalent of:

1. στρατεύω _____ 6. ὑπὸ τοῦ παιδός _____
2. ὁ ἔνοικος _____ 7. συναγείρω _____
3. καὶ δὴ καί _____ 8. ἡ συμφορά _____
4. ἑκατόν _____ 9. ποῦ γῆς _____
5. κεῖμαι _____ 10. οὐδαμοῦ _____

117

Exercise 16γ

Give the Greek equivalent of:

1. later _____   6. I am able _____
2. ally _____   7. how much? _____
3. I end _____   8. I overtake _____
4. two hundred _____ 9. to many parts _____
5. I understand _____

Exercise 16δ

Give the imperfect, future, and aorist of:

1. στρατεύω _____   5. καταλαμβάνω _____
   _____   _____
   _____   _____

2. τελευτάω _____   6. συναγείρω _____
   _____   _____
   _____   _____

3. δύναμαι _____   7. κεῖμαι _____
   _____   _____
   no aorist middle   no aorist

4. ἐπίσταμαι _____

   _____
   no aorist middle

Exercise 16ε

Translate into English on a separate sheet of paper:

Ο ΟΔΥΣΣΕΥΣ ΥΠΟ ΤΗΣ ΚΑΛΥΨΟΥΣ ΚΑΤΕΧΕΤΑΙ

[1] ἐπεὶ ὅ τε Ὀδυσσεὺς καὶ οἱ ἑταῖροι ἀπὸ τῆς τοῦ Ἡλίου νήσου ἀπέπλεον, ὁ Ζεὺς χειμῶνα δεινὸν πέμψας τὴν ναῦν κεραυνῷ ἔβαλεν. οἱ μὲν οὖν ἑταῖροι ἐκ τῆς νεὼς ἐκπεσόντες πάντες ἐν τοῖς κύμασιν ἀπέθανον· ὁ δὲ Ὀδυσσεὺς τοῦ ἱστοῦ λαβόμενος μόνος σῴζεται. ἐννέα οὖν ἡμέρας διὰ τῶν κυμάτων τῷ ἀνέμῳ ἐφέρετο τοῦ ἱστοῦ λαμβανόμενος. τῇ δὲ δεκάτῃ νῆσον εἶδεν οὐ πολὺ ἀπέχουσαν· τὸν οὖν ἱστὸν καταλιπὼν πρὸς τὴν νῆσον ἔνευσεν. ἐκεῖ δὲ ᾤκει Καλυψώ, θεὰ δεινή· ἡ δὲ αὐτὸν εὐμενῶς ἐδέξατο· ἐφίλει γὰρ αὐτὸν καὶ ἔτρεφε καὶ ἔλεγεν ὅτι αὐτὸν ἀθάνατον ποιήσει. ἐβούλετο γὰρ κατέχειν αὐτὸν ἐν τῇ νήσῳ καὶ πόσιν ἑαυτῇ ποιεῖν. ἀλλ᾽ οὐδέποτε αὐτὸν ἔπεισεν· ἐβούλετο γὰρ εἰς τὴν πατρίδα γῆν ἐπανιέναι καὶ τὴν γυναῖκα ὁρᾶν.

[**ΚΑΛΥΨΟΥΣ**, *Calypso* **ΚΑΤΕΧΕΤΑΙ**, *Is Held Back* **κεραυνῷ**, *thunderbolt* **τοῦ ἱστοῦ**, *the mast* **πολὺ**, *very* **ἀπέχουσαν**, *being far away* **ἔνευσεν** (from νέω), *he swam* **εὐμενῶς**, *kindly* **ἔτρεφε**, *she was nourishing* **ἀθάνατον**, *immortal* **πόσιν**, *husband* **οὐδέποτε**, *never*]

[2] ἕπτα οὖν ἔτη ὁ Ὀδυσσεὺς ἐν τῇ νήσῳ ἔμενεν, ὑπὸ τῆς Καλυψοῦς κατεχόμενος. μόνος δὲ ἐν τῇ ἀκτῇ ἐκαθίζετο, ἀεὶ δακρύων· "φεῦ, φεῦ," ἔφη, "βούλομαι εἰς τὴν πατρίδα γῆν ἐπανιέναι, ἀεὶ δὲ κατέχομαι ὑπὸ τῆς Καλυψοῦς."

[**ἔτη**, *years* **κατεχόμενος**, *being held back* **τῇ ἀκτῇ**, *the promontory*]

[3] ὁ δὲ Ζεύς, ἐκ τοῦ οὐρανοῦ πρὸς τὴν γῆν βλέπων, τὸν Ὀδυσσέᾱ εἶδεν ἐν τῇ ἀκτῇ καθήμενον δακρύοντα· ἠλέαιρεν οὖν αὐτόν, καὶ τὸν Ἑρμῆν καλέσᾱς, "ἴθι δή, Ἑρμῆ," φησίν, "πέτου πρὸς τὴν νῆσον Ὠγυγίᾱν· ἐκεῖ γὰρ ὁ Ὀδυσσεὺς ὑπὸ τῆς Καλυψοῦς κατέχεται. κέλευε οὖν αὐτὴν ἀποπέμψαι αὐτόν. εἰ δὲ μὴ ἀποπέμψει αὐτόν, ἐγὼ κολάσω αὐτήν."

[**τῇ ἀκτῇ**, *the promontory* **καθήμενον**, *sitting* **ἠλέαιρεν** (from ἐλεαίρω), *he was pitying* **τὸν Ἑρμῆν**, *Hermes* **πέτου** (from πέτομαι), *fly!* **Ὠγυγίᾱν**, *Ogygia* **κατέχεται**, *is being held back* **κολάσω**, *I will punish*]

[4] ὁ μὲν οὖν Ἑρμῆς τῷ Διὶ πειθόμενος ἐπέτετο πρὸς τὴν Ὠγυγίᾱν· ἐπεὶ δὲ ἀφίκετο, ἐζήτει τὴν Καλυψώ. εὑρὼν δὲ αὐτὴν ἐν τῇ οἰκίᾳ καθημένην, "χαῖρε, ὦ θεά," ἔφη· "ὑπὸ τοῦ Διὸς κελεύει τὸν Ὀδυσσέᾱ ἀποπέμψαι· πολὺν γὰρ χρόνον κατέχεται ὑπὸ σοῦ εἰς τὴν πατρίδα γῆν ἐπανιέναι βουλόμενος." ἡ δὲ Καλυψώ, "φεῦ, φεῦ," ἔφη, "τί λέγεις; βούλομαι αὐτὸν ἀεὶ κατέχειν καὶ πόσιν ἐμαυτῇ ποιεῖν. φιλῶ γὰρ αὐτόν." ὁ δὲ Ἑρμῆς, "δεῖ σε τῷ Διὶ πείθεσθαι· εἰ δὲ μή, κολάσει σε." οὕτως εἰπὼν ἀποπέτεται.

[**ἐπέτετο**, *was flying* **καθημένην**, *sitting* **κατέχειν**, *to hold X back* **πόσιν**, *husband* **κολάσει**, *he will punish* **ἀποπέτεται**, *he flies away*]

[5] ἡ δὲ Καλυψὼ πολλὰ ὀδῡρομένη τὸν Ὀδυσσέᾱ ἐζήτει. εὗρε δὲ αὐτὸν ἐν τῇ ἀκτῇ καθήμενον, δακρύοντα, καί, "θάρρει, ὦ Ὀδυσσεῦ," ἔφη, "μὴ δάκρῡε. κελεύομαι γὰρ ὑπὸ τοῦ Διός σε οἴκαδε ἀποπέμψαι. ἄγε δή· σχεδίᾱν ποιήσομεν." ἡγήσατο οὖν αὐτῷ εἰς τὴν τῆς νήσου ἐσχατιᾱν ὅπου πολλὰ δένδρα ἦν. ὁ οὖν Ὀδυσσεὺς εἴκοσι δένδρα κατατεμὼν σχεδίᾱν παρεσκεύαζεν. τρεῖς μὲν οὖν ἡμέρᾱς ἐπόνει τὴν σχεδίᾱν παρασκευάζων, τῇ δὲ τετάρτῃ πάντα ἕτοιμα ἦν, τῇ δὲ πέμπτῃ ἡ Καλυψὼ ἀπέπεμψεν αὐτὸν ἀπὸ τῆς νήσου. ὁ δὲ χαίρων ἀπέπλευσεν.

[**ὀδῡρομένη**, *lamenting* **τῇ ἀκτῇ**, *the promontory* **καθήμενον**, *sitting* **θάρρει**, *cheer up!* **σχεδίᾱν**, *raft* **ἐσχατιᾱν**, *edge* **κατατεμὼν** (from κατατέμνω), *having cut down*]

[6] πρῶτον μὲν οὖν ἀνέμῳ πράῳ ἐφέρετο διὰ τῶν κῡμάτων, ἔπειτα δὲ ὁ Ποσειδῶν ἰδὼν αὐτόν, "ὦ πόποι," ἔφη, "τὸν Ὀδυσσέᾱ ὁρῶ διὰ τῶν κῡμάτων ῥᾳδίως φερόμενον. ἐὰν μὴ κωλύσω αὐτόν, εἰς τὴν πατρίδα γῆν ἀβλαβὴς ἀφίξεται." οὕτως

εἰπὼν δεινὸν χειμῶνα ἔπεμψε πάντας τοὺς ἀνέμους ἐκλύσας. κῦμα δὲ μέγιστον τὴν σχεδίᾶν βαλὸν κατέθραυσεν. ὁ δὲ Ὀδυσσεὺς εἰς τὰ κύματα εἰσπεσὼν μάλα ἐφοβεῖτο ἀλλὰ τῇ σχεδίᾳ μόλις προσνεύσᾶς τῶν ἐρειπίων ἐλάβετο. δύο οὖν ἡμέρᾶς δύο τε νύκτας τοῖς ἀνέμοις ἔνθα καὶ ἔνθα ἐφέρετο ἀεὶ θάνατον προσδοκῶν. τέλος δὲ ἡ Ἀθηνᾶ, ἰδοῦσα αὐτὸν καὶ ἐλεαίρουσα, πάντας τοὺς ἄλλους ἀνέμους ἔπαυσε, μόνον δὲ Βορέᾶν πρᾶον ἔπεμψεν· τούτῳ δὲ τῷ ἀνέμῳ ὁ Ὀδυσσεὺς πρὸς τὴν Φαιᾱκίᾶν ἐφέρετο, ὅπου ἔμελλε ὑπὸ τῆς Ναυσικᾶᾱς σῴζεσθαι.

[**πρᾱ́ῳ**, *gentle* **πόποι**, *dear me* (exclamation of surprise or anger) **ἐὰν μὴ κωλύσω**, *If I do not hinder/prevent* **ἀβλαβὴς**, *unharmed* **τὴν σχεδίᾶν**, *the raft* **κατέθραυσεν** (from καταθραύω), *broke in pieces, shattered* **προσνεύσᾶς** (from προσνέω) + dat., *having swum toward* **τῶν ἐρειπίων**, *the wreckage* **ἔνθα καὶ ἔνθα**, *hither and thither* **θάνατον**, *death* **προσδοκῶν**, *expecting* **ἐλεαίρουσα**, *pitying* **Βορέᾶν**, *Boreas* **Φαιᾱκίᾶν**, *Phaeacia* **τῆς Ναυσικᾶᾱς**, *Nausicaa*]

Grammar

Review of Prepositions

The following list includes all of the prepositions that have occurred in the α and β stories and the tail readings in Book I. Prepositions generally have a range of meanings that must be learned by observation of their use in context. The number and Greek letter after the entry for a preposition indicate the chapter in which the preposition occurs in a vocabulary list; e.g., the entry "**ἀνά** + acc. (5α)" indicates that this preposition occurs in Vocabulary 5α. The absence of a number and Greek letter after an entry means that the preposition does not occur in any vocabulary list; these prepositions are used in the stories and glossed when they occur. The phrases given as examples usually contain the first occurrences of the prepositions in the stories; a preposition often occurs in a story before it is formally introduced in a vocabulary list.

ἅμα + dat.
 together with: ἅμα τῷ παιδί (5α:21)
ἀνά + acc. (5α)
 up: ἀνὰ τὴν ὁδόν (5α:4)
ἀπό + gen. (4α)
 from: ἀπὸ τοῦ ἄστεως (4α:20)
διά + gen. (9α)
 through: δι᾽ ὀλίγου = *through little (time)* = *soon* (5α:8)
διά + acc.
 because of: διὰ τοῦτο
ἐγγύς + gen. (13β)
 near: ἐγγὺς τῆς οἰκίᾶς (9 tail reading:8)
εἰς + acc. (2β)

into: εἰς τὸν ἀγρόν (2β:3)

to: εἰς τὴν κρήνην (4 tail reading:1)

at (with verbs such as ἀφικνέομαι): εἰς τὴν νῆσον (6α:14)

for: εἰς πολλὰς ἡμέρᾱς (6β:5–6)

ἐκ, ἐξ + gen. (3α)

out of: ἐκ τοῦ ἀγροῦ (1β:2), ἐξ ἔργων (8α:23)

ἐν + dat. (3β)

in: ἐν ταῖς Ἀθήναις (1α:1–2)

on: ἐν τῇ ὁδῷ (4β:9)

among: ἐν τοῖς δούλοις (11 tail reading: 5)

ἐντός + gen.

within: λιμένος πολυβενθέος ἐντός (16β:29)

ἐπί + dat. (5β)

upon, on: ἐπὶ τῇ γῇ (5β:16)

ἐπί + acc. (5β and 9α)

at; against: ἐπ' αὐτόν (5β:8)

onto (with ἀναβαίνω): ἐπὶ ἄκρᾱν τὴν ἀκτήν (7 tail reading:4)

upon: ἐπὶ τὸν ὄχθον (15 tail reading:3)

κατά + acc. (5α and 11β)

down: κατὰ τὴν ὁδόν (5 tail reading:5)

distributive: κατ' ἔτος, *each year* (6α:5)

by: κατὰ θάλατταν (11β:38)

on: κατὰ τοῦτο τοῦ ὄρους (14 tail reading:6)

μετά + gen. (6α)

with: μετὰ τῶν ἑταίρων (6α:11)

μετά + acc. (of time and place) (6α)

after (of time): μετὰ τὸ δεῖπνον (3β:7)

after (of place): μετ' αὐτούς (5α:9)

ὄπισθεν + gen.

behind: ὄπισθεν τοῦ ἱεροῦ (9α:35)

παρά + acc. (11α)

to (of persons only): παρὰ ἰᾱτρόν τινα (11α:4)

along, past: παρὰ τὴν Σικελίᾱν (10 tail reading: 2)

περί + gen. (7α)

about, concerning: περὶ ἀνδρὸς πολυτρόπου (7α:6)

περί + acc. (7α)

around: περὶ Τροίᾱν (7α:8)

πλήν + gen.

except: πλὴν ἑνός (8 tail reading:7)

πρό + gen. (10β)

before (of time or place): πρὸ τῆς νυκτός (10β:9–10)

πρός + dat. (4α)

    at: πρὸς τῇ κρήνῃ (4:title)

    near, by: πρὸς τῇ ὁδῷ (5 tail reading:9)

πρός + acc. (1β and 11β)

    to, toward: πρὸς τὸ ἕρμα (1β:3)

    against: πρὸς τοὺς λίθους (11β:3–4)

    upon, onto: πρὸς τὸν τοῦ Δικαιοπόλιδος πόδα (3α:18)

σύν + dat.

    with: σὺν θεῷ (12β:30–31)

ὑπέρ + gen. (8β)

    on behalf of, for: ὑπὲρ σοῦ (7 tail reading:2)

    above: ὑπὲρ Θερμοπυλῶν (14 tail reading, title)

ὑπέρ + acc.

    over: ὑπὲρ τὸ ὄρος (14 tail reading:1)

ὑπό + gen. (16α)

    by (of agent): ὑφ' ἡμῶν (16α:16)

    under: ὑπὸ τῶν προβάτων (7β:33)

ὑπό + dat. (5β)

    under: ὑπὸ τῷ δένδρῳ (1β:5)

ὑπό + acc. (5β)

    under (with verbs of motion): ὑπὸ τὸ ζυγόν (2β:7–8)

Exercise 16ζ

Translate the underlined English phrases into Greek using the noun and preposition supplied:

1.   He sleeps <u>under the tree</u>. τὸ δένδρον: ὑπό   _____

2.   He awakens <u>before the day</u>. ἡ ἡμέρᾱ: πρό   _____

3.   He climbs <u>onto the promontory</u>. ἡ ἀκτή: ἐπί   _____

4.   He walks <u>with his friends</u>. οἱ φίλοι: μετά   _____

5.   He walked <u>down the hill</u>. τὸ ὄρος: κατά   _____

6.   They talked <u>about the young man</u>. ὁ νεᾱνίᾱς: περί   _____

7.   They marched <u>toward the town</u>. τὸ ἄστυ: πρός   _____

8.   He lives <u>in Athens</u>. αἱ Ἀθῆναι: ἐν   _____

9.   She went <u>over the mountain</u>. τὸ ὄρος: ὑπέρ   _____

10.   I hope that he goes <u>with god</u>. θεός: σύν   _____

11.   They went <u>up the road</u>. ἡ ὁδός: ἀνά   _____

12.   A gloom sits <u>on the city</u>. ἡ πόλις: ἐπί   _____

13.   I'm doing this <u>on behalf of my father</u>. ὁ πατήρ: ὑπέρ   _____

14. They are resting <u>near the spring</u>. ἡ κρήνη: πρός _____
15. They departed <u>after the festival</u>. ἡ ἑορτή: μετά _____
16. They traveled <u>into the town</u>. τὸ ἄστυ: εἰς _____
17. They ran <u>under the tree</u>. τὸ δένδρον: ὑπό _____
18. The enemy are fighting <u>around Athens</u>.
    αἱ Ἀθῆναι: περί _____
19. They sailed <u>past the island</u>. ἡ νῆσος: παρά _____
20. They went <u>out of the house</u>. ἡ οἰκίᾱ: ἐκ, ἐξ _____
21. They left <u>from the spring</u>. ἡ κρήνη: ἀπό _____
22. They worked <u>because of the money</u>. τὸ ἀργύριον: διά _____
23. They resided <u>near the town</u>. τὸ ἄστυ: ἐγγύς _____
24. He slept <u>through the night</u>. ἡ νύξ: διά _____
25. They lived <u>behind the temple</u>. τὸ ἱερόν: ὄπισθεν _____

(β)

Exercise 16η

Translate the following English phrases and words with the correct form (present or imperfect) of the Greek verb supplied:

1. κεῖμαι: he/she lies _____
2. κεῖμαι: they lie _____
3. δύναμαι: they are able _____
4. κεῖμαι: you (sing.) lie _____
5. ἐπίσταμαι: do you (sing.) understand? _____
6. κεῖμαι: to lie _____
7. δύναμαι: to be able _____
8. δύναμαι: we were able _____
9. ἐπίσταμαι: he/she was understanding _____
10. κεῖμαι: (αὐτοὺς) lying _____
11. κεῖμαι: you (pl.) are lying _____
12. ἐπίσταμαι: we understand _____
13. δύναμαι: I was able _____
14. δύναμαι: you (pl.) are able _____
15. ἐπίσταμαι: (ἡ γυνὴ) understanding _____

16. δύναμαι: we are able   _____

17. κεῖμαι: they were lying   _____

18. δύναμαι: he was able   _____

19. ἐπίσταμαι: they understand   _____

20. κεῖμαι: lie! (pl.)   _____

21. ἐπίσταμαι: to understand   _____

22. κεῖμαι: you (sing.) were lying   _____

23. δύναμαι: you (sing.) were able   _____ or

          _____

24. κεῖμαι: we lie   _____

25. δύναμαι: be able! (sing.)   _____

26. ἐπίσταμαι: understand! (pl.)   _____

27. δύναμαι: they were able   _____

28. ἐπίσταμαι: you (sing.) were
    understanding   _____ or

          _____

29. κεῖμαι: we were lying   _____

30. δύναμαι: he/she is able   _____

Exercise 16θ

Give an English equivalent of:

1. ἄξιος   _____   4. ὁ ποταμός   _____

2. αἱ σπονδαί   _____   5. πολιορκέω   _____

3. ἥκιστά γε   _____   6. τὸ ἔτος   _____

Exercise 16ι

Give the Greek equivalent of:

1. life   _____   5. I vex   _____

2. spirit   _____   6. libation   _____

3. death   _____   7. peace   _____

4. I am distressed   _____

Exercise 16κ

Give the imperfect, future, and aorist of:

1. πολιορκέω _____   2. λῡπέω _____
   _____   _____
   _____   _____

Exercise 16λ

Translate the following on a separate sheet of paper:

Ο ΟΔΥΣΣΕΥΣ ΥΠΟ ΤΗΣ ΝΑΥΣΙΚΑΑΣ ΣΩΙΖΕΤΑΙ

[1] δύο τ' οὖν ἡμέρᾱς δύο τε νύκτας ἐπλανᾶτο ὁ Ὀδυσσεὺς τῷ ἀνέμῳ φερόμενος. τῇ δὲ τρίτῃ ἡμέρᾳ ἐπ' ἄκρῳ κύματι αἰρόμενος νῆσόν τινα εἶδε οὐ πολὺ ἀπέχουσαν. τὰ οὖν τῆς σχεδίᾱς ἐρείπια καταλιπὼν τῇ νήσῳ προσνεῖν ἐπειρᾶτο. ἐπεὶ δὲ τῇ νήσῳ προσεχώρησεν, πανταχοῦ ἦσαν πέτραι μεγάλαι, ὥστε οὐ δυνατὸν ἦν ἐκεῖ ἐκ τῆς θαλάττης ἐκβῆναι. παρένει οὖν τῷ αἰγιαλῷ, τόπον ζητῶν ὅπου ὁμαλὸς ἦν ὁ αἰγιαλός. τέλος δὲ πρὸς ποταμοῦ στόμα ἐφέρετο· ἐκεῖσε οὖν ἔνευσεν. οὕτως οὖν μόλις ἐξέβη εἰς τὴν γῆν. πολλὰ δὲ καὶ δεινὰ παθὼν μάλα ἔκαμνεν· πολὺν οὖν χρόνον ἐν τῷ αἰγιαλῷ ἡσύχαζεν. τέλος δὲ ἀνέστη καί, "οἴμοι," ἔφη, "τί δεῖ με ποιεῖν; εἰς τίνων γῆν ἥκω; ἆρα φιλάνθρωποί εἰσιν οἱ ἐνθάδε οἰκοῦντες ἢ βάρβαροί τε καὶ ξένοις ἐχθροί; μάλα γὰρ φοβοῦμαι εἰς γῆν ἀλλοτρίᾱν ἀφικόμενος. κρύψομαι οὖν." οὕτως εἰπὼν εἰς ὕλην τινὰ ἔσπευσεν οὐ πολὺ ἀπέχουσαν καὶ κρυψάμενος ἐν τοῖς θάμνοις ἐκάθευδεν.

[**ἐπλανᾶτο**, *was wandering*   **πολύ**, *very*   **ἀπέχουσαν**, *being far away*   **τῆς σχεδίᾱς**, *the raft*   **ἐρείπια**, *wreckage*   **προσνεῖν** (from προσνέω) + dat., *to swim toward*   **πέτραι**, *rocks*   **παρένει** + dat., *he was swimming beside*   **τῷ αἰγιαλῷ**, *the shore*   **τόπον**, *a place*   **ὁμαλός**, *level*   **ἔνευσεν** (from νέω), *he swam*   **φιλάνθρωποί**: deduce from φιλέω and ἄνθρωπος   **ἐχθροί** + dat., *hostile (to)*   **ἀλλοτρίᾱν**, *foreign*   **κρύψομαι**, *I will hide (myself)*   **ὕλην**, *woods*   **τοῖς θάμνοις**, *the bushes*]

[2] οὐ πολὺ δὲ ἀπεῖχεν ἡ πόλις ἡ τῶν Φαιάκων, ὧν ἐβασίλευεν ὁ Ἀλκίνους. τῷ δὲ Ἀλκίνῳ ἦν θυγάτηρ τις καλλίστη, ὀνόματι Ναυσικάᾱ. ἡ δὲ Ναυσικάᾱ ἐβούλετο τὰ ἱμάτια πλῡνειν. ἐπεὶ οὖν πρῶτον ἀνέτειλεν ὁ ἥλιος, πρὸς τὸν Ἀλκίνουν ἔσπευσε καί, "πάππα φίλε," ἔφη, "βούλομαι τὰ ἱμάτια εἰς τὸν ποταμὸν φέρειν καὶ πλῡνειν· πολλὰ γὰρ ἄλουτά ἐστιν καὶ τὰ ἐμὰ καὶ τὰ τῶν ἀδελφῶν. ἆρα οὖν ἐθέλεις τοὺς δούλους κελεύειν ἅμαξάν μοι παρασκευάζειν; πολὺ γὰρ ἀπέχει ὁ ποταμός, πολλὰ δὲ ἱμάτια δεῖ ἐκεῖσε φέρειν."

[**πολύ**, *very*   **ἀπεῖχεν**, *was far away*   **τῶν Φαιάκων**, *the Phaeacians*   **Ἀλκίνους**, *Alcinous*   **τὰ ἱμάτια**, *the clothes*   **πλῡνειν**, *to wash*   **ἀνέτειλεν** (from ἀνατέλλω), *rose*   **ἄλουτά**, *unwashed*   **ἅμαξάν**, *wagon*]

[3] ὁ δὲ Ἀλκίνους, "μάλιστά γε, ὦ θύγατερ φιλτάτη," ἔφη, "τοὺς δούλους εὐθὺς κελεύσω ἄμαξάν σοι παρασκευάζειν." οἱ δὲ δοῦλοι τῷ Ἀλκίνῳ πειθόμενοι ἄμαξαν καλὴν ἐξήγαγον. ἡ μὲν οὖν Ναυσικάᾱ ἐξήνεγκε τὰ ἱμάτια, ἡ δὲ μήτηρ σῖτόν τε παρεσκεύασε καὶ οἶνον. ἡ δὲ Ναυσικάᾱ τὰς ἀμφιπόλους ἐκάλεσεν καὶ ἐπὶ τὴν ἄμαξαν ἀναβᾶσα τὰς ἡμιόνους ἐκέντησεν. αἱ δὲ ἡμίονοι κεντούμεναι ταχέως ἔδραμον τήν τε Ναυσικάᾱν φέρουσαι καὶ τὰ ἱμάτια, αἱ δὲ ἀμφίπολοι εἵποντο ὄπισθεν τῆς ἀμάξης.

[φιλτάτη, *dearest* ἄμαξάν, *wagon* ἐξήνεγκε: from ἐκ- + φέρω τὰ ἱμάτια, *the clothes* τὰς ἀμφιπόλους, *her handmaids* ἐκέντησεν, *she goaded* ὄπισθεν + gen., *behind*]

[4] ἐπεὶ δὲ εἰς τὸν ποταμὸν ἀφίκοντο, τὰ ἱμάτια ἐξελόντες ἐκ τῆς ἀμάξης ἐν τῷ ποταμῷ ἐξέπλῡναν. ἐπεὶ δὲ πάντα ἐξέπλῡναν, ἐκαθίζοντο ἐπὶ τῷ αἰγιαλῷ καὶ ἐδείπνησαν. ἔπειτα δὲ ἡ Ναυσικάᾱ σφαῖραν λαβοῦσα ἔβαλε πρὸς τὰς ἀμφιπόλους· αἱ δὲ τὴν σφαῖραν εἷλον. οὕτως οὖν πολὺν χρόνον ἔπαιζον τὴν σφαῖραν ἀλλήλαις βάλλουσαι. τέλος δὲ ἡ Ναυσικάᾱ τὴν σφαῖραν ἔβαλε πρὸς ἀμφίπολόν τινα, ἡ δὲ σφαῖρα τῆς μὲν ἀμφιπόλου ἥμαρτεν, εἰς δὲ τὸν ποταμὸν εἰσέπεσεν. πᾶσαι οὖν αἱ κόραι μέγα ἐβόησαν καὶ ἔκλαγον.

[τὰ ἱμάτια, *the clothes* ἐξελόντες: from ἐκ- + αἱρέω τῆς ἀμάξης, *the wagon* ἐξέπλῡναν, *they washed X thoroughly* τῷ αἰγιαλῷ, *the shore* ἐδείπνησαν, *they ate* σφαῖραν, *ball* τὰς ἀμφιπόλους, *her handmaids* ἔπαιζον, *they were playing* ἥμαρτεν (from ἁμαρτάνω) + gen., *missed* αἱ κόραι, *the girls* ἔκλαγον (from κλάζω), *screamed*]

[5] ἐν δὲ τούτῳ ὁ Ὀδυσσεὺς ἐν τοῖς θάμνοις καθεύδει. ἐξαίφνης δὲ ἐγείρεται ὑπὸ τῶν κορῶν κλαζουσῶν. "οἴμοι," ἔφη, "τίνων εἰς γῆν ἥκω; ἆρα νύμφαι εἰσίν, αἳ ἐν τοῖς τε ὄρεσιν οἰκοῦσι καὶ τοῖς ποταμοῖς, ἢ κόραι ἀνθρώπιναι; ἀλλ' ἄγε· τοὺς θάμνους καταλείψω καὶ μαθήσομαι τίνες εἰσίν."

[τοῖς θάμνοις, *the bushes* ἐξαίφνης, *suddenly, immediately* κλαζουσῶν, *screaming* νύμφαι, *nymphs* (nature spirits) ἀνθρώπιναι, *human*]

[6] οὕτως οὖν εἰπὼν ἐκ τῶν θάμνων ἐξῆλθε καὶ ταῖς κόραις προσεχώρησεν. αἱ δὲ ἄνθρωπον ἰδοῦσαι προσχωροῦντα γυμνόν τ' ὄντα καὶ ξένον ἐφοβοῦντο καὶ πᾶσαι ἔφυγον· μόνη δὲ ἔμεινεν ἐν τῷ αἰγιαλῷ ἡ Ναυσικάᾱ. ὁ δὲ Ὀδυσσεὺς τὴν Ναυσικάᾱν ἰδὼν μένουσαν, βραδέως προσεχώρησε καί, "ἆρα τῶν θεῶν τις εἶ," ἔφη, " ἢ θνητή; εἰ μὲν γάρ τις τῶν θεῶν εἶ οἳ οὐρανὸν ἔχουσιν, Ἄρτεμίς μοι εἶναι φαίνει, ἡ τοῦ Διὸς παῖς· εἰ δέ τις τῶν θνητῶν, μακάριοι μέν εἰσί σοί γε πατὴρ καὶ μήτηρ, μακάριοι δὲ καὶ οἱ ἀδελφοί. οὐδέποτε γὰρ τοιοῦτον εἶδον οὔτ' ἄνδρα οὔτε γυναῖκα. οἴκτῑρέ με, ἄνασσα, ὃς πολλὰ παθὼν εἰς τὴν σὴν γῆν ἥκω. ἱκετεύω σε ἱμάτιά τέ μοι παρέχειν καὶ ἄγειν με πρὸς τὸ ἄστυ."

[τῶν θάμνων, *the bushes* ταῖς κόραις, *the girls* γυμνόν, *naked* τῷ αἰγιαλῷ,

the shore   θνητή, *mortal*   μακάριοι, *blessed; happy*   οὐδέποτε, *never*   τοιοῦτον, *such*   οἴκτῑρέ, *pity!*   ἄνασσα, *queen; lady*   ἱκετεύω, *I beseech*   ἱμάτιά,
clothes]

[7] ἡ δὲ Ναυσικάᾱ ἠλέησεν αὐτὸν καί, "μηδὲν φοβοῦ, ὦ ξένε," ἔφη· "οἰκτίρω γάρ
σε, ὃς πολλὰ παθὼν εἰς τὴν ἡμετέρᾱν γῆν ἥκεις. ἱμάτιά τε σοι παρέξω καὶ
ἡγήσομαι πρὸς τὸ ἄστυ." οὕτως εἰποῦσα τὰς ἀμφιπόλους ἐκάλεσε καί, "ἔλθετε
δεῦρο, ὦ ἀμφίπολοι," ἔφη· "τί ἀπεφύγετε ἄνδρα ἰδοῦσαι; ἐπανέλθετε καὶ λούσατε
τὸν ξένον ἐν τῷ ποταμῷ."

[ἠλέησεν (from ἐλεέω), *pitied*   οἰκτίρω, *I pity*   ἱμάτιά, *clothes*   τ ὰ ς   ἀ μ φ ι-
πόλους, *her handmaids*   λούσατε, *wash!*]

[8] αἱ οὖν ἀμφίπολοι τῇ Ναυσικάᾱ πειθόμεναι τὸν Ὀδυσσέᾱ εἰς τὸν ποταμὸν
ἤγαγον καὶ αὐτῷ ἱμάτια ἐκόμισαν κάλλιστα καὶ καταλιποῦσαι αὐτὰ παρὰ τῷ
Ὀδυσσεῖ ἀπῆλθον. ὁ δὲ Ὀδυσσεὺς λουσάμενος ἐν τῷ ποταμῷ καὶ ἐνδῡσάμενος τὰ
ἱμάτια ταῖς κόραις προσεχώρησεν.

[ἀμφίπολοι, *handmaids*   ἱμάτια, *clothes*   λουσάμενος, *having washed (himself)*
ἐνδῡσάμενος, *having put on*   ταῖς κόραις, *the girls*]

[9] ἡ δὲ Ναυσικάᾱ ἰδοῦσα αὐτὸν προσχωροῦντα ἐθαύμασε καί, "ὦ ἀμφίπολοι,"
ἔφη, "ὡς καλός ἐστιν ὁ ξένος· θεῷ γὰρ ἔοικεν. εἰ γὰρ τοιοῦτος πόσις μοι γένοιτο.
ἀλλὰ παράσχετε αὐτῷ σῖτόν τε καὶ οἶνον." αἱ οὖν ἀμφίπολοι σῖτόν τε καὶ οἶνον
αὐτῷ παρέσχον· ὁ δὲ πάντα κατέφαγεν· μάλα γὰρ ἐπείνη.

[ἀμφίπολοι, *handmaids*   ἔοικεν + dat., *he is like*   ε ἰ   γ ὰ ρ . . . μ ο ι   γ έ ν ο ι τ ο
(optative), *may there be for me, may I have*   τοιοῦτος, *such*   πόσις, *a husband*
κατέφαγεν (from κατεσθίω), *he ate up*   ἐπείνη (from πεινάω; irregular in that -α- +
-ε > η instead of ᾱ), *he was hungry*]

[10] ἔπειτα δὲ ἡ Ναυσικάᾱ, "ἄγε δή, ὦ ξένε," ἔφη, "νῦν σοι εἰς τὸ ἄστυ
ἡγήσομαι." ἐπὶ οὖν τὴν ἄμαξαν ἀναβᾶσα τὰς ἡμιόνους ἐκέντησεν. αἱ δὲ ἡμίονοι
κεντούμεναι ταχέως ἔδραμον, ὁ δὲ Ὀδυσσεὺς καὶ αἱ ἀμφίπολοι ὄπισθεν εἵποντο. δι'
ὀλίγου οὖν τῷ ἄστει προσεχώρησαν. ἡ δὲ Ναυσικάᾱ αὐτῷ, "μὴ εἴσελθε εἰς τὸ ἄστυ
σὺν ἐμοί, ὦ ξένε," ἔφη, "ἀλλὰ μένε ἐνταῦθα. ἐὰν γάρ τις τῶν Φαιάκων ἴδῃ σε ἐμοὶ
ἑπόμενον, θαυμάσει καὶ ἐρεῖ, 'τίς ὅδε Ναυσικάᾱ ἕπεται καλός τε μέγας τε ξένος;
ποῦ δὲ αὐτὸν εὗρεν; πόσις δὲ αὐτῇ ἔσται;' ἐγὼ μὲν οὖν εἰς τὸ ἄστυ σπεύσω, σὺ δὲ
μόνος εἴσελθε καὶ τὴν τοῦ πατρὸς οἰκίᾱν ζήτει. τὴν δὲ οἰκίᾱν εὑρὼν ἴθι εὐθὺς εἰς τὸ
μέγαρον. ἐκεῖ ὄψει τὴν ἐμὴν μητέρα. ἴθι οὖν εὐθὺς πρὸς αὐτὴν καὶ ἱκέτευε αὐτήν
σε οἰκτίρειν καὶ εὐμενῶς δέξασθαι."

[τὴν ἄμαξαν, *the wagon*   ἐκέντησεν, *she goaded*   ὄπισθεν, *behind*   σὺν + dat.,
with   ἐὰν . . . ἴδῃ (subjunctive), *if . . . sees*   τῶν Φαιάκων, *the Phaeacians*   πόσις,
husband   τὸ μέγαρον, *the megaron* or *great hall* (the chief room in a Homeric palace)
ἱκέτευε, *beg!*   οἰκτίρειν, *to pity*   εὐμενῶς, *kindly*]

[11] ἡ μὲν οὖν Ναυσικάᾱ εἰς τὸ ἄστυ ἔσπευσεν, ὁ δὲ Ὀδυσσεὺς ὀλίγον χρόνον

μείνᾱς εἰς τὸ ἄστυ εἰσῆλθε καὶ πάντα ἐποίησεν ὅσα ἡ Ναυσικάᾱ ἐκέλευσεν. τὴν οὖν τοῦ Ἀλκίνου οἰκίᾱν εὑρὼν καὶ εἰς τὸ μέγαρον εἰσελθὼν τόν τε Ἀλκίνουν εἶδε καὶ πολλοὺς βασιλέᾱς δειπνοῦντας καὶ τὴν τῆς Ναυσικάᾱς μητέρα ἐπὶ τῇ ἐσχάρᾳ καθημένην. εὐθὺς οὖν πρὸς αὐτὴν ἔσπευσε καὶ ἱκέτευεν αὐτὴν οἰκτίρειν τε ἑαυτὸν καὶ εὐμενῶς δέξασθαι. πάντες οὖν ἐθαύμασαν καὶ ἐσίγησαν. τέλος δὲ ὁ Ἀλκίνους, "ὦ ξένε," ἔφη, "οἰκτίρω σε καὶ εὐμενῶς δέξομαι. καθίζου παρὰ ἐμοί." ἀμφίπολον οὖν ἐκέλευσε σῖτόν τε καὶ οἶνον αὐτῷ παρέχειν. τοῖς δὲ βασιλεῦσιν, "νῦν μέν," ἔφη, "πάντες οἴκαδε ἄπιτε· αὔριον δὲ βουλεύσομεν ὅπως τοῦτον τὸν ξένον εἰς τὴν πατρίδα γῆν πέμψομεν."

[ὅσα, *as many as* τὸ μέγαρον, *the megaron* or *great hall* (the chief room in a Homeric palace) δειπνοῦντας, *dining* τῇ ἐσχάρᾳ, *the hearth* καθημένην, *sitting down* ἱκέτευεν, *began to beg* οἰκτίρειν, *to pity* εὐμενῶς, *kindly* παρὰ + dat., *beside* ἀμφίπολον, *a handmaid* βουλεύσομεν, *we will deliberate, plan* ὅπως, *how*]

[12] πάντες οὖν οἱ βασιλῆς οἴκαδε ἀπῆλθον. ὁ δὲ Ἀλκίνους τῷ Ὀδυσσεῖ, "εἰπέ μοι, ὦ ξένε," ἔφη, "πῶς εἰς τὴν ἡμετέρᾱν γῆν ἥκεις;" ὁ δὲ Ὀδυσσεὺς πάντα αὐτῷ εἶπεν ὅσα ἔπαθεν ὑπὸ τῆς Καλυψοῦς κατεχόμενος καὶ ὅπως εἰς τὴν Φαιᾱκίᾱν τοῖς ἀνέμοις φερόμενον ἑαυτὸν ἔσωσεν ἡ Ναυσικάᾱ. ὁ δὲ Ἀλκίνους ἀκούσᾱς ἐθαύμασε καί· "νῦν μὲν δεῖ σε καθεύδειν· μάλα γὰρ κάμνεις. αὔριον δὲ βουλεύσομεν ὅπως σε εἰς τὴν πατρίδα γῆν ἀποπέμψομεν."

[βουλεύσομεν, *we will deliberate, plan* ὅπως, *how*]

[13] τῇ δὲ ὑστεραίᾳ ὁ Ἀλκίνους πάντας τοὺς βασιλέᾱς εἰς δαῖτα συνεκάλεσεν. ὁ δὲ Ὀδυσσεὺς εἰς τὸν δαῖτα ἰέναι παρασκευασάμενος, λουσάμενος καὶ χλαῖναν καλλίστην ἐνδῡσάμενος, πρὸς τὸ μέγαρον ἔσπευδεν· ἀλλ' ἰδού, ἐν τῇ ὁδῷ ἔμενεν ἡ Ναυσικάᾱ καί, "χαῖρε, ὦ ξένε," ἔφη· "σὺ μὲν εἰς τὴν πατρίδα γῆν ἐπανελθὼν μή μου ἐπιλανθάνου· ἐγὼ γάρ σε ἔσωσα." ὁ δέ, "Ναυσικάᾱ," ἔφη, "οὐδέποτε σου ἐπιλήσομαι· ἀληθῆ γὰρ λέγεις· σύ με ἔσωσας." οὕτω δ' εἰπὼν εἰς τὸ μέγαρον εἰσῆλθεν.

[δαῖτα, *banquet, feast* συνεκάλεσεν, *called together* λουσάμενος, *having washed (himself)* χλαῖναν, *cloak* ἐνδῡσάμενος, *having put on* τὸ μέγαρον, *the megaron* or *great hall* (the chief room in a Homeric palace) ἐπιλανθάνου + gen., *forget!* οὐδέποτε, *never*]

[14] ἐνταῦθα δὴ πάντες τῷ δαιτὶ ἔχαιρον. ὁ δὲ Ὀδυσσεὺς πάντα τε αὐτοῖς ἐξηγήσατο ὅσα ἔπαθεν ἐν τῇ Τροίᾳ μαχόμενος καὶ πάντα ὅσα ἔπαθεν ἐκ τῆς Τροίᾱς οἴκαδε ἐπανιέναι πειρώμενος· οἱ δὲ ἔχαιρον ἀκούοντες. ὁ δὲ Ἀλκίνους, "αὔριον," ἔφη, "τὸν ξένον οἴκαδε πέμψομεν· ὑμεῖς οὖν πάντες δῶρα φέρετε εἰς τὴν ναῦν. νῦν δὲ οἴκαδε σπεύδετε."

[τῷ δαιτὶ, *the banquet, feast* ἔχαιρον + dat., *were rejoicing over, were enjoying* ὅσα, *as many as* δῶρα, *gifts*]

[15] τῇ οὖν ὑστεραίᾳ ἐπεὶ πρῶτον ἀνέτειλεν ὁ ἥλιος, πάντες πρὸς τὴν θάλατταν κατῆλθον, δῶρα φέροντες· τὰ μὲν οὖν δῶρα εἰς τὴν ναῦν εἰσέθεσαν, ὁ δὲ Ὀδυσσεὺς τὸν Ἀλκίνουν χαίρειν κελεύσᾱς εἰς τὴν ναῦν ἀνέβη. οἱ δὲ ναῦται τὴν ναῦν λύσαντες εἰς τὴν θάλατταν ἤλασαν. ταχέως οὖν ἔπλευσαν. ὁ δὲ Ὀδυσσεὺς οὕτως ἔκαμνεν ὥστε ἐκάθευδεν ἐν τῷ καταστρώματι. δι᾽ ὀλίγου δὲ εἰς τὴν Ἰθάκην ἀφίκοντο. οἱ δὲ ναῦται ἦραν αὐτὸν ἔτι καθεύδοντα καὶ κατέθεσαν αὐτόν τε καὶ τὰ δῶρα ἐν τῷ αἰγιαλῷ.

[ἀνέτειλεν (from ἀνατέλλω), rose   δῶρα, gifts   εἰσέθεσαν (from εἰστίθημι), they put in   ἤλασαν (from ἐλαύνω), they rowed   τῷ καταστρώματι, the deck   τὴν Ἰθάκην, Ithaca   κατέθεσαν (from κατατίθημι), put X down   τὰ δῶρα, the gifts   τῷ αἰγιαλῷ, the shore]

VOCABULARY
CHAPTERS 14–16

VERBS

-ω Verbs

ἀγγέλλω,
ἀγγελῶ,
ἤγγειλα — *I announce; I tell*

ἀναγκάζω,
ἀναγκάσω,
ἠνάγκασα — *I compel*

ἀντέχω,
ἀνθέξω,
ἀντέσχον — + dat., *I resist*

βλάπτω,
βλάψω,
ἔβλαψα — *I harm, hurt*

γράφω, γράψω,
ἔγραψα — *I write*

διαφθείρω,
διαφθερῶ,
διέφθειρα — *I destroy*

εἴκω, εἴξω,
εἶξα — + dat., *I yield*

ἐλπίζω, ἐλπιῶ,
ἤλπισα — *I hope; I expect; I suppose*

ἐμπῖπτω,
ἐμπεσοῦμαι,
ἐνέπεσον — + dat., *I fall into; I fall upon; I attack*

ἐπιπέμπω,
ἐπιπέμψω,
ἐπέπεμψα — *I send against; I send in*

καταλαμβάνω,
καταλήψομαι,
κατέλαβον — *I overtake, catch*

πιστεύω,
πιστεύσω,
ἐπίστευσα — + dat., *I trust, am confident (in); I believe;* + ὡς, *I believe* (that)

πράττω, πράξω,
ἔπραξα — intransitive, *I fare;* transitive, *I do* X

προσβάλλω,
προσβαλῶ,
προσέβαλον — + dat., *I attack*

στρατεύω,
στρατεύσω,
ἐστράτευσα — active or middle, *I wage war, campaign;* + ἐπί + acc., *I campaign* (against)

συμβάλλω,
συμβαλῶ,
συνέβαλον — *I join battle;* + dat., *I join battle with*

συμπῖπτω,
συμπεσοῦμαι,
συνέπεσον — *I clash;* + dat., *I clash with*

συναγείρω,
συναγερῶ,
συνήγειρα — active, transitive, *I gather* X; middle, intransitive, *I gather together*

φράζω, φράσω,
ἔφρασα — *I show; I tell; I tell of, explain*

Deponent -ω Verbs

διέρχομαι,
δίειμι,
διῆλθον — *I come through; I go through*

παραγίγνομαι,
παραγενή-
σομαι, παρ-
εγενόμην — *I arrive*

συνέρχομαι,
σύνειμι,
συνῆλθον — *I come together*

-άω Contract Verbs

πειράω,
πειράσω,
ἐπείρασα — active or middle, *I try, attempt*

130

τελευτάω,
τελευτήσω,
ἐτελεύτησα   *I end; I die*

Deponent -άω Contract Verbs

χράομαι,
χρήσομαι,
ἐχρησάμην   + dat., *I use; I enjoy*

-έω Contract Verbs

ἀναχωρέω,
ἀναχωρήσω,
ἀνεχώρησα   *I retreat, withdraw*
ἐπιπλέω,
ἐπιπλεύσομαι,
ἐπέπλευσα   + dat. or + εἰς + acc., *I sail against*

λῡπέω, λῡπήσω,
ἐλύπησα   *I grieve, vex, cause pain to* X; *passive, I am grieved, distressed*

ναυμαχέω,
ναυμαχήσω,
ἐναυμάχησα   *I fight by sea*
πολιορκέω,
πολιορκήσω,
ἐπολιόρκησα   *I besiege*

-όω Contract Verbs

δηλόω,
δηλώσω,
ἐδήλωσα   *I show*
ἐλευθερόω,
ἐλευθερώσω,
ἠλευθέρωσα   *I free, set free*

Athematic Presents and Imperfects

δύναμαι,
δυνήσομαι   *I am able; I can*
ἐπίσταμαι,
ἐπιστήσομαι   *I understand; I know*
κατάκειμαι   *I lie down*
κεῖμαι,
κείσομαι   *I lie*

-μι Verbs

ἀνέστην   *I stood up*

NOUNS

1st Declension

ἀπορίᾱ, -ᾱς, ἡ   *perplexity; difficulty; the state of being at a loss*
ἀρετή, -ῆς, ἡ   *excellence; virtue; courage*
εἰρήνη, -ης, ἡ   *peace*
θόρυβος, -ου, ὁ   *uproar, commotion*
κόσμος, -ου, ὁ   *good order*
νίκη, -ης, ἡ   *victory*
ὁπλῑ́της, -ου, ὁ   *hoplite (heavily-armed foot soldier)*
πύλαι, -ῶν, αἱ   pl., *double gates; pass (through the mountains)*
σπονδαί,
-ῶν, αἱ   pl., *peace treaty*
σπονδή, -ῆς, ἡ   *libation*
σπουδή, -ῆς, ἡ   *haste; eagerness*
στρατιώτης,
στρατι-
ώτου, ὁ   *soldier*
συμφορά̄, -ᾶς, ἡ   *misfortune; disaster*
τύχη, -ης, ἡ   *chance; luck; fortune*
φυγή, -ῆς, ἡ   *flight*

2nd Declension

βίος, -ου, ὁ   *life*
ἔνοικος, -ου, ὁ   *inhabitant*
θάνατος, -ου, ὁ   *death*
θῡμός, -οῦ, ὁ   *spirit*
ναύαρχος, -ου, ὁ   *admiral*
νεκρός, -οῦ, ὁ   *corpse*
νοῦς, νοῦ, ὁ   *mind*
πέπλος, -ου, ὁ   *robe; cloth*
πολέμιοι, -ων, οἱ   *the enemy*
πόλεμος, -ου, ὁ   *war*
ποταμός, -οῦ, ὁ   *river*
πρόγονος, -ου, ὁ   *ancestor*
στενά, -ῶν, τά   *narrows; straits; mountain pass*
στόλος, -ου, ὁ   *expedition; army; fleet*
στρατηγός, -οῦ, ὁ   *general*
στρατός, -οῦ, ὁ   *army*
σύμμαχος, -ου, ὁ   *ally*

3rd Declension

ἀγών, ἀγῶνος, ὁ	struggle; contest
ἔτος, ἔτους, τό	year
μέρος, μέρους, τό	part
πατρίς, πατρίδος, ἡ	fatherland
πλῆθος, πλήθους, τό	number; multitude

ADJECTIVES

1st/2nd Declension

ἄξιος, -ᾱ, -ον	worthy; + gen., worthy of
δεξιός, -ά, -όν	right (i.e., on the right hand)
διᾱκόσιοι, -αι, -α	two hundred
μόνος, -η, -ον	alone; only
ὅδε, ἥδε, τόδε	this here; pl., these here
ὀλίγος, -η, -ον	small; pl., few
οὗτος, αὕτη, τοῦτο	this; pl., these
πεζός, -ή, -όν	on foot
πολέμιος, -ᾱ, -ον	hostile; enemy
πόσος; -η; -ον;	how much? pl., how many?
στενός, -ή, -όν	narrow

3rd and 1st Declension

ἅπᾱς, ἅπᾱσα, ἅπαν	all; every; whole

Indeclinable

ἑκατόν	a hundred

PREPOSITIONS

ὑπό	+ gen., under; of agent, by; + dat., under; + acc., under

ADVERBS

μηκέτι	+ imperative, don't . . . any longer; + infin., no longer
μόνον	only

ὅπου	where
οὐδαμοῦ	nowhere
πανταχοῦ	everywhere
πολλαχόσε	to many parts
ὕστερον	later

CONJUNCTIONS

ἕως	until
ἤ	with comparatives, than
οὐ μόνον . . . ἀλλὰ καί	not only . . . but also
ὡς	that
ὡς	when

EXPRESSIONS

ἐν μέσῳ	+ gen., between
ἥκιστά γε	least of all, not at all
καὶ δὴ καί	and in particular; and what is more
κατὰ γῆν	by land
κόσμῳ	in order
μάλιστά γε	certainly, indeed
ποῦ γῆς;	where (in the world)?
τῇ προτεραίᾳ	on the day before

PROPER NAMES & ADJECTIVES

Αἰσχύλος, -ου, ὁ	Aeschylus
Ἀρτεμίσιον, -ου, τό	Artemisium
Ἀσίᾱ, -ᾱς, ἡ	Asia (i.e., Asia Minor)
Ἀττική, -ῆς, ἡ	Attica
Βοιωτίᾱ, -ᾱς, ἡ	Boeotia
Ἐφιάλτης, -ου, ὁ	Ephialtes
Εὔβοια, -ᾱς, ἡ	Euboea
Θεμιστοκλῆς, Θεμιστο- κλέους, ὁ	Themistocles
Θερμοπύλαι, -ῶν, αἱ	Thermopylae
Κόρινθος, -ου, ἡ	Corinth
Λακεδαιμόνιοι, -ων, οἱ	the Lacedaemonians, Spartans
Λεωνίδης, -ου, ὁ	Leonidas
Πελοπόννησος, -ου, ἡ	the Peloponnesus

Περσικός,
-ή, -όν — *Persian*
Ξέρξης, -ου, ὁ — *Xerxes*
Πέρσαι, -ῶν, οἱ — *the Persians*
Σιμωνίδης, -ου, ὁ — *Simonides*

Σπαρτιάτης,
-ου, ὁ, — *a Spartan*
Φάληρον, -ου, τό — *Phalerum* (the old
harbor of Athens)

ANSWER KEY

ANSWERS: CHAPTER 1

Exercise 1α
1. ὁ κλῆρος. 2. τὸν ἄνθρωπον. 3. τὸν ἀγρόν. 4. ὁ σῖτος. 5. ὁ οἶκος. 6. τὸν πόνον. 7. ὁ αὐτουργός. 8. ὁ ἀγρός.

Exercise 1β and Exercise 1γ
1. ὁ οἶκός (S) ἐστι (LV) μῑκρός (C). 2. ὁ ἄνθρωπός (S) ἐστι (LV) μακρός (C). 3. ὁ ἀγρὸς (S) παρέχει (TV) πολὺν σῖτον (DO). 4. ὁ ἄνθρωπος (S) τὸν οἶκον (DO) φιλεῖ (TV). 5. μῑκρός (C) ἐστιν (LV) ὁ πόνος (S).

Exercise 1δ
1. toil, work. 2. much. 3. house; home; dwelling. 4. he/she says; he/she tells; he/she speaks. 5. he/she rejoices. 6. he/she works. 7. field. 8. he/she loves. 9. but. 10. and, but. 11. beautiful. 12. and.

Exercise 1ε
1. οἰκεῖ. 2. ὁ σῖτος. 3. γάρ. 4. μακρός. 5. πονεῖ. 6. οὐ, οὐκ, οὐχ. 7. οὖν. 8. ὁ αὐτουργός. 9. μῑκρός. 10. οὖν. 11. ὁ ἄνθρωπος. 12. ἐστί(ν). 13. λέγει. 14. ἐν ταῖς Ἀθήναις.

Exercise 1ζ
1. ἀγρός. 2. βαδίζει. 3. μακρός ἐστι. 4. πολύς. 5. οἶκος. 6. οἰκεῖ. 7. χρόνος πολύς. 8. ὁ αὐτουργὸς ἰσχῡρός ἐστιν. 9. μακρός. 10. ἥλιος. 11. ἀγρὸς μῑκρός. 12. ὁ Δικαιόπολίς ἐστιν αὐτουργός. 13. ὁ χρόνος ἐστὶ μακρός. 14. ὁ σῖτός ἐστι πολύς.

Exercise 1η
1. S. 2. IV. 3. DO. 4. TV. 5. C. 6. LV. 7. S. 8. C. 9. DO. 10. TV. 11. DO. 12. TV. 13. TV. 14. C. 15. S. 16. IV. 17. IV. 18. S. 19. TV. 20. DO. 21. IV. 22. IV. 23. TV. 24. DO. 25. IV. 26. IV. 27. S. 28. IV. 29. S. 30. IV.

Exercise 1θ
1. time. 2. he/she carries. 3. him. 4. to, toward. 5. he/she lifts. 6. to/toward the sun.

Exercise 1ι
1. χαλεπός. 2. βαδίζει. 3. καθίζει. 4. ὁ ἥλιος. 5. ἰσχῡρός. 6. βαδίζει.

Exercise 1κ

THE HOME
   The home is small but beautiful. So the man loves his home. In the field the work is difficult, and Dicaeopolis is always very tired. For the field is small, but the work is long. For the man digs his field and works for a long (for much) time. And in his house he rests and no longer works. So in his house Dicaeopolis rejoices.

ANSWERS: CHAPTER 2

Exercise 2α
1. λύει. 2. φιλῶ. 3. εἶ. 4. καλεῖ. 5. ἔκβαινε. 6. σπεύδει. 7. καθεύδεις. 8. ἐλαύνω. 9. πάρεστι(ν). 10. κάλει. 11. ἐκβαίνω. 12. ἔλαυνε. 13. μὴ σπεῦδε.

Exercise 2β
1. ἐκβαίνει. 2. σπεῦδε. 3. ἐστιν. 4. ἐλαύνω. 5. φέρε. 6. φέρει. 7. ἔλαυνε. 8. πονεῖ.

Exercise 2γ
1. οὐκ ἔστιν. 2. οὐκ εἰμί. 3. οὐκ εἰμί. 4. οὐ πονεῖς. 5. οὐκ ἔστιν.

Exercise 2δ
1. the strong man/human being/person. 2. the long time. 3. the lazy slave. 4. the small plow. 5. the difficult work/toil. 6. the small house/home/dwelling.

Exercise 2ε

1. lazy. 2. plow. 3. don't . . . 4. thus, so. 5. he/she drives. 6. I. 7. on the one hand . . . and/but on the other hand . . . 8. he/she sleeps.

Exercise 2ζ

1. πάρεστι(ν). 2. καλεῖ. 3. τί; 4. ὁ δοῦλος. 5. πάρεστι(ν). 6. ἐλθέ. 7. σπεύδει. 8. ἐκβαίνει.

Exercise 2η

1. τὸν μακρὸν χρόνον. 2. τοῦ μακροῦ χρόνου. 3. τῷ μακρῷ χρόνῳ. 4. ὦ μακρὲ χρόνε. 5. τὸ ἰσχυρὸν δένδρον. 6. τοῦ ἰσχυροῦ δένδρου. 7. τῷ ἰσχυρῷ δένδρῳ. 8. ὦ ἰσχυρὸν δένδρον.

Exercise 2θ

1. τοῦ. 2. οἴκου. 3. δοῦλός. 4. ἰσχυρὸς. 5. ἄνθρωπος. 6. ἀργὸς. 7. τῷ. 8. οἴκῳ. 9. αὐτὸν. 10. δοῦλε. 11. τοῦ. 12. οἴκου. 13. χαλεπός. 14. ἀργός. 15. τὸν. 16. ἀγρόν. 17. μῑκρὸς. 18. ἀγρός. 19. πόνος.

Exercise 2ι

1. καθίζεις. 2. φέρει. 3. βαδίζω. 4. λέγεις. 5. φέρω. 6. βάδιζε. 7. λέγε. 8. βαδίζεις. 9. καθίζω. 10. ἐκβαίνεις. 11. λέγει. 12. φέρεις. 13. ἐκβαίνω. 14. λέγω. 15. ἐκβαίνει. 16. καθίζει. 17. κάθιζε. 18. καθεύδω. 19. φέρε. 20. ἔκβαινε.

Exercise 2κ

1. I look; I see. 2. slowly. 3. ox. 4. tree. 5. I lead; I take. 6. then, thereafter.

Exercise 2λ

1. ἤδη. 2. βαίνω. 3. εἰσάγω. 4. συλλαμβάνω. 5. ὁ δεσπότης. 6. ἄγω. 7. εἰς. 8. λαμβάνω, ἄγω.

Exercise 2μ

AFTER NOONTIME

[1] And after noontime Dicaeopolis says: "I am going to my home; for I am very tired. But you, Xanthias, stay in the field and lift the stones." So Dicaeopolis goes to his home and sleeps. But Xanthias remains in the field and lifts the stones.

[2] But the sun is blazing and wears out the slave. But in the field there is a large tree. And the tree provides shade. So the slave looks toward the large tree. And then he slowly walks toward the tree; for Dicaeopolis is not present. So Xanthias sits under the tree. And the slave does not work but sleeps under the tree. But Dicaeopolis comes out of the house and drives the oxen to the field. And in the field he sees his slave sleeping under the tree. So he says: "You cursed slave, why are you now sleeping under the tree? Why are you not lifting the stones? Why are you not carrying the stones out of the field? Xanthias, you are strong, but very lazy, and you don't love your work." And Xanthias gets up and says: "I am not lazy, but I am very tired; for the work is long, and the sun is blazing. And you are a difficult master. For the field is beautiful and provides much food. So you hurry to the field, and you drive the oxen, and you take the plow. For you are a master, and you love the field very (much); but I am a slave, and I do not love the field very (much). Don't be difficult, master; look, I am lifting the stones."

ANSWERS: CHAPTER 3

Exercise 3α

1. λύει. 2. λύουσι(ν). 3. φιλῶ. 4. λύετε. 5. εἶ. 6. προσχωρεῖν. 7. κάθευδε. 8. προσχωροῦσι(ν). 9. καλεῖ. 10. φιλεῖτε. 11. λάμβανε. 12. φιλεῖν. 13. σπεύδει. 14. πίπτουσι(ν). 15. καθεύδεις. 16. πίπτειν. 17. ἐλαύνω. 18. πίπτετε. 19. πάρεστι(ν). 20. μένουσι(ν). 21. κάλει. 22. μένειν. 23. ἐκβαίνω. 24. εἰσί(ν).

Exercise 3β

1. μένουσιν. 2. σπεύδετε. 3. ἐκφέρουσιν. 4. ἐστιν. 5. ἐκφέρειν. 6. ἐλαύνετε.
7. ἕλκουσιν. 8. αἴρειν.

Exercise 3γ

1. I fall. 2. big, large; great. 3. no longer. 4. out of the house/home/dwelling. 5. stone. 6. I
go toward, approach. 7. here, hither. 8. both . . . and. 9. responsible (for); to blame. 10. O
Zeus.

Exercise 3δ

1. μένω. 2. αὖθις. 3. δυνατός. 4. ὦ Ζεῦ. 5. φησί(ν). 6. αὐτόν. 7. ἔτι. 8. αὐτό or
αὐτόν.

Exercise 3ε

1. ἄνθρωπον. 2. ἀνθρώπων. 3. οἴκους. 4. οἴκοι. 5. δοῦλον. 6. δούλῳ.

Exercise 3ζ

1. the beautiful fields. 2. the long/large works/toils. 3. the lazy slaves. 4. the beautiful
dinners. 5. the brave farmers. 6. the small houses/homes/dwellings.

Exercise 3η

1. τὸ ἰσχῡρὸν ἄροτρον. 2. τῷ ἰσχῡρῷ ἀρότρῳ. 3. τοῦ ἰσχῡροῦ ἀρότρου. 4. ὦ ἰσχῡρὸν
ἄροτρον. 5. τοὺς ἀνδρείους ἀνθρώπους. 6. τοῖς ἀνδρείοις ἀνθρώποις. 7. τῶν ἀνδρείων
ἀνθρώπων. 8. ὦ ἀνδρεῖοι ἄνθρωποι 9. τὰ καλὰ δεῖπνα. 10. τοῖς καλοῖς δείπνοις. 11. τῶν
καλῶν δείπνων. 12. ὦ καλὰ δεῖπνα. 13. τὸν ἀργὸν δοῦλον. 14. τῷ ἀργῷ δούλῳ. 15. τοῦ
ἀργοῦ δούλου. 16. ὦ ἀργὲ δοῦλε.

Exercise 3θ

1. I loosen, loose. 2. you. 3. so great. 4. Philip. 5. boy; son; child. 6. when. 7. in the field.
8. so great/so many stones.

Exercise 3ι

1. ἡ παῖς. 2. τὸ δεῖπνον. 3. ἀνδρεῖος. 4. μηκέτι μένε. 5. λείπω. 6. πολλοί. 7. ὁ πατήρ.

Exercise 3κ

PHILIP FALLS FROM THE TREE

For a long time both the father and his son work in the field. Then Philip climbs up
onto many trees and shakes down the fruits; and the fruits fall from the trees, and
Dicaeopolis collects them. And finally Dicaeopolis leads Philip to a very large tree and
says, "Look, Philip, this tree has much fruit. So climb up and shake down the fruit." And
Philip says, "It is not possible, father, to climb up onto so great a tree. For I am very
tired." But Dicaeopolis says, "Do not be lazy, son, for it is possible to climb up onto the
tree. Hurry!" So Philip approaches the tree and slowly climbs up. But suddenly he slips
and falls to the ground and stays there motionless. Then fear seizes (takes) Dicaeopolis.
But Philip gets up and says, "Don't be afraid (have fear); for I am well." And Dicaeopolis
says, "you are very brave, son. But now don't work any longer; for you are tired. It is
time to go home (to home) and to rest." And when they enter (go into) their home, they
rest and eat dinner.

ANSWERS: CHAPTER 4

Exercise 4α

1. λύω. 2. φιλοῦσι(ν). 3. ἐσμέν. 4. ἐθέλεις. 5. χαίρετε, ὦ φίλοι/φίλαι. 6. ἔχουσι(ν).
7. θεωρεῖ. 8. ποιοῦμεν. 9. ἀκούετε. 10. ἔχω. 11. ἐθέλομεν. 12. ἀκούει. 13. χαίρομεν.
14. ἔχει. 15. ποιοῦσι(ν). 16. ἐθέλετε. 17. φιλεῖτε. 18. λύεις. 19. θεωρεῖς. 20. ἴσθι.
21. ἄκουε. 22. χαίρειν. 23. φιλῶ. 24. πονεῖτε. 25. οἰκεῖν. 26. προσχώρει. 27. ἔστε.
28. εἶ. 29. εἶναι. 30. ἐστέ.

Exercise 4β

1. τὰς θαλάττᾱς. 2. αἱ μέλιτται. 3. τῶν μαχαιρῶν. 4. τὰ ἄροτρα. 5. αἱ οἰκίαι. 6. τὰς

κρήνᾱς. 7. ταῖς ὑδρίαις. 8. τῶν καιρῶν. 9. αἱ ἑορταί. 10. τοῖς φίλοις. 11. αἱ μάχαιραι. 12. τῇ μελίττῃ. 13. τῆς ὑδρίᾱς. 14. τὸν καιρόν. 15. τῇ ἑορτῇ. 16. τῆς φίλης or τοῦ φίλου. 17. τὴν θάλατταν. 18. τῆς μελίττης. 19. τῇ μαχαίρᾳ. 20. τῷ ἀρότρῳ. 21. τὴν οἰκίᾱν. 22. τῆς ἑορτῆς.

Exercise 4γ

1. I listen (to); I hear. 2. man; husband. 3. look! 4. very. 5. dance; chorus. 6. woman; wife. 7. greetings! 8. mother. 9. not working, idle, lazy. 10. from the field. 11. Are you sleeping? 12. festival. 13. even; also, too. 14. I have; I hold. 15. I watch; I see. 16. the festival of Dionysus.

Exercise 4δ

1. πρῶτον. 2. φίλος, φίλη, φίλον. 3. ἡ κρήνη. 4. ἐθέλω. 5. ἀκούω. 6. ἐν νῷ ἔχω. 7. ὁ ἀνήρ. 8. ἡ φίλη. 9. ταχέως. 10. ποιέω. 11. ὁ καιρός. 12. ἡ ὑδρίᾱ. 13. μόλις. 14. ὁ ἄγγελος. 15. ἡ θυγάτηρ. 16. χαίρω.

Exercise 4ε

1. τὴν θάλατταν. 2. τὸν δεσπότην. 3. τὴν μάχαιραν. 4. τὸν νεᾱνίᾱν. 5. τὴν ὁδόν. 6. τοὺς νεᾱνίᾱς. 7. τὰς ὑδρίᾱς. 8. τοὺς καιρούς. 9. τὰς ἑορτάς. 10. τοὺς δεσπότᾱς. 11. τῷ Ξανθίᾳ. 12. τῇ ὑδρίᾳ. 13. τῷ πολίτῃ. 14. τῇ ἑορτῇ. 15. τῷ φίλῳ. 16. ταῖς θαλάτταις. 17. τοῖς δεσπόταις. 18. ταῖς μαχαίραις. 19. τοῖς νεᾱνίαις. 20. ταῖς νήσοις. 21. τῆς θαλάττης. 22. τοῦ δεσπότου. 23. τῆς μαχαίρᾱς. 24. τοῦ Ξανθίου. 25. τῆς ὁδοῦ. 26. τῶν δεσποτῶν. 27. τῶν ὑδριῶν. 28. τῶν καιρῶν. 29. τῶν ἑορτῶν. 30. τῶν φίλων.

Exercise 4ζ

1. πολλαῖς. 2. μεγάλους. 3. πολλῶν. 4. ῥᾳδίοις. 5. μεγάλων. 6. καλοί. 7. ῥᾴδιαι. 8. πολλῶν. 9. πολλοῖς. 10. καλούς or καλά.

Exercise 4η

1. καλή. 2. καλαί. 3. μεγάλη. 4. μεγάλαι. 5. μακρᾶς. 6. μακρῶν. 7. φίλης. 8. φίλων. 9. ῥᾳδίᾱν. 10. ῥᾳδίᾱς. 11. μεγάλᾱς. 12. πολλαί. 13. μεγάλης. 14. μεγάλαις. 15. μεγάλη. 16. μεγάλην. 17. πολύν. 18. πολλά. 19. ῥᾳδίου. 20. ῥᾳδίων. 21. πολλῶν. 22. φίλῳ. 23. καλοῖς. 24. πολλά.

Exercise 4θ

1. I groan. 2. easy. 3. most, most of all; very much; especially. 4. always. 5. homeward, to home. 6. truly. 7. lazily. 8. ἡ ὁδός. 9. τί; 10. πείθω. 11. καλῶς. 12. ἄλλος, ἄλλη, ἄλλο. 13. ἡ γῆ. 14. τί;

Exercise 4ι

THE MISTRESS AND THE SLAVE

[1] A certain woman, Phaedra by name, approaches the spring. A slave follows. And the slave carries a large water jar. And the slave is tired and says, "Mistress, don't walk so quickly; for the water jar is large, and it is not easy to hurry." But Phaedra says, "Don't talk nonsense, slave, but hurry. For it is time for you to go to the master and to carry water to him."

[2] So the slave walks slowly to the spring. But the mistress—for a large stone is in the road—approaches and sits on the large stone. And then she looks from the large stone toward her slave. But she no longer walks toward the spring but toward a large tree. So the mistress calls her and says, "What are you doing, (you) lazy (one)? Why are you not hurrying toward the spring? Do you have in mind to sit under the large tree and sleep?" But the slave looks toward her mistress and says, "Don't be so difficult, mistress; for the work is great (much), and I have in mind to sit for a short (not much) time. Look, the sun is blazing and wears me down."

[3] But the mistress says, "Don't talk nonsense; it is not time to rest. For there is no water in the house, and I am about to hurry home and prepare dinner for the master. So

hurry!" But Myrrhine says, "Don't be difficult, Phaedra; for the slave is tired. For the sun is blazing and wears her down. Don't you know that (both) many slave women and many slave men tire, when the sun is blazing, and they do not wish to work?" So allow her to rest for a short (small) time in the shade!"

ANSWERS: CHAPTER 5

Exercise 5α
1. τῑμᾶτε. 2. ζητοῦσι(ν). 3. ζητεῖν. 4. βοῶμεν. 5. τίμᾱ. 6. ὁρῶ. 7. φιλεῖς. 8. τῑμῶσι(ν). 9. τῑμᾶν. 10. ὁρῶμεν. 11. τῑμᾷ. 12. ζητεῖτε. 13. βοᾷς. 14. φιλοῦσι(ν). 15. τῑμᾶτε. 16. βοῶ. 17. οἰκεῖ. 18. ζήτει.

Exercise 5β
1. λύει. 2. φίλε-ε > φίλει. 3. φεύγουσι(ν). 4. φιλέ-ει > φιλεῖ. 5. λύετε. 6. ποιέ-ομεν > ποιοῦμεν. 7. τῑμά-ετε > τῑμᾶτε. 8. ὁρά-εις > ὁρᾷς. 9. τῑμα-ε > τίμᾱ. 10. δίωκε.

Exercise 5γ
1. ἡ. 2. οἱ. 3. ὁ. 4. αἱ.

Exercise 5δ
1. ἆρ' ἀκούεις; 2. καθ' ὁδόν. 3. ἀλλ' ἐθέλουσιν. 4. μεθ' ὑμῶν.

Exercise 5ε
1. I shout. 2. up the mountain/hill. 3. wolf. 4. careless. 5. I guard. 6. so that, that, so as to. 7. I see. 8. sheep. 9. neither . . . nor. 10. I run. 11. hare. 12. top (of). 13. I seek, look for. 14. soon.

Exercise 5ζ
1. ἄπειμι. 2. διώκω. 3. ἴθι. 4. ὁ κύων or ἡ κύων. 5. οὐδέ. 6. τῑμάω. 7. κατὰ τὸ ὄρος. 8. ὁ πάππος. 9. ποῦ; 10. φεύγω. 11. ἡ οἰκία. 12. ἄκρον τὸ ὄρος.

Exercise 5η
1. Inf. 2. Ind. 3. Inf. 4. Ind. 5. Inf. 6. Ind. 7. Ind.

Exercise 5θ
1. ἐστιν. 2. ἐστιν. 3. εἰσίν. 4. ἐστίν. 5. εἰσι. 6. ἐστιν. 7. εἰσιν. 8. ἐστι.

Exercise 5ι
1. αὐτόν. 2. αὐτούς. 3. ἐμέ or με. 4. ἡμᾶς. 5. αὐτοὶ. 6. αὐτάς. 7. αὐτούς. 8. ἐμοί or μοι. 9. αὐτῶν. 10. αὐτῆς. 11. αὐτοῦ. 12. αὐτῆς. 13. σὺ. 14. ἡμεῖς, ὑμεῖς. 15. αὐτόν. 16. αὐτοῖς or αὐταῖς. 17. ἡ ἐμὴ. 18. σοῦ, σου. 19. ὑμῶν. 20. μου. 21. ἡμῶν. 22. αὐτῶν. 23. αὐτοῦ. 24. αὐτῆς. 25. ὑμῖν. 26. σοί, σοι. 27. ἡ ἡμετέρᾱ. 28. ἡ σὴ. 29. αὐτῇ. 30. αὐταῖς. 31. αὐτὴ. 32. αὐτός. 33. ὁ αὐτὸς. 34. ἡ ὑμετέρᾱ. 35. αὐτήν. 36. αὐτάς. 37. τὴν αὐτὴν. 38. σέ, σε. 39. ὑμᾶς. 40. αὐτοῖς. 41. αὐτῷ.

Exercise 5κ
Column B: 6, 1, 4, 2, 3, 5.

Exercise 5λ
1. ὁ οἶκος ὁ <u>μέγας</u> 2. <u>μέγας</u> ὁ οἶκος 3. ὁ <u>ἀγαθὸς</u> φίλος 4. ὁ φίλος <u>ἀγαθός</u> 5. <u>καλὸν</u> τὸ δένδρον 6. τὸ <u>καλὸν</u> δένδρον

Exercise 5μ
1. attributive. 2. predicate. 3. attributive. 4. predicate.

Exercise 5ν
1. I have come. 2. at that very moment, then. 3. good. 4. both . . . and. 5. I flee away, escape. 6. on the road. 7. now. 8. I suffer; I experience. 9. first. 10. the same woman/wife.

Exercise 5ξ
1. γιγνώσκω. 2. ὑπὸ τῷ δένδρῳ. 3. τύπτω. 4. ὅτι. 5. ὁ μῦθος. 6. ἡμεῖς. 7. θαυμάζω. 8. ὑμεῖς. 9. ἄγριος. 10. αὐτός, αὐτή, αὐτό.

Exercise 5o

THE SLAVE DOESN'T LOVE THE DOG

[1] So Philip and Melissa wish to hear a story from Myrrhine. And the mother says: "And what? What kind of story do you wish to hear?" And Philip (says): "I wish to hear a story about a terrible and great wild beast." But Melissa (says): "Why about a terrible and great wild beast? Why not about a beautiful girl? Don't you wish to tell us such a story, mother?"

[2] And the mother (says): "Don't shout; for grandfather is sleeping. But come to me and sit near me; for I am about to tell you a beautiful story; and in the story is a beautiful woman and a brave man and a great and terrible wild beast. So don't make a commotion but listen!"

[3] And meanwhile Philip says, "Stop, mother; for Xanthias is running toward us. But what is the man doing? He is taking stones and pelting the dog. Zeus! You fool, what are you doing? Don't pelt the dog!"

[4] And the slave says: "Are you calling me, boy? But I am driving the dog away from me. For the dog is always staying near me and barking; and if I walk, he chases me and rushes at me. He often desires to bite me. So what do I do? So call the dog to you." So Philip calls Argus: "Argus, come here to us! Sit here with us! Don't go away from us but you, too, listen to the story! For mother always tells us beautiful stories. But you, Xanthias, go away to the field and work!" And the mother (says): "But now be silent, children, and listen to the story."

ANSWERS: CHAPTER 6

Exercise 6α

1. πλεῖ. 2. πλεῖτε. 3. πλεῖς. 4. πλεῖν. 5. πλέομεν. 6. πλέουσι(ν). 7. πλέω. 8. πλεῖ.

Exercise 6β

1. δέχεται. 2. ἔρχονται. 3. ἐρχόμεθα. 4. δέχου. 5. πείθει or πείθῃ. 6. ἀφικνεῖσθε. 7. γίγνονται. 8. ἀφικνοῦ. 9. ἀφικνοῦμαι. 10. φοβεῖσθε. 11. φοβεῖται. 12. φοβοῦ. 13. βούλεσθε. 14. ἀφικνεῖσθαι. 15. ἀφικνοῦνται. 16. ἀπέρχεται. 17. ἀφικνούμεθα. 18. λύεσθαι. 19. λύει or λύῃ. 20. δέχεσθε.

Exercise 6γ

5. τῑμᾷ. 6. τῑμᾶσθε. 8. τῑμῶ. 9. τῑμῶμαι. 10. τῑμᾶσθε. 11. τῑμᾶται. 14. τῑμᾶσθαι. 15. τῑμῶνται. 17. τῑμώμεθα.

Exercise 6δ

Column B: 8, 4, 6, 1, 2, 5, 7, 3.

Exercise 6ε

1. they rule. 2. comrade, companion. 3. we receive. 4. night. 5. terrible. 6. there. 7. he/she kills. 8. you (pl.) want; you (pl.) wish or want! wish! 9. island. 10. you (sing.) flee out, escape. 11. I come; I go. 12. with the friends.

Exercise 6ζ

1. ἡ ἡμέρᾱ. 2. ἀφικνέομαι. 3. πλέω. 4. σῴζω. 5. πείθομαι. 6. ἡ παρθένος. 7. φοβέομαι. 8. μετὰ τὸ δεῖπνον. 9. βοηθέω. 10. γίγνομαι. 11. ὁ βασιλεύς. 12. ἡ ναῦς. 13. γίγνεται. 14. φοβέομαι. 15. πέμπω. 16. ὦ πάππα. 17. φοβέομαι.

Exercise 6η

Column B: 3, 6, 2, 1, 4, 10, 9, 5, 8, 7.

Exercises 6θ and 6ι

1. μοι (F). 2. ταῖς κόραις (A). 3. τῆς νήσου (H). 4. ὑμῖν (B). 5. τῇ ὑστεραίᾳ (E). 6. τῷ λίθῳ (D). 7. τῶν φίλων (H). 8. τῷ φίλῳ (F). 9. τῷ λίθῳ (G). 10. τῇ ὁδῷ (G). 11. τοῦ ἀγροῦ (H). 12. τῷ οἴκῳ (G). 13. τῷ ἀνθρώπῳ (F). 14. τῷ δούλῳ (A), 15. ὀνόματι (C).

16. τῆς οἰκίας (H). 17. τῷ δένδρῳ (G). 18. τῇ δεξιᾷ (D). 19. τῷ λαβυρίνθῳ (G). 20. τῷ νεανίᾳ (F).

Exercise 6κ
1. I lead. 2. indeed, in fact. 3. I go forward; I come forward, advance. 4. they say. 5. double gates. 6. how! 7. I hand over; I supply, provide. 8. many times, often.

Exercise 6κ
1. γε. 2. οὐδαμῶς. 3. ἐξέρχομαι. 4. μάχομαι. 5. πολλάκις. 6. πορεύομαι.

Exercise 6μ

DICAEOPOLIS IS DISPLEASED

[1] So mother is silent for a short (small) time and looks toward her children. And Melissa says, "(But) what, mother? Why are you silent? What happens then? For I want to hear the story. Don't you too want to hear the story, Philip?" "Certainly; for I want to learn what Theseus does. Mother, how beautiful is the story!"

[2] And meanwhile the children see Xanthias and Dicaeopolis; for Xanthias is running toward the house and approaches the children, and Dicaeopolis is chasing him and shouting loudly and says, "Where are you fleeing, you cursed creature? Why aren't you staying in the field and helping? Do you want to sleep already? Why don't you obey me? Look, take (receive) the seed and follow me to the fields and work!"

[3] And Xanthias (says): "I have already been working (I am already working) in the field for a long (much) time. It is now noontime. And the sun is blazing, and I am very tired; so I want to rest a short (small) time." But Dicaeopolis says, "It is not possible to rest; for the work is long. Look, do you see this stick? Aren't you afraid?" But Xanthias (says): "Certainly; I see the stick and am very afraid. But the sun wears me down and it is not possible to follow you to the field."

[4] And Myrrhine (says) to her husband: "Don't shout like that (so, thus), husband; for grandfather is very tired; so he is sleeping and does not want to wake up. Don't lead the slave to the field at noontime, but let him rest a little while (time)." So Dicaeopolis is silent and sits in the shade, and Xanthias himself also sits and is soon sleeping; for he fears Dicaeopolis, but he is very tired.

[5] Then Philip says, "Mother, why don't you tell father about the wolf?" But Myrrhine (says): "No, Philip; for now he is very tired and is displeased; and I want to tell him everything (all things) at home after work."

ANSWERS: CHAPTER 7

Exercise 7α
1. (the) good (men/people) . . . good (things). 2. many (women). 3. many terrible (things), lit., many and terrible (things). 4. (the) evil (men/people) . . . evil (things). 5. many (men, people).

Exercise 7β
1. παῖδες. 2. παιδί. 3. παῖδας. 4. ὀνόματος. 5. ὀνόματα. 6. ὀνόμασι(ν). 7. φύλαξ. 8. φύλακα. 9. φυλάκων. 10. αἰγός. 11. αἰγί. 12. αἶγας. 13. ἐλπίδες. 14. ἐλπίδα. 15. ἐλπίσι(ν). 16. ἐλπίδας.

Exercise 7γ
1. ἐμαυτὸν or ἐμαυτήν. 2. ἑαυτὰς. 3. ἡμᾶς αὐτοὺς. 4. σεαυτῷ. 5. σεαυτὸν. 6. ἑαυτούς. 7. ἑαυτῷ. 8. σεαυτῇ. 9. ἑαυτῆς. 10. ὑμᾶς αὐτοὺς. 11. ἑαυτὴν. 12. ἑαυτοῦ. 13. ἡμῖν αὐταῖς. 14. ὑμῶν αὐτῶν. 15. σεαυτὴν.

Exercise 7δ
1. I lift, raise. 2. no one; no. 3. sea. 4. goat. 5. what man? 6. I order, tell. 7. who? 8. very big, very large; very great; biggest, largest; greatest. 9. I prepare. 10. about, concerning; around.

Exercise 7ε

1. αἱρέω. 2. τὸ ὄνομα. 3. ἰέναι. 4. ἡ πόλις. 5. ἐπαίρω ἐμαυτόν. 6. ἐμαυτοῦ, ἐμαυτῆς.
7. τις. 8. εὑρίσκω. 9. ἀνήρ τις. 10. περί.

Exercise 7ζ

1. χειμῶνες. 2. χειμῶνι. 3. χειμῶνας. 4. χειμῶσι(ν). 5. κλῶπας. 6. κλωψί(ν). 7. κλῶπα.
8. κλωπός. 9. κλώψ. 10. κυνί. 11. κύων. 12. κυσί(ν). 13. κυνῶν. 14. ῥήτορσι(ν).
15. ῥήτορι. 16. ῥήτορες. 17. σῶφρων. 18. σώφρονι. 19. σώφρονας. 20. σώφροσι(ν).

Exercise 7η

1. τίς. 2. τίνος. 3. τίνα. 4. τινα. 5. τίνες. 6. τίνα. 7. τί. 8. τίσι. 9. τινας. 10. τις.
11. τι. 12. τίνι.

Exercise 7θ

1. I am about (to); I am destined (to); I intend (to). 2. wine. 3. two. 4. fire. 5. I start, rush.
6. of sound mind; prudent; self-controlled. 7. from where? whence? 8. I stop X. 9. all
men, human beings, persons.

Exercise 7ι

1. ὁ Κύκλωψ. 2. πῶς; 3. ὁ ὀφθαλμός. 4. ὁ ξένος. 5. βάλλω. 6. βάλλω. 7. ἕν.
8. ἀποκρίνομαι. 9. ἐνθάδε. 10. ὁρμάομαι.

Exercise 7κ

THE END OF THE STORY

[1] And when Philip ends the story, Melissa says, "And what happens after this to
Odysseus and his comrades? To what island do they then sail? Do they arrive at their
fatherland? Who of his companions are saved from the sea? Don't stop, Philip, but tell
me all the story about Odysseus!"

[2] And Philip (says): "They do not arrive at their fatherland, since the Cyclops's
father becomes hostile to them and does not allow them to return home by sea, nor is
Odysseus able to bring them safely from the sea to the harbor (to save them from the sea
to the harbor)."

[3] And Melissa (says): "What are you saying? Whose son is the Cyclops?" And
Philip (says): "Of Poseidon, the god of the sea. For Odysseus sails away from the shore
of the island but from the midst (middle) of the sea he shouts thus: 'Cyclops, you are
terrible, but I am brave and strong. Why do you not receive strangers well into your
dwelling (house)? Do you not know that Zeus always saves strangers? And now you no
longer have an eye in the middle of your forehead. And I am responsible, and my name
is Odysseus. I am Odysseus of many counsels, the son of Laertes, and I have (my) home
in Ithaca.' And the Cyclops lifts a great stone from the mountain and throws it at
Odysseus's ship. Then the stone falls into the sea, and Odysseus and his comrades
escape.

[4] "But the Cyclops calls Poseidon, his father, and says: 'Father Poseidon, master
and king of the sea, see what I suffer at the hand of Odysseus; so come to my aid and
don't allow him to return home. And if this is not possible, kill all his comrades.'" And
Melissa (says): "What in fact happens? Does Poseidon make a storm on the sea? Is
Odysseus saved from (out of) the storm? Do his comrades die in the storm? Are all safe
when the storm stops? Tell me, Philip, tell me, and don't stop."

[5] And Philip (says): "Melissa, don't make a commotion but listen to the end of the
story; for I want to tell the story, but you be silent and listen to me!"

[6] And Melissa is silent, and Philip says, "Odysseus and his comrades suffer many
terrible things, they often suffer storms, and some are saved, but others die in the sea.
And finally they arrive at the island of Aeolus."

ANSWERS: CHAPTER 8

Exercises 8α and 8β

1. ἐργαζόμεναι (C). 2. θεωμένῳ (A). 3. πορευομένους (A). 4. ἐργαζόμενοι (S).
5. διαλεγομένων (C). 6. λῡόμενος (C). 7. ἑπομένους (A). 8. φοβούμεναι (C). 9. μαχόμενοι
(A). 10. ἐργαζόμεναι (S). 11. ἑπόμενος (A). 12. ἐργαζομένη (A). 13. παυόμενοι (C).
14. βουλομένη (C). 15. μαχόμενοι (S). 16. ἡγούμενος (A). 17. ἐργαζόμενον (A).
18. πορευόμενος (C). 19. φοβούμενοι (C). 20. πειθόμενος (C).

Exercise 8γ

1. I see, watch, look at. 2. city. 3. I talk to, converse with. 4. god. 5. at home. 6. good! well
done! 7. nevertheless. 8. to that place, thither. 9. while. 10. Dionysus.

Exercise 8δ

1. ἕπομαι. 2. εὖ. 3. ὥσπερ. 4. ἡ ἑσπέρα. 5. τὸ ἔργον. 6. ἐργάζομαι. 7. ἡ θύρᾱ. 8. ὁ
ποιητής.

Exercise 8ε

THE GODS LOVE THOSE WHO WORK

[1] And Philip comes into the house and sees Myrrhine and Melissa and Dicaeopolis
talking to one another. Then Dicaeopolis stops talking and looks toward his son; and
Melissa stops working and runs to Philip. And Myrrhine says, "Look, Dicaeopolis, the
wolf-slayer is coming in. Don't you want to honor the wolf-slayer?" And Dicaeopolis,
replying, says: "But I indeed certainly wish to honor the wolf-slayer. Come here, son, and
tell me, who wish to honor you, everything (all the things) about the wolf." And Philip,
obeying his father, sits down and tells everything (all things) again.

[2] And then Dicaeopolis (says): "Well done, son; for you are very brave and strong.
So I want to honor you, because you have killed so great a wolf, a terrible and fierce wild
beast. So we are about to go to the city; for there the Athenians are celebrating a festival
for Dionysus. Don't you want to see the contests and the choruses in the festival?"

[3] And Philip (says): "I do want (to do so), father; for we go so rarely to the city that
it is impossible for me who work in the fields to see the festivals and the contests. So take
(lead) us to Athens, father." And Dicaeopolis says, "Then let it be so! For I too want to
honor Dionysus. And you, son, do not speak badly of/belittle those working in the
fields/country; for farming makes men strong. And the gods do not love lazy men and
men of the sort who don't work; but the gods are always friendly to the man who works."

[4] And Philip says, "but I wish to work, and I want also to go to the city and see the
contests."

[5] And when night comes, Dicaeopolis says, "Now it is time to sleep; for tomorrow
we intend to go to the city at dawn (together with the day). So sleep."

[6] Then soon (after not much time) sleep overcomes (takes) Philip. And in his
dreams the boy sees himself watching the contests in Athens. And while he is watching
the contests, look, the god himself is present in the theater. Then Dionysus shouts loudly
and says: "Boy, I rejoice seeing that you are watching the choruses in the theater and that
you honor me thus. And I also honor both you and your father; for he always works very
(hard) in the fields and takes care of the grape vines and makes much wine. For I always
watch you, even if you do not see me; for I am present everywhere and honor the good
(men) and those who work, but the bad and the lazy I do not honor. So always be true
(beautiful) and good, boy, since I and all other gods are always watching you."

[7] And the boy is very afraid and wants to reply but no longer sees the god. And
there is darkness everywhere, and the boy says: "Alas, what is happening? Father, where
are you? Save me!"

[8] And meanwhile his father approaches his son and says, "What is happening to
you, son? Get up! Why are you shouting? Cheer up!"

[9] And Philip wakes up from sleep very frightened and says, "Father, hereafter I intend always to work with you in the fields; for the god does not honor the lazy."

[10] And Dicaeopolis (says): "But rest now, son, and sleep a sweet sleep; for the god is propitious to you and rejoices if men honor him and go to the city wishing to see his festival."

Exercise 8ζ

1. ἀνδρός. 2. μητέρες. 3. θυγατέρα. 4. ἀνδράσι(ν). 5. πάτερ. 6. γυναικός. 7. χεῖρες. 8. μητέρα. 9. ἄνδρας. 10. θυγατρί. 11. πατράσι(ν). 12. χεῖρας. 13. γυναικῶν. 14. χειρί. 15. πατρί. 16. μητέρας. 17. θυγατράσι(ν). 18. γυναῖκα. 19. ἄνδρες. 20. θυγατέρων. 21. μητέρες. 22. χειρός. 23. πατέρα. 24. ἀνδρί.

Exercises 8η and 8θ

1. πᾶσαν (P), the whole sea. 2. παντός (A), (of) the whole work. 3. πάντες (P), all the men. 4. πᾶσα, every woman. 5. πάντα (P), all the plows. 6. πάσᾱς (P), all the women. 7. πᾶν, every work. 8. πάντων (P), (of) all men. 9. πάσαις (P), (to/for) all mothers. 10. πάσης (A), (of) the whole woman. 11. πάντας (P), all the fathers. 12. πᾱσῶν (P), (of) all the maidens. 13. πᾶν (A), the whole/entire city. 14. πᾶσαι (P), all the mothers. 15. πάντα (A), the whole/entire house, home, dwelling. 16. παντί (P), (by) the whole work or (by) all the work. 17. πᾶς (P), the whole work/toil or all the work/toil. 18. πᾶσι (P), (to/for) all men. 19. πάσῃ, (to/for) every daughter. 20. πᾶς, every man/human being.

Exercise 8ι

1. 4th. 2. 7. 3. 9th. 4. 6. 5. 10th. 6. 8. 7. 2nd. 8. 3. 9. 10. 10. 5th. 11. 8th. 12. 5. 13. 1. 14. 3rd. 15. 1st. 16. 1. 17. 2. 18. 7th. 19. 6th. 20. 4. 21. 9. 22. 1.

Exercise 8κ

1. ἕν. 2. εἷς. 3. μία. 4. ἕνα. 5. μιᾶς. 6. ἑνός. 7. οὐδενί. 8. οὐδέν. 9. οὐδεμίαν. 10. δύο. 11. δυοῖν. 12. δυοῖν. 13. δύο. 14. δύο. 15. τρεῖς. 16. τρισίν. 17. τρεῖς. 18. τριῶν. 19. τρεῖς. 20. τέτταρες. 21. τέτταρας. 22. τεττάρων. 23. τέτταρσιν. 24. τέτταρα.

Exercise 8λ

1. B, for three days. 2. C, within three days. 3. A, on the third day. 4. C, within five days. 5. B, all day or the whole day. 6. A, on the fifth day. 7. A, on the next day. 8. B, for a long time.

Exercise 8μ

1. I wake X up. 2. on behalf of/for the mother. 3. altar. 4. young man. 5. meanwhile. 6. I go up, get up; I climb, go up onto.

Exercise 8ν

1. τέλος. 2. τῇ ὑστεραίᾳ. 3. ἡ ἀγορά. 4. ἡ χείρ. 5. ὁ πολίτης. 6. εὔχομαι. 7. καθίζω. 8. καθίζομαι.

Exercise 8ξ

POLEMARCHUS AND HIS CHILDREN

[1] Then the father leads them into the city; and the grandfather leaning upon his staff goes with him slowly. And the mother, very fearful on behalf of her children, looks around at the crowd and follows her husband; and she leads her daughter and her son. And her daughter says, "Mother, where is everyone (are all) going? Why are they hurrying so?" And Myrrhine replies: "Everyone is (All are) hurrying to the Acropolis, just as we (are), daughter, wanting to honor the gods. For we too wish to honor the gods, all (of them), and especially Zeus, the father of all the other gods, and Athena, his daughter, and Dionysus; for the Athenians are celebrating a festival for Dionysus, and all the citizens want to see the festival. Look, fathers are leading both their sons and daughters to the festival, coming from the country, just as we (are); and all the boys and all the girls are following their fathers and their mothers, since the crowd is great (much),

and great (much) the commotion, and it is not easy to walk to the Acropolis through so many men and women, both citizens and foreigners. And so don't you abandon us but always follow together with us."

[2] And meanwhile a certain man runs toward Dicaeopolis through the crowd and takes hold of his hand. "Dicaeopolis," he says, "how are you? What are you doing in Athens? Where are you going and from where?" And Dicaeopolis, replying to him, (says): "I have come, Polemarchus, from the country to the city, wishing to pray to all the gods and at the same time to see the festival. And I am leading my father and my wife, and my daughter and my son." And Polemarchus says, "Hither indeed, sitting down tell me everything (all things) both about your home and about the country. And you, too, sit down. Are you Philip? Zeus, how handsome (beautiful) a boy you are; but your father so rarely leads you to the city that I scarcely recognize you."

[3] And meanwhile three boys come out of a certain house and shout to Polemarchus: "Father, why aren't we going to the festival? Lead us there, just as all other fathers are leading their own children (the children of themselves)." And Dicaeopolis (says): "One, two, three; but indeed the fourth, dear Polemarchus, where is he?"

[4] "What are you saying, Dicaeopolis? Zeus, how rarely you come to the city; for no longer do I have four children, but now five (for no longer are there four, but now five children for me); but the fifth stays with his mother in the house. And the first is already a teenager, and he is now spending time with all the other teenagers on the Acropolis, wanting to see the festival. So I have many children, but not as many as your friend Ctesippus. How many children does he have now?"

[5] And Dicaeopolis replies: "Who is able to say exactly (to a number)? Six, seven, eight, nine, ten—for he is always begetting (making) children, just as some bull, so that now he has a village, not a house (so that now a village, not a house, is for him)."

[6] And Polemarchus says, "But I, after my fifth, no longer want to beget (make) other children; for life is hard, and it is not easy to provide food for all my sons. And I have one daughter (there is one daughter for me)."

[7] And Dicaeopolis replying says, "But you and I drag the same yoke, Polemarchus. For life is difficult for all, and the field does not provide much food. But what are the names of (your) children?"

[8] "For the first the name is Nicobulus, and for the second Hiero, and for the third Melanippus, and for the fourth Philotimus, and for the fifth Diagoras; and for my one daughter the name is Hebe."

[9] "Yes, by Zeus, how difficult life is, Polemarchus. For we seek good women for a long time; for no one wants to beget (make) children from a bad woman. Then we beget (make) children. And the husband provides food for his wife; and the wife carries her little child for a long time within herself and often suffers great dangers concerning her own life (the life of herself). And when she gives birth, no woman abandons her own little child (the little child of herself), but nourishes (it) for a long (much) time and always labors day and night and flees no labor. But often, when the children grow up and become teenagers and young men, they obey neither their father nor their mother nor anyone else (no one other); for they heed no one. For if (their) father orders them (to do) anything, they do not wish to do it (they wish to do nothing)."

[10] But Zeus is propitious both to you and to me, Dicaeopolis; for no one of our sons acts like this (does thus), but they are all fine (beautiful) and good."

[11] For a long time Dicaeopolis and Polemarchus converse thus with one another. And finally Dicaeopolis says, "It is time now for us to go to the agora and to the Acropolis. Farewell, dear Polemarchus; see you later (to again)."

ANSWERS: CHAPTER 9

Exercise 9α and 9β

1. φιλοῦσα (C). 2. τρέχουσιν (A). 3. φιλοῦντες (A). 4. πονούντων (A). 5. τῑμῶντι (A).
6. ὁρῶντες (C). 7. καλῶν (A). 8. ἀκούουσα (C). 9. καθεύδων (C). 10. τῑμῶσαι (S).
11. σπεύδοντα (A). 12. πίνων (C). 13. ἐσθίοντας (A). 14. καθεύδοντος (A). 15. ἀκούοντι
(A). 16. καθεύδοντες (S). 17. βοωσῶν (A). 18. ὄντες (C). 19. βοῶσα (C). 20. πονοῦντα
(A). 21. τῑμῶντα (C). 22. τῑμῶν (A).

Exercise 9γ

1. I eat. 2. through. 3. I come back, return. 4. most beautiful, very beautiful. 5. left hand.
6. temple.

Exercise 9δ

1. ἄγε or ἄγετε. 2. κάμνω. 3. πίνω. 4. ἡ θεός. 5. ἡ δεξιά. 6. ἐπί. 7. ὁ κίνδῡνος. 8. ἡ
Νίκη.

Exercise 9ε

1. βασιλῆς. 2. πόλει. 3. ναῦς. 4. ἄστεως. 5. βουσί(ν). 6. πόλιν. 7. βασιλεύς.
8. γέροντα. 9. ἄστεων. 10. νεώς. 11. βοῦν. 12. γέρουσι(ν). 13. πόλις. 14. βοός.
15. γέροντι. 16. ἄστη. 17. βασιλέᾱς. 18. πόλεσι(ν). 19. βοῶν. 20. νῆες. 21. ἄστυ.
22. ναυσί(ν). 23. γερόντων. 24. βασιλεῖ.

Exercise 9ζ and 9η

1. The stranger's name is Admetus (A). 2. We have come from the field (C). 3. We will
finish the work within two days (E). 4. We hear the greatest poet (D). 5. The young man
loves the maiden (D). 6. He is the best of the poets (B). 7. We are fighting for/on behalf of
our city (C). 8. I take hold of the big rock (D). 9. We hear the words of the messenger (A).
10. Many of the farmers are away (B).

Exercise 9θ

1. The men in the agora. 2. Some (men) . . . others. 3. The friends. 4. the man working in
the field. 5. The men waiting. 6. The woman watching the dances. 7. The man in the
road. 8. The women running toward the spring. 9. The enemy. 10. disgrace/dishonor.
11. the men of old. 12. the things inside. 13. the truth. 14. The one (girl/woman) . . . the
other.

Exercise 9ι

1. I increase. 2. old. 3. sacrificial victim. 4. propitious. 5. priest. 6. I am silent.
7. procession. 8. middle (of).

Exercise 9κ

1. καίω or κᾱ́ω. 2. ἕτοιμος. 3. τέρπομαι. 4. ὁ κῆρυξ. 5. ὁ οὐρανός. 6. ὁ γέρων. 7. ὁ
δῆμος. 8. ἄριστος. 9. ὁ οὐρανός. 10. ὁ Βρόμιος.

Exercise 9λ

MELISSA'S DREAM

[1] There is now a great (much) silence at the gates. And Dicaeopolis and the others
are sleeping on the ground; and a few (not many) are still reveling in the city, being
drunk and shouting. But it is not possible for Melissa to rest. For seeing many terrible
things in her dreams she is very frightened; for she seems to herself to be the daughter of
Chryses, the priest of a certain village near Troy. For her grandfather often speaks about
Chryses and about Troy. And in her sleep Melissa sees many kings of the Greeks talking
with one another near a burning fire; and among the kings is Agamemnon, a strong man,
but difficult and very terrible. And all the other kings fear him since he is so difficult
(being so difficult); for Agamemnon is the greatest of the kings, and the others all honor
him. And the daughter of Chryses is now a slave of Agamemnon, the greatest king; and
her father, being a priest of Apollo, coming to his daughter's aid, wants to save her. And
the kings of the Greeks receive the priest and listen to him speaking. And the priest says

these things to all the kings, and especially to Agamemnon: "Kings of the Greeks, I am a priest of Apollo. So if you release my daughter, the gods who have their homes on Mount Olympus and especially Apollo are destined to come to aid you who want (wanting) to take Troy and to bring you safely (save you) to your fatherland. And I bring you much gold and hand (it) over (to you); so receive it and release (loosen) my dear daughter to me."

[2] Then all the other kings wish to honor the priest and want, obeying the priest, both to receive the gold and to release the girl. But Agamemnon, being angry, orders the old priest to go away and not to return again. And he says these things to the priest: "I do not intend to release (loosen) your daughter; for now she is my slave, and in Argos she is destined to grow old in my house with my other slave women. So go away, if you want to return home safely."

[3] So the old priest is frightened and goes away in silence, and his daughter, seeing her father going away, groans and cries. The other kings pity the priest, and his daughter, groaning, says, "Father, priest of the great Apollo, do not desert me here with the foreigners being a slave; save me, father!"

[4] "Save me, save me," groaning, Melissa shouts and wakes up. And Myrrhine, awakened by the shout of her daughter, says, "What's the matter (What are you suffering), daughter? There is no danger now; but resting, sleep beside me; for the sun is soon about to rise, and we are about to go to the theater. Don't you want to see the choruses and the contests? So don't cry but rest beside me!"

ANSWERS: CHAPTER 10

Exercise 10α
1. λύσουσι(ν). 2. λύσομεν. 3. ἐθελήσετε. 4. λύσεται. 5. γενησόμεναι. 6. πέμψω.
7. δέξει or δέξῃ. 8. λέξουσι(ν). 9. πείσει. 10. παρασκευάσεις. 11. γράψων. 12. γράψει.
13. φυλάξει. 14. ἕξεις. 15. σχήσεις. 16. σπεύσουσι(ν). 17. κομιεῖ. 18. κομιοῦσι(ν).
19. κομιοῦμαι. 20. ἡγήσεσθε. 21. τῑμήσουσι(ν). 22. φιλήσω. 23. νῑκήσειν. 24. ὄψομαι.
25. βήσεσθαι. 26. βησόμεθα. 27. ἀκούσεσθε. 28. πλεύσομαι. 29. γνώσεσθε.
30. πῐόμεθα. 31. δραμούμεθα. 32. βαδιοῦνται. 33. πεσεῖται. 34. θαυμάσει or
θαυμάσῃ. 35. βλεψόμεθα. 36. πεσούμενον. 37. φεύξομαι. 38. πείσονται.
39. διωξόμεθα. 40. ἔσται. 41. ἔσεσθε. 42. ἔσεσθαι. 43. παρεσόμεθα.

Exercise 10β
1. I defeat; I win. 2. I become. 3. I find. 4. I see, watch, look at. 5. alas! 6. well. 7. I arrive. 8. I arrive at the theater.

Exercise 10γ
1. θεάσομαι. 2. νῑκήσω. 3. ἀφίξομαι. 4. γενήσομαι. 5. εὑρήσω.

Exercise 10δ

GOOD CITIZENS
[1] There is much commotion in the city. For many people, men and women, children, citizens and foreigners, do not stop coming to the city from the country and from the Piraeus. And many farmers are already going away out of the city, wanting to return to their farms. For when festivals take place in Athens and other cities, the countrymen always hurry into the cities to see the choruses and to revel. But soon (after not much time), longing seizes them for the country life, and they return out of the cities into the country. For no country man loves cities. For those living in the country love peace and quiet very much, and in cities there is much commotion. "O city, city!" groans Dicaeopolis, "I look away to the country, loving peace and quiet, hating the city, and longing for my farm. For everyone who lives in the city (all living in the city) seem to me (to be) evil. For if some god is about to benefit some city, he makes good men in it; but if a

city is about to suffer bad things, god takes out the good men from this city. And in the city of Athens where are the good men now? Alas, alas for the city!"

[2] And grandfather says, "By the will of the gods, dear child, the city will have good men (there will be good men for the city)."

[3] And meanwhile Dicaeopolis sees a certain friend coming forward with difficulty through the crowd, and he says, "Greetings, dear Hieronymus, how rarely I see you."

[4] And Hieronymus says, "For it is not possible for me, Dicaeopolis, to go to the country. For the citizens, if they wish to accomplish anything with other cities, always come to me first. For I seem to them to be a competent messenger; and in the other cities I listen to the words of the citizens, and then I bring messages out of the other cities to Athens. So I often journey also to other cities, as (being) a messenger of Athens. Soon indeed I will go to Lacedaemon; so because of this I rarely have leisure to go to the country."

[5] And Dicaeopolis says, "But you are a good man; for you are competent to benefit your own city."

[6] And Hieronymus, replying, says, "A good citizen (a beautiful and good man) will want to learn how men will manage both their homes and their cities well, and they will honor their own parents (the parents of themselves), and they will both receive and send away citizens and foreigners well. But how rarely are there (do there become) good men in the cities now, dear Dicaeopolis."

[7] So the men converse with one another for a short time concerning both the city and good citizens. And finally Hieronymus (says): "Farewell, friend. I will pray that the gods will provide you with many good things (will provide many good things to you). Go, indeed, rejoicing. For it is time for me to go away. And perhaps I will see you soon again either in the city or somewhere else."

Exercise 10ε

1. μενοῦμεν. 2. ἀρεῖν. 3. μαχεῖ or μαχῇ. 4. ἐγερεῖ. 5. ἐγερεῖν. 6. ἀρεῖ. 7. ἀποκτενοῦσι(ν). 8. μαχεῖσθαι. 9. ἀποκρινοῦμαι. 10. καμεῖσθε. 11. ἀποκτενῶ. 12. βαλοῦσι(ν). 13. ἐλῶμεν. 14. βαλοῦντα. 15. μενοῦσιν. 16. ἀποκρινουμένη.

Exercise 10ζ

1. ἔρχεται. 2. ἔρχει or ἔρχῃ. 3. ἐρχόμεθα. 4. ἰέναι. 5. ἴθι. 6. ἰοῦσα. 7. εἶμι. 8. ἴᾱσι(ν). 9. ἴμεν. 10. ἴτε. 11. εἶ. 12. εἶμι. 13. εἰσι(ν). 14. εἴσιμεν. 15. εἴσιθι. 16. εἰσιέναι. 17. ἐπάνειμι. 18. ἐπανιέναι. 19. ἐπανιών. 20. ἐπανέρχονται. 21. ἔξεισι(ν). 22. ἐξιέναι. 23. ἔξιθι. 24. ἐξερχόμεθα. 25. ἐξιοῦσα. 26. ἀπίᾱσι(ν). 27. ἀπιέναι. 28. ἀπέρχονται. 29. ἄπιθι. 30. προσιέναι. 31. πρόσιτε. 32. πρόσειμι. 33. προσέρχεσθε. 34. ἴτε. 35. ἐρχόμεθα.

Exercise 10η

1. Grandfather approaches Dicaeopolis to persuade him to stay in the city. 2. Is it allowed/possible for us to stay in the city? 3. We must work/It is necessary for us to work in the fields. 4. We must return/It is necessary for us to return home to accomplish many works/deeds. 5. I wish to go home to hear what is happening.

Exercise 10θ

Column B: 5, 7, 8, 9, 1, 10, 2, 3, 4, 6, 6.

Exercise 10ι

1. I flee away, escape. 2. before. 3. it is necessary. 4. straightway, immediately, at once. 5. shout. 6. I stay; I wait; I wait for. 7. parents. 8. I strike, hit.

Exercise 10κ

1. ἀποκτείνω. 2. ἡ κεφαλή. 3. καταλείπω. 4. τὸ ὕδωρ. 5. ποτέ. 6. εὐθύς. 7. τρέπω. 8. ἔξεστι(ν). 9. ποτέ. 10. αἴρω. 11. καταλείπω. 12. μένω. 13. ἀποφεύγω. 14. ποτέ.

Exercise 10λ

1. ἀποφεύξομαι. 2. τρέψω. 3. ἀρῶ. 4. καταλείψω. 5. ἀποκτενῶ. 6. μενῶ.

Exercise 10μ

PHILIP IS BLIND

[1] Then Dicaeopolis approaches his son and says, "Don't be afraid, dear son. For a certain dizziness and vertigo seized you when you fell down and struck you head against the ground. But now rest for a short time. For doubtless you will regain your sight soon. For thus it often happens to others suffering these things."

[2] But Philip, seeing nothing, is not able to keep quiet but groaning and crying says these things: "Alas, wretched me! For the gods, wishing to punish me, sent me this misfortune and made me blind for the rest of my life." And Dicaeopolis, answering, says, "Don't think these things, Philip, but cheer up! For now I will go to the agora to seek some doctor; for doubtless a doctor will be able to help you and to heal your eyes. So stay here. For soon I will return." "Where are you going, father? Will I stay here without you? But who will stay together with me? For I am afraid, since I see nothing (seeing nothing); but everywhere there seems to me to be darkness." And Myrrhine, crying, says, "Do not fear (Fear nothing), son, for I will stay with you, and I will not go away. And there will be with you your grandfather and Melissa; be brave; for none of us will desert you. Then your father will return after a short (not much) time and will bring a doctor. And we will guard you from dangers and will lead you to the colonnade, where it will be possible to rest a short time. So take hold of my hand!" And Philip says, "Dear mother, call my father, and don't let him go away!"

[3] Then the mother, taking hold of her husband's hand, whispers these things: "What is the matter with the child? Why do his eyes see nothing except darkness? Will he truly regain his sight soon?" And Dicaeopolis, answering, (says), "Philip suffers a great misfortune, dear wife, and I do not know what will happen. For now he is blind. So we must pray to all the gods."

ANSWERS: CHAPTER 11

Exercise 11α

1. ἀφίκετο. 2. ἔσχον. 3. ἀπέθανον. 4. ἀποθανεῖν. 5. μάθετε. 6. ἐβάλομεν. 7. βάλε.
8. λαβεῖν. 9. λιπεῖν. 10. ἐγενόμην. 11. ἔπεσον. 12. ἐπάθετε. 13. φύγετε.
14. καταλιπεῖν. 15. ἐλάβετε. 16. ἔφυγε(ν). 17. γενέσθαι. 18. ἐπίομεν. 19. ἔπαθε(ν).
20. ἄγαγε. 21. ἤγαγες. 22. ηὗρε(ν) or εὗρε(ν). 23. ἀφικόμενος. 24. εὑρών.
25. μαθοῦσα. 26. ἀφίκου. 27. ἐγενόμεθα. 28. ἀφίκεσθε. 29. γενοῦ. 30. γένεσθε.

Exercise 11β

1. led (A). 2. Standing (P), decided (A), to knock (A). 3. did (A), opening (A), greeted (A).
4. are (P), asked (A). 5. explains (P), happened (A), asks (P), to stay (P). 6. hearing (A), led (A). 7. Come in (A), stay (P), wish (P). 8. entering (A), expressed (A).

Exercise 11γ

1. παθοῦσα. 2. λαβόντα. 3. βαλόντος. 4. φυγούσᾱς. 5. ἀγαγόντες. 6. λιπούσῃ.
7. ἀφικομένων. 8. σχοῦσι(ν). 9. γενομένης. 10. πιόντας. 11. μαθοῦσαι.
12. ἀποθανόντι. 13. εὑρουσῶν. 14. ἀποθανόν. 15. μαθών. 16. λιπούσαις.
17. ἀφικόμενον. 18. γενομένῳ. 19. πεσόντος. 20. λαβούσᾱς.

Exercise 11δ

1. I cry, weep. 2. brother. 3. blind. 4. I lead in; I take in. 5. I strike; I knock on (a door). 6. I leave. 7. it seems (good). 8. he/she said. 9. word; story. 10. How are you? 11. tomorrow.
12. to the doctor.

Exercise 11ε

1. αἰτέω. 2. ὁ ἰᾱτρός. 3. σοφός, -ή, -όν. 4. κομίζω. 5. μανθάνω. 6. πάσχω.

7. ἀποθνῄσκω. 8. λαμβάνω. 9. καλῶς ἔχω. 10. εἰ. 11. σκοπέω. 12. δοκεῖ.

Exercise 11ζ

1. μαθήσομαι, ἔμαθον. 2. δόξει, ἔδοξε(ν). 3. κομιῶ, ἐκόμισα. 4. σκέψομαι, ἐσκεψάμην. 5. αἰτήσω, ᾔτησα. 6. εἰσάξω, εἰσήγαγον. 7. λείψω, ἔλιπον. 8. πείσομαι, ἔπαθον. 9. δακρύσω, ἐδάκρυσα. 10. κόψω, ἔκοψα. 11. ἀποθανοῦμαι, ἀπέθανον. 12. λήψομαι, ἔλαβον.

Exercise 11η

1. εἷλε(ν). 2. εἴδετε. 3. ἦλθον. 4. ἑλεῖν. 5. εἴπετε. 6. ἦλθε(ν). 7. ἔδραμες. 8. εἰπεῖν. 9. ἤνεγκον. 10. ἰδεῖν. 11. δραμεῖν. 12. ἔλετε. 13. εἶπον. 14. εἶδον. 15. ἰδοῦσα. 16. ἑλών. 17. ἐνεγκεῖν. 18. ἔνεγκε. 19. ἔφαγε(ν). 20. φάγετε.

Exercise 11θ

1. λίπε. 2. φύγε. 3. ἔλθετε. 4. ἰδέ. 5. εἰπέ. 6. λάβετε. 7. δράμε. 8. εἴπετε. 9. ἴδετε. 10. εὑρέ. 11. εὕρετε. 12. δράμετε. 13. βάλετε. 14. ἐνέγκετε. 15. ἐλθέ.

Exercise 11ι

1. ηὔξ-. 2. ὥρμα-. 3. ηὐχ-. 4. ὠφελε-. 5. ἤγειρ-. 6. ἤκου-.

Exercise 11κ

1. I come; I go. 2. to/toward/against the land. 3. alas! 4. I help; I benefit. 5. reward; pay. 6. I am sick, ill. 7. drachma. 8. by sea.

Exercise 11λ

1. λέγω. 2. ὁράω. 3. προσέρχομαι. 4. ὁ ὀβολός. 5. τὸ ἀργύριον. 6. αἱρέω.

Exercise 11μ

1. ὄψομαι, εἶδον. 2. αἱρήσω, εἷλον. 3. λέξω or ἐρῶ, ἔλεξα or εἶπον. 4. εἶμι, ἦλθον.

Exercise 11ν

IN THE CAVE

[1] It is night, but Philip does not want to sleep; for, crying, he says: "Alas, poor me, who was responsible for this misfortune of mine (for me)? Doubtless someone of the gods; for when I lifted myself up in the road, having become blind, immediately I understood that the gods hated me. Why did I not die then? For I do not want to be blind all my life. Dear father, mother, come to my aid, since I've suffered this (having suffered these things)."

[2] And his mother (says): "Don't cry, child, but listen to me. Do you know Chaerephon, your father's friend and companion?"

[3] And the child said, "Yes, by Zeus, for he has a field not far from our home, and father often took me there."

[4] And Myrrhine (said): "Do you know what misfortune he experienced when (being) still a child?"

[5] And Philip said, "I indeed don't, mother, but tell me."

[6] "Listen indeed. Chaerephon, when (being) still a child, having gone forth (forward) once a little away from his own farm, found a certain cave such as Homer told (about)."

[7] And Philip, taking up (the conversation), said, "Do you mean (say) the one of the Cyclops?"

[8] "Yes. Then taking two companions he went into the cave, wanting to look around at everything (all things)."

[9] "And what companions did he have?" said Philip.

[10] Dicaeopolis said, taking up (the conversation), "After finding the cave, he took us (as) companions, my brother and me, when we were still children (still being children)."

[11] "Then what happened? Tell me, father!"

[12] "Then taking torches we all went together to look for the cave. And I, wanting to find the way again, left stones after me as I was walking. And having found the cave, we

went in, as mother told you. Am I telling the truth, brother?"

[13] And his brother (said): "For how (are you) not (telling the truth)?" I took two torches; for you did not take (any), having small stones in your hands. And Chaerephon, thinking (he was) going into some battle, just as Odysseus against the Cyclops, took a sword in his right hand, and in his left hand he was holding a torch. Thus we went into the darkness of the cave.

[14] "And we took our dog with us, who was (being) a large and handsome animal, called Cerberus."

[15] The mother said, taking up (the conversation), "But you did not take food and water, as if going on a long journey, and because of this there was great danger of your dying (for you to die) in the cave. For, son, they took nothing except the sword and the torches."

[16] "And going forward," said Dicaeopolis's brother, "we scarcely saw anything in the darkness of the cave, although having torches. Then Chaerephon, the one going ahead, suddenly stumbled; and he fell down into a certain chasm of the earth. And I, wanting to come to his aid after he had fallen (after falling), threw away the torches. And they, falling, went out.

[17] "Everywhere there was suddenly darkness around us. Then great fear seized (took) us. And we went down slowly into the chasm, although seeing nothing, wanting to learn what ever Chaerephon experienced having fallen into the chasm.

[18] "And with difficulty we found him lying in the far corner of the chasm. And soon he moves and recovers. And finally he gets up (lifts himself) and says, 'Why is there darkness everywhere? Am I blind?' And your father said, 'No, for you are not blind, but in the darkness of the cave we are all as if blind. For we no longer have torches. So it is necessary for us to walk in the darkness, if we want to find the entrance of the cave again.'

[19] "Then I, being the oldest of all, became the leader of the others in the darkness. And you, Dicaeopolis, were (became) responsible for the salvation of all of us. For your father, child, said to the dog, 'Go on, Cerberus, find the way.' And the dog, catching the scent of the way, returned home. And meanwhile we, being very afraid, were (became) scarcely able to go forward in the darkness. Child, to no one did such a great misfortune ever happen as (happened) to us then, as it seems to me."

[20] And Philip said, "Were you too able to find the entrance of the cave?"

[21] "No," said his mother, "they were not capable of walking (to walk) through the darkness and of finding (to find) the way."

[22] "All night long (All the night)," Dicaeopolis said, taking up (the conversation), "we went around the cave in a circle, not being able to go out, as if having fallen into a labyrinth. And finally we hear the dog barking; and our father, shouting, calls us. And shortly (after not much time) we saw the light of a torch and our father coming in. For having seen the stones on the way and following the dog, he found the cave. But then indeed we perceived that Chaerephon was blind. For he saw nothing, neither the light, nor the dog, nor our father.

[23] "Then, taking him, we led him out of the cave crying and groaning and took him to his home.

[24] "And his father, when he saw his son having become blind, first he groaned, and then he said that we must take the child to the temple of Asclepius in Epidaurus. But we were not able (to do so); so he himself took his son. And when he arrived at the god (i.e., at the temple of the god), leading his own son, first he led him to the sea and washed him. Then they went to the sacred precinct of the god. There he laid his son down, and on the next day he woke up seeing. Even you just now saw him seeing everything (all things)."

[25] And the mother said, "So do not fear, dear son; for soon you too will regain your sight. But now sleep quietly; for it is late."

ANSWERS: CHAPTER 12

Exercise 12α

1. ἔλῡσε(ν). 2. κέλευσον. 3. ἐλύσαντο. 4. λύσασθε. 5. ἐπέμψαμεν. 6. φύλαξαι.
7. πεῖσαι. 8. γράψον. 9. ἔπεισε(ν). 10. πέμψον. 11. δέξασθαι. 12. ἔλεξε(ν).
13. ἔσπευσας. 14. δεξαμένη. 15. κομίσᾱς. 16. ἐτίμησαν. 17. τῑμήσατε. 18. ἐφίλησα.
19. βοῆσαι. 20. φιλῆσαι. 21. ἡγησάμεθα. 22. ἡγήσατο. 23. θεᾱσάμενος.
24. ἐθεᾱσάμην. 25. ἤκουσα. 26. ἐπλεύσατε. 27. ἐδίωξας. 28. ἐθαύμασε(ν).
29. βαδίσατε. 30. ἐβάδισαν. 31. ἠργασάμεθα or εἰργασάμεθα. 32. ἠργάσω or εἰργάσω.

Exercise 12β

1. λῡσάμενος. 2. διώξαντες. 3. λῡσᾶσαν. 4. φιλησᾶσαις. 5. σπεύσαντας.
6. παρασκευάσαντα. 7. βλεψᾶσης. 8. ἀκουσάντων. 9. δεξαμένῳ. 10. τῑμήσαντας.
11. λέξᾱσα. 12. εὐξάμενος.

Exercise 12γ

1. mule. 2. as quickly as possible. 3. crowd. 4. wall. 5. I worry; I care. 6. I bid X farewell, I bid farewell to X. 7. bad, evil. 8. either . . . or.

Exercise 12δ

1. τάχιστα. 2. ἤ. 3. ὁ λιμήν. 4. καίπερ. 5. ἀπορέω. 6. ὀρθός, -ή, -όν. 7. γεραιός, -ά, -όν. 8. ὀρθός, -ή, -όν.

Exercise 12ε

1. φροντιῶ, ἐφρόντισα. 2. φυλάξω, ἐφύλαξα. 3. πέμψω, ἔπεμψα. 4. ἀπορήσω, ἠπόρησα. 5. βοήσομαι, ἐβόησα. 6. πείσω, ἔπεισα.

Exercise 12ζ

1. ἦρα. 2. ἐγείρατε. 3. ἔμεινε(ν). 4. μεῖνον. 5. ἀποκτεῖναι. 6. ἄρατε.
7. ἀποκρίνασθαι. 8. ἦρω. 9. ἀπεκρίνατο. 10. ἠράμεθα. 11. ἀπεκρῑνάμεθα.
12. ἐμείναμεν. 13. ἠράμην. 14. ἤγειρας. 15. ἦραν. 16. ἀπεκρίνασθε.
17. ἀπεκτείνατε. 18. ἀποκρίνασθε. 19. μείνᾱσα. 20. ἀποκρῑνάμενος.

Exercise 12η

1. ἔκαυσε(ν). 2. ἔπλευσαν. 3. ἤλασας. 4. ἠθελήσατε. 5. ἐκάλεσας. 6. μαχέσασθαι.
7. ἐλάσᾱσα.

Exercise 12θ

1. ἐξέβαλον. 2. εἰσέπεμψα. 3. ἀπεχώρησα. 4. κατέφυγον. 5. ἀπέλιπον. 6. προσέπεσον.
7. ἐξεκόμισα. 8. συνέπεμψα.

Exercise 12ι

1. I ask. 2. more. 3. then. 4. ship's captain. 5. certainly, indeed. 6. I relate.

Exercise 12κ

1. φαίνομαι. 2. πλεῖστος, -η, -ον. 3. ὁ ἔμπορος. 4. ὁ ναύτης. 5. μέγα. 6. Ἀθήνᾱζε.

Exercise 12λ

1. ἐρωτήσω, ἠρώτησα or ἠρόμην. 2. ἐξηγήσομαι, ἐξηγησάμην. 3. φανοῦμαι.

Exercise 12μ

GOD IS GREAT

[1] And while Dicaeopolis's brother and Myrrhine were returning to the city, a certain man (who was) walking to the Piraeus observed them from afar and told his slave to run ahead and to tell them to wait. And the slave, having run ahead and calling, said, "Cephalus tells you to wait." And the brother said, "Where is (the man) himself?" "He's approaching," replied the slave, "but wait!" So Dicaeopolis's brother and the wife waited. And the woman was not ceasing to cry (was not stopping crying). And a little

later both Cephalus arrived and Adeimantus, the brother of Cephalus, and Niceratus and some others.

[2] Seeing the woman crying and the man distressed, Cephalus said: "(My) dear, what ever is the matter (what ever are you suffering)? We, having prayed to the god and at the same time having seen the festival, are now happily (rejoicing) returning homeward. For the procession of the Athenians seemed to us to be beautiful, and the choruses and the contests (seemed to us to be) beautiful. Did you not see the festival? For I looked for you throughout the agora and was amazed that I was not able to find (you). How indeed (is it that) you are walking from the Piraeus to the city? You seem to me to be distressed. What is wrong with you (What are you suffering) and the woman with you? What is it?"

[3] "Dear Cephalus," replied Dicaeopolis's brother, "this (woman), who is (being) my brother's wife, suffered something terrible. You were looking for me, but I was not in the city; for I went down to the harbor with my brother and his wife and his son. For his son, who is a fine and good child (being a beautiful and good child), having become blind because of a misfortune in the city, sailed to Epidaurus together with his father. For his father wants to pray to Asclepius, if somehow he (i.e., Asclepius) is willing to heal him."

[4] "But cheer up, woman," said Cephalus, "for the god in Epidaurus is great, and he is able to heal all those who are sick, if he wishes. Do you remember Ambrosia, the blind (one)?"

[5] And Myrrhine (said): "(Yes,) for how (do I) not (remember her)?"

[6] And Cephalus (said): "So Ambrosia, being blind, went once to the god in Epidaurus. And walking through the sacred precinct, she heard many (people) saying that the god (had) made them well. But to Ambrosia it seemed impossible that lame and blind (people) became well, only having seen a dream. But while sleeping she saw a vision; the god seemed to say to the woman that he would make her well. 'But it is necessary,' Asclepius said, 'for you to provide a reward to the temple—a silver pig.' And then the god healed the sick eyes for her (her sick eyes). On the next day she woke up well and went out of the temple rejoicing. So don't fear, woman, for your child; for doubtless the god will heal him."

[7] Cephalus and the others with him, having bid (them) farewell, went away toward the harbor, and Dicaeopolis's brother led his (i.e., Dicaeopolis's) wife to Athens.

ANSWERS: CHAPTER 13

Exercise 13α

1. ἔλυε(ν). 2. ἔμενον. 3. ἔλεγον. 4. ἐπέμπομεν. 5. ἠκούετε. 6. ἔπειθες. 7. ἐλύοντο. 8. ἐγίγνεσθε. 9. ἐφίλουν. 10 ἐθεῶ. 11. ἐθεᾶσθε. 12. ἡγεῖτο. 13. ἐφοβοῦ. 14. ᾔρει. 15. ἐθεᾶτο. 16. ἐφοβούμεθα. 17. ἐθεώμην. 18. ἐθεώμεθα. 19. ἐθεῶντο. 20. ἐφιλοῦμεν. 21. ἦσαν. 22. ἦτε. 23. ᾔειν or ᾔει. 24. ἦσαν or ᾔεσαν. 25. ἦν. 26. ἦ or ἦν. 27. ᾔεισθα or ᾔεις. 28. ᾖα or ᾔειν. 29. ἦμεν. 30. ἦτε. 31. ἦμεν. 32. ἦσθα. 33. ἑώρα. 34. εἰπόμην. 35. ἑώρων. 36. ἠργαζόμην or εἰργαζόμην. 37. ἠργάζοντο or εἰργάζοντο. 38. εἶχον. 39. εἷλκε(ν). 40. ἑώρων. 41. ἑώρας. 42. ἑωρῶμεν. 43. ἑωρᾶτε.

Exercise 13β

1. I. 2. I. 3. A. 4. I or A. 5. A. 6. I. 7. A. 8. I or A. 9. A, I. 10. I.

Exercise 13γ

1. sails. 2. I row. 3. firm, steady. 4. quick, swift.

Exercise 13δ

1. ὁ ἄνεμος. 2. ἡσυχάζω. 3. ἀλλήλων. 4. λαμπρός, -ή, -όν.

Exercise 13ε

1. ἡσύχαζον, ἡσυχάσω, ἡσύχασα. 2. ἤρεσσον, no future, ἤρεσα. 3. εἶλκον, ἕλξω,

εἵλκυσα. 4. εἶχον, ἕξω or σχήσω, ἔσχον. 5. ἠργαζόμην or εἰργαζόμην, ἐργάσομαι, ἠργασάμην or εἰργασάμην. 6. εἰπόμην, ἕψομαι, ἑσπόμην. 7. ἑώρων, ὄψομαι, εἶδον. 8. ᾖα or ᾔειν, εἶμι, ἦλθον.

Exercise 13ζ

1. ὅς. 2. ἅς. 3. ᾧ. 4. ἥ. 5. ὧν. 6. ᾧ. 7. ἅ. 8. ὄν. 9. οἵ. 10. ἧς. 11. αἷς. 12. ᾧ. 13. οἷς. 14. ὅ. 15. ὅς. 16. ἥν. 17. οἵ. 18. ὅ. 19. ᾗ. 20. ὧν.

Exercise 13η

1. τείχους. 2. τριήρεις. 3. ἀληθεῖς. 4. ψευδῶν. 5. ὄρη. 6. τείχει. 7. τριήρεις. 8. ὁρῶν. 9. τριήρεσι(ν). 10. τείχη. 11. ἀληθεῖς. 12. ψευδοῦς. 13. τριήρη. 14. τείχεσι(ν). 15. ψευδῆ. 16. ἀληθεῖ. 17. ὄρει. 18. ψευδῆ. 19. τριήρων. 20. ὄρεσι(ν). 21. τριήρει. 22. ὄρους. 23. ἀληθοῦς. 24. τεῖχος.

Exercise 13θ

1. ταχέσι(ν). 2. βραδεῖαν. 3. ταχύν. 4. βραδείᾱς. 5. ταχέα. 6. ταχεῖαν. 7. βραδέος. 8. ταχεῖς. 9. βραδέων. 10. ταχείαις.

Exercise 13ι

1. freedom. 2. the truth (= true things). 3. fight; battle. 4. wave. 5. when. 6. I ward off X, I defend myself against X. 7. trireme. 8. who (emphatic). 9. no one, no. 10. I ward off X from Y. 11. near the house. 12. false. 13. in truth. 14. who. 15. as it seems.

Exercise 13κ

1. τὰ ψευδῆ. 2. ὡς. 3. ἡ μάχη. 4. ὅς. 5. τὸ ναυτικόν. 6. αἵ. 7. ἡ Ἑλλάς. 8. ἐκεῖνο. 9. ὀργίζομαι. 10. ἡ ἀρχή. 11. ἀληθής, ἀληθές. 12. ὁ βάρβαρος. 13. τὰ στενά. 14. ἅμα.

Exercise 13λ

1. ὠργιζόμην, ὀργιοῦμαι. 2. ἤμῡνον, ἀμυνῶ, ἤμῡνα. 3. ἠμῡνόμην, ἀμυνοῦμαι, ἠμῡνάμην.

Exercise 13μ

VIRTUE ALWAYS OVERCOMES INSOLENCE

[1] And the old sailor said, "First I want to speak to you about the Athenians' virtue and courage. For I, who was present, will clearly reveal to you the true cause that provided freedom to all the Greeks. For we, who (had) lived our lives in every freedom, thought that we must fight the barbarians for the freedom of all Greeks.

[2] "For our ancestors established a fine (beautiful) government. But the governments of other peoples were tyrannies and oligarchies. But we were not thinking it fitting to be slaves or masters of one another, but we were seeking equality of political rights according to law. For we were friends to one another and all free, and we were yielding/submitting to no other thing except to a true notion of virtue.

[3] "But tyrants and those having been reared in tyranny are always without a taste of freedom and true friendship. For insolence always holds (takes) the souls of tyrants; and insolence bursting into bloom produces the fruit of recklessness/sin/ruin, and from it men pluck nothing other than tears and sorrow. For Zeus, who sees all (all things), punishes the insolence of tyrants, who, (although) being mortal, dare to contend against the gods.

[4] "And we, just as our ancestors who conquered the barbarians at Marathon, thinking (that) a beautiful death leaves behind an immortal reckoning concerning good men, were not afraid of the multitude of the enemy but trusted in our own virtue (the virtue of ourselves). So in the dangers of war having left the city behind, and having gotten into our triremes, we set our souls/lives, (although) being few, against the multitude of Asia. So on the one hand we showed to all men, (by) winning victory in the naval battle, that it is better to run risks with a few on behalf of freedom than to fight with many slaves on behalf of their own slavery (the slavery of themselves). On the other

hand we showed that even in naval dangers, just as in (dangers of) infantry, virtue always overcomes number, thinking that in truth men are a city (men to be a city), and not walls nor yet triremes empty of men. For walls and homes and temples without the virtue of men are like (just as) a motionless body.

[5] "And first we warded off the barbarians from the land and from all Greece, and then we prepared to rebuild the city and the walls. And thus our city put a stop to military forces coming insolently against Europe. And it is necessary to recount all the deeds from the beginning; so listen."

ANSWERS: CHAPTER 14

Exercise 14α
1. σώφρων. 2. πολλοί. 3. ἀληθής. 4. κακίων. 5. καλλίων. 6. σωφρονεστέρᾱ. 7. χαλεπώτατος. 8. ἀνδρειότερος. 9. ἀμείνων. 10. ἀληθέστατος. 11. κάκιστος. 12. μείζων. 13. ἄριστος. 14. καλή. 15. ἀνδρειότατος. 16. ἐλάττων. 17. κακίων. 18. χαλεπώτεροι. 19. μείζων. 20. χαλεπός. 21. μῑκρά. 22. πλεῖστος. 23. μέγιστος. 24. ὀλιγίστη. 25. καλλίστη. 26. πλείων or πλέων.

Exercise 14β
1. truly. 2. more bravely. 3. best. 4. badly. 5. more, rather. 6. most. 7. worst. 8. most bravely. 9. bravely. 10. well. 11. more truly. 12. worse. 13. most, most of all; very much; especially. 14. much. 15. better. 16. very. 17. more. 18. most truly.

Exercise 14γ
1. μείζων τοῦ ἀδελφοῦ or μείζων ἢ ὁ ἀδελφός. 2. πολλῷ σωφρονέστεραι. 3. ὡς ἀνδρειότατα. 4. καλλίων. 5. μεγίστη πᾱσῶν. 6. ἐλάττων τοῦ πατρός or ἐλάττων ἢ ὁ πατήρ. 7. κάκιστοι.

Exercise 14δ
1. hoplite. 2. than. 3. soldier. 4. number; multitude. 5. between. 6. I fare; I do. 7. I join battle (with). 8. this. 9. I come together.

Exercise 14ε
1. ὁ στόλος. 2. τὰ στενά. 3. ὁ στόλος or ὁ στρατός. 4. στενός, -ή, -όν. 5. χράομαι. 6. χράομαι. 7. τὰ στενά. 8. ἐπιπέμπω. 9. ἐλπίζω. 10. ὀλίγος, -η, -ον. 11. προσβάλλω. 12. ἐλπίζω. 13. ὁ στόλος. 14. κατὰ γῆν.

Exercise 14ζ
1. προσέβαλλον, προσβαλῶ, προσέβαλον. 2. ἐπέπεμπον, ἐπιπέμψω, ἐπέπεμψα. 3. ἤλπιζον, ἐλπιῶ, ἤλπισα. 4. ἐχρώμην, χρήσομαι, ἐχρησάμην. 5. συνῇα or συνῄειν, σύνειμι, συνῆλθον. 6. συνέβαλλον, συμβαλῶ, συνέβαλον. 7. ἔπρᾱττον, πρᾱ́ξω, ἔπρᾱξα.

Exercise 14η
Answers are not provided for this exercise.

Exercise 14θ
1. οὗτος. 2. τοῦτον. 3. ἐκείνην. 4. ἐκείνους. 5. τούτῳ. 6. τόδε. 7. αἵδε. 8. ταύτης. 9. ἐκεῖνο. 10. τῇδε. 11. τῇδε. 12. οὗτοι. 13. ἐκείνων. 14. τούτου. 15. ἐκείνῳ. 16. τᾱ́σδε. 17. τούτοις. 18. τοῦδε. 19. ἐκείναις. 20. αὕτη.

Exercise 14ι
1. ποῖ; 2. πόθεν; 3. που. 4. ποτε. 5. πῶς; 6. ποι. 7. πως. 8. ποῦ; 9. πότε; 10. ποθεν.

Exercise 14κ
1. all; every; whole. 2. I come through; I go through. 3. when. 4. double gates; (mountain) pass. 5. I show; I tell; I tell of, explain. 6. war. 7. I announce; I tell. 8. the enemy.

Exercise 14λ
1. ἕως. 2. τῇ προτεραίᾳ. 3. ὅδε, ἥδε, τόδε. 4. ὅπου. 5. πολέμιος, -ᾱ, -ον. 6. γράφω. 7. ἀναχωρέω. 8. ἀντέχω. 9. παραγίγνομαι. 10. ἀναχωρέω.

Exercise 14μ

1. διῇα or διῄειν, δίειμι, διῆλθον. 2. ἀντεῖχον, ἀνθέξω, ἀντέσχον. 3. ἔφραζον, φράσω, ἔφρασα. 4. ἤγγελλον, ἀγγελῶ, ἤγγειλα. 5. ἀνεχώρουν, ἀναχωρήσω, ἀνεχώρησα. 6. ἔγραφον, γράψω, ἔγραψα. 7. παρεγιγνόμην, παραγενήσομαι, παρεγενόμην.

Exercise 14ν

TWO MEN QUARREL

[1] And while the old sailor was speaking about the barbarians sailing into Phalerum, suddenly everyone on the ship heard men shouting loudly. For two men quarreling with one another were raising their voices loudly.

[2] The one said, "No by Zeus, you will not escape unpunished for saying this." And the other, answering, said, "Go and be hanged!" And everyone (all) in the ship, having heard these shouts and this commotion, came close to the men who were quarreling, wanting to learn the cause of this quarrel. The men, breaking into laughter, were saying, "Strike, strike the rogue!" and the women, screaming, (were saying), "Stop, stop the men quarreling."

[3] And Dicaeopolis (said), "What is (it)? What is this commotion? What is this matter? Who are the ones shouting?"

[4] And the old sailor said, "I do not know; but it is necessary for us to learn what is happening. Come on, then, come with me." And saying this he got up (raised himself up) and went toward the ones who were quarreling.

[5] And the steersman, running toward (them), said, "Hercules, what [is] this? What ever is this bad thing? By Poseidon, you are out of your minds, as it seems to me. Stop, stop quarreling with one another and tell me from the beginning how you got into this quarrel (from where this quarrel happened for you)."

[6] Then the one man said, "This (fellow) first was saying many bad things (speaking many things badly) and in a loud voice, and then he even struck me, and he made such a great shouting and commotion that even you and all these others came. This man is insane, as it seems to me."

[7] And the other (man), taking up (the conversation), said, "Tell me, you worst of all men; do you dare to say this even while looking me in the face (looking at me)?"

[8] And he, answering, said, "Be quiet, you rogue; for you took a stick against me, who am (being) a free man, and you struck me. Isn't this great (much) insolence?"

[9] And the other (man) (said): "By Zeus, and I did well striking you, since you are (you being) not only a thief but also a spy of the Lacedaemonians and not really (in truth) an Athenian merchant."

[10] And he (said): "What do you say, men? Isn't this rogue insulting me?"

[11] And the other (man said): "Do you want to be quiet? And listen, steersman; for this was the beginning of the quarrel. This (fellow) did such things because of which he is now with reason hated by me. But it is necessary even for you all, Athenians, to hear all these matters. For this man is not an Athenian merchant, as he wishes to appear, but, being a spy of the Lacedaemonians, he lives in our city plotting against us. For the father of (for) this man spoke with a foreign accent and was not able to speak Attic Greek well. And I saw both this (man) himself and a certain foreigner conversing in the agora in the Doric dialect. And now indeed I heard this (fellow) speaking on behalf of the Lacedaemonians; for he was saying that the city of the Spartans is stronger than ours and that the Lacedaemonians were always braver than the Athenians in battles and that the Lacedaemonians are the most self-controlled of all the Greeks and much more self-controlled than the Athenians and many other such things."

[12] And the steersman (said): "You worst and most wicked of men, do you indeed dare to say these things to us?"

[13] And the merchant, being very afraid, said, "No, steersman; but I hate the Lacedaemonians very much and know (I do not not know) that the Athenians are the best of the Greeks, having an empire by sea and more triremes than the Lacedaemonians. For they have a larger army than we on land, but many (by much) fewer ships and sailors. For no one does not know that the Athenians are better in naval skill than all the other Greeks. I was only saying this, that the Lacedaemonians, with whom we are always displeased, are not responsible for everything bad (all bad things).

[14] "How am I not most truly an Athenian? For I am your citizen, friends, being Athenian both on the side of my father and my mother. For this man slanders my father, since he spoke (was speaking) with a foreign accent. But he, taken by the enemy in war, became a slave and stayed in a foreign land for a long time and because of this was no longer able to speak Attic Greek well. But he was in truth a citizen, and not a foreigner, as this man says talking nonsense (talks nonsense), and his father Charisius and his mother were Athenians. And concerning his mother I want to say these things to you: I had a grandfather (there was a grandfather for me), Athenian men, the father of my mother, who was one of those who campaigned at Marathon and died (there), and his brother died at Salamis campaigning with Themistocles.

[15] "You heard this man saying that he saw me in the agora conversing with a certain foreigner in the Doric dialect. But what? For being a merchant I often set out from this city and sailed from this sea into many other lands, 'I saw the cities and came to know the mind of many men,' just as Homer says about Odysseus. So it is in no way strange that I learned also the dialects of very many men. So don't believe this man telling lies and slanders, steersman.

[16] "And, men, why must I say more (things) to you? For I think that now you know all (you do not know nothing), since you (have) heard the truth."

[17] And the steersman said, "But now, rest and do not cause a commotion and do not fight against one another; for we must sail calmly and arrive at Epidaurus. So you, merchant, don't speak on behalf of the Lacedaemonians, and you, sailor, do not be vexed but be quiet!" Having said these things, he went away, and soon all the others too sat down.

[18] And Dicaeopolis (said): "Look, old man, how great is the change of affairs in this our land; for you were describing to us how all the Greeks, both the Lacedaemonians and the Athenians, fought together against the barbarians on behalf of freedom; but now men living in the same city hate one another and seek some cause for hatred and fighting (battle). For then the Greeks thought all Greece to be a common fatherland, but now they care only for their own homes. So our ancestors carefully guarded both concord toward the Greeks and hatred toward the barbarians; for concord used to seem to be the greatest good for cities. And now not only do the Athenians hate the Lacedaemonians and the Lacedaemonians hate the Athenians, but also the Athenians themselves have hatred toward one another. Alas, alas for this city!"

[19] And Philip, taking up (the conversation), said, "But I want to hear how the Athenians fought against the barbarians at Salamis. So do not stop describing (these events), sailor, but tell us what happened when the barbarians were lying at anchor in the harbor."

[20] And the sailor said, "So be quiet and listen."

ANSWERS: CHAPTER 15

Exercise 15α

1. ἔβη. 2. βᾶσα. 3. στῆθι. 4. βῆναι. 5. ἔγνως. 6. ἔγνων. 7. ἔστησαν. 8. στῆτε. 9. γνῶναι. 10. γνούς. 11. ἔβητε. 12. ἔβησαν. 13. ἔστην. 14. ἔστητε. 15. γνῶτε.

16. ἔβης. 17. ἔγνω. 18. ἔστης. 19. ἔβημεν. 20. γνοῦσα. 21. στάς. 22. ἔστη.
23. ἔγνωσαν. 24. στᾶσα. 25. ἔβην. 26. στῆναι. 27. βῆθι. 28. γνῶθι. 29. βάς.
30. ἔγνωτε. 31. βῆτε. 32. ἔστημεν.

Exercise 15β
1. Περικλέᾱ. 2. Ἡρακλεῖ. 3. Σοφόκλεις. 4. Περικλέους. 5. Θεμιστοκλεῖ.
6. Θεμιστοκλέᾱ. 7. Περίκλεις. 8. Ἡρακλέους.

Exercise 15γ
1. perplexity; difficulty; the state of being at a loss. 2. I yield. 3. I compel. 4. only. 5. mind.
6. flight.

Exercise 15δ
1. ὁ ναύαρχος. 2. ὁ στρατηγός. 3. μόνος, -η, -ον. 4. μηκέτι. 5. διαφθείρω. 6. οὐ
μόνον . . . ἀλλὰ καί.

Exercise 15ε
1. διέφθειρον, διαφθερῶ, διέφθειρα. 2. ἠνάγκαζον, ἀναγκάσω, ἠνάγκασα. 3. εἶκον,
εἴξω, εἶξα.

Exercise 15ζ
1. δηλοῦσι(ν). 2. δηλοῦ. 3. ἐλευθεροῦμεν. 4. ἐλευθεροῦσθαι. 5. δουλῶ. 6. δουλοῖ.
7. ἐδήλου. 8. ἐλευθεροῦνται. 9. δουλοῦν. 10. δούλου. 11. δηλοῦσα. 12. ἠροῦτε.
13. ἐδούλουν. 14. ἀροῦν. 15. ἠλευθέρους. 16. ἐλευθεροῦσθε. 17. ἀροῖς. 18. ἠροῦμεν.
19. πληροῦτε. 20. πληροῦτε. 21. ἐπλήρουν. 22. ἐλευθεροῦται. 23. δουλούμεθα.
24. ἐδηλούμην. 25. ἠλευθερούμεθα. 26. δηλούμενος. 27. ἠλευθεροῦντο. 28. δηλοῖ.
29. ἠλευθεροῦτο. 30. ἐδουλοῦσθε.

Exercise 15η
1. νοῖ. 2. νοῖς. 3. νοῦ. 4. νοῦ. 5. νῶν. 6. νῷ. 7. νοῦς. 8. νοῦν.

Exercise 15θ
1. 100. 2. 12th. 3. 40. 4. 20. 5. 10,000. 6. 1000th. 7. 11. 8. 500. 9. 100th. 10. 80. 11. 12.
12. 11th.

Exercise 15ι
1. as quickly as possible. 2. to sleep, in order to sleep. 3. when. 4. as it seems. 5. that.
6. how. 7. that.

Exercise 15κ
1. ancestor. 2. right. 3. I trust, am confident (in); I believe. 4. corpse. 5. everywhere. 6. I
clash (with). 7. I try, attempt. 8. part. 9. haste, eagerness. 10. I fight by sea. 11. uproar,
commotion. 12. I free, set free.

Exercise 15λ
1. ὁ πέπλος. 2. πεζός, ή, -όν. 3. ὁ ἀγών. 4. ἡ πατρίς. 5. ἡ νίκη. 6. ἡ ἀρετή.
7. ἐμπίπτω. 8. ὡς. 9. ὁ κόσμος. 10. δηλόω. 11. ἡ τύχη. 12. ἐπιπλέω. 13. βλάπτω.
14. ἀνέστην. 15. κόσμῳ.

Exercise 15μ
1. συνέπιπτον, συμπεσοῦμαι, συνέπεσον. 2. ἐναυμάχουν, ναυμαχήσω, ἐναυμάχησα.
3. ἠλευθέρουν, ἐλευθερώσω, ἠλευθέρωσα. 4. ἔβλαπτον, βλάψω, ἔβλαψα. 5. ἐνέπιπτον,
ἐμπεσοῦμαι, ἐνέπεσον. 6. ἐπείρων, πειράσω, ἐπείρᾱσα. 7. ἐπίστευον, πιστεύσω,
ἐπίστευσα. 8. ἐπέπλεον, ἐπιπλεύσομαι, ἐπέπλευσα. 9. ἐδήλουν, δηλώσω, ἐδήλωσα.

Exercise 15ν

THE GODS PUNISHED XERXES

[1] And the old sailor said, "For we ran risks on behalf of our fatherland and on
behalf of the freedom of all Greeks; and because of this we in truth enjoy immortal praise,
not because we won but much more because the cause of our fighting (battle) was just.
For fighting and setting our fatherland free not only were we showing to all men of that
time (τότε) what virtue is, but we were also putting an end to (stopping) for all future

(ἔπειτα) time the Greeks fearing a multitude of ships and men. For the gods always punish insolence, honor virtue, and provide great glory to those fighting on behalf of freedom.

[2] "For in that time all Asia was subject to Xerxes, now the fourth king of the Persians. For the first, Cyrus by name, having set free the Persians, his own citizens, at the same time also enslaved his masters the Medes and ruled the rest of Asia as far as Egypt. And his son Cambyses attacked many other lands of Egypt and Libya, enslaving them. And third Darius with his infantry (army on foot) went into the lands of the Scythians, and with (his) ships he took control of the sea and the islands. And he attacked the Athenians at Marathon but did not win. And Xerxes, the fourth king of the Persians, was enslaving many other peoples, but he did not have (was not having) loyal and free men but only a great multitude of slaves. And always desiring things belonging to others, Xerxes decided to make war upon the Greeks, and crossed into Europe. And using what lawful (claim) did he wage war against the Greeks? Just as in all his life, so also then he was showing his insolence, thinking (himself) to be immortal and despising the gods, who (had) presented him with such a great empire (provided such a great empire to him). For insolence is the greatest evil for men and begets tyrants. And what else is insolence if not to think (oneself) to be better than gods and to want to enslave all men? Because of this Zeus punished Xerxes; for it is not possible for mortals to fight against the immortals.

[3] "And our fathers and we ourselves from childhood (from children) lived our life in total freedom, hating slavery. And because of this we were doing many fine (beautiful) deeds in our whole life both in private and in public. And in particular, fighting and subduing the power of all Asia, we were making clear to all men that virtue and daring always conquer insolence. And when we attacked the enemy, we did not turn our attention to the dangers of war but we had in mind to save our fatherland and our children and our wives.

[4] "So we showed bravery and virtue with intelligence (mind)—for when man does anything without intelligence (mind), he always suffers something bad. For our intelligence (mind) is in each (of us) a god—and because of this all the gods came to our aid, and punished the barbarians. For the gods, if it is necessary to tell the truth, ordained our victory and the barbarians' defeat.

[5] "So know, child, the deeds of our fathers and their daring, and show even yourself always in all your life the same virtue, if you want to be a friend to the gods and wish to become worthy of your fatherland."

ANSWERS: CHAPTER 16

Exercise 16α

1. is woken up. 2. ransoms. 3. stop. 4. was being washed. 5. wakes himself up, wakes up. 6. being destroyed. 7. was being loosened, loosed. 8. is not being learned. 9. washes herself, washes. 10. are being loosed. 11. is being struck. 12. stops. 13. were being woken up. 14. was washing himself, was washing. 15. were not stopping.

Exercise 16β

1. I wage war, campaign (against). 2. inhabitant. 3. and in particular; and what is more. 4. a hundred. 5. I lie. 6. by the boy. 7. I gather. 8. misfortune; disaster. 9. where (in the world)? 10. nowhere.

Exercise 16γ

1. ὕστερον. 2. ὁ σύμμαχος. 3. τελευτάω. 4. διᾱκόσιοι, -αι, -α. 5. ἐπίσταμαι. 6. δύναμαι. 7. πόσος; πόση; πόσον; 8. καταλαμβάνω. 9. πολλαχόσε.

Exercise 16δ

1. ἐστράτευον, στρατεύσω, ἐστράτευσα. 2. ἐτελεύτων, τελευτήσω, ἐτελεύτησα.
3. ἐδυνάμην, δυνήσομαι. 4. ἠπιστάμην, ἐπιστήσομαι. 5. κατελάμβανον,
καταλήψομαι, κατέλαβον. 6. συνήγειρον, συναγερῶ, συνήγειρα. 7. ἐκείμην, κείσομαι.

Exercise 16ε

ODYSSEUS IS HELD BACK BY CALYPSO

[1] When Odysseus and his comrades were sailing from the island of Helios, Zeus, sending a terrible storm, hit his ship with a thunderbolt. Then the comrades, having fallen out of the ship, all died in the waves; and Odysseus, taking hold of the mast, alone is saved. Then he was being carried nine days through the waves by the wind, holding onto the mast. And on the tenth (day) he saw an island being not very far away; then leaving the mast behind he swam toward the island. And Calypso was living there, a terrible goddess; and she received him kindly, for she was loving him and was nourishing (him) and was saying that she would make him immortal. For she was wanting to hold him back on the island and to make (him) husband to herself. But she never persuaded him; for he was wanting to return to his fatherland and to see his wife.

[2] So for seven years Odysseus was remaining on the island, being held back by Calypso. And he used to sit alone on the promontory, always crying: "Alas, alas," he said, "I want to return to my fatherland, but I am always held back by Calypso."

[3] And Zeus, looking from heaven toward the land, saw Odysseus sitting on the promontory weeping; so he was pitying him, and, having called Hermes, he says, "Go on, Hermes, fly to the island Ogygia; for there Odysseus is being held back by Calypso. Then order her to send him away. And if she does (will) not send him away, I will punish her."

[4] Then Hermes, obeying Zeus, was flying toward Ogygia; and when he arrived, he was looking for Calypso. And, after finding her sitting in her house, he said, "Greetings, goddess, you are being ordered by Zeus to send Odysseus away; for he has been (is) held back for a long time by you, wanting to return to his fatherland." And Calypso said, "Alas, alas, what are you saying? I want to hold him back always and make (him) husband to myself. For I love him." But Hermes (said), "You must obey Zeus; and if (you do) not, he will punish you." So saying, he flies away.

[5] And Calypso, lamenting greatly (many things), was looking for Odysseus. And she found him sitting on the promontory, crying, and she said, "Cheer up, Odysseus, do not cry. For I am ordered by Zeus to send you away homeward. Come on; we will make a raft." Then she led him to the edge of the island where there were many trees. Then Odysseus, having cut down twenty trees, was preparing a raft. Then he was working for three days, preparing the raft, and on the fourth (day) everything was ready, and on the fifth (day) Calypso sent him away from the island. And he, rejoicing, sailed away.

[6] Then at first he was being carried through the waves by a gentle wind, but then Poseidon, seeing him, said, "Dear me, I see Odysseus being carried easily through the waves. If I do not hinder/prevent him, he will arrive at his fatherland unharmed." So saying, he sent a terrible storm, having unleashed (loosened) all the winds. And a very great wave, hitting the raft, shattered (it). And Odysseus, having fallen out into the waves, was very afraid but with difficulty having swum to the raft took hold of the wreckage. Then for two days and two nights he was being carried hither and thither, always expecting death. And finally Athena, seeing him and pitying (him), stopped all the other winds, and she sent only gentle Boreas; and by this wind Odysseus was being carried toward Phaeacia, where he was destined to be saved by Nausicaa.

Exercise 16ζ

1. ὑπὸ τῷ δένδρῳ. 2. πρὸ τῆς ἡμέρας. 3. ἐπὶ τὴν ἀκτήν. 4. μετὰ τῶν φίλων. 5. κατὰ τὸ ὄρος. 6. περὶ τοῦ νεανίου. 7. πρὸς τὸ ἄστυ. 8. ἐν ταῖς Ἀθήναις. 9. ὑπὲρ τὸ ὄρος.

10. σὺν θεῷ. 11. ἀνὰ τὴν ὁδόν. 12. ἐπὶ τῇ πόλει. 13. ὑπὲρ τοῦ πατρός. 14. πρὸς τῇ κρήνῃ. 15. μετὰ τὴν ἑορτήν. 16. εἰς τὸ ἄστυ. 17. ὑπὸ τὸ δένδρον. 18. περὶ τὰς Ἀθήνας. 19. παρὰ τὴν νῆσον. 20. ἐκ τῆς οἰκίᾱς. 21. ἀπὸ τῆς κρήνης. 22. διὰ τὸ ἀργύριον. 23. ἐγγὺς τοῦ ἄστεως. 24. διὰ τῆς νυκτός. 25. ὄπισθεν τοῦ ἱεροῦ.

Exercise 16η

1. κεῖται. 2. κεῖνται. 3. δύνανται. 4. κεῖσαι. 5. ἐπίστασαι; 6. κεῖσθαι. 7. δύνασθαι. 8. ἐδυνάμεθα. 9. ἠπίστατο. 10. κειμένους. 11. κεῖσθε. 12. ἐπιστάμεθα. 13. ἐδυνάμην. 14. δύνασθε. 15. ἐπισταμένη. 16. δυνάμεθα. 17. ἔκειντο. 18. ἐδύνατο. 19. ἐπίστανται. 20. κεῖσθε. 21. ἐπίστασθαι. 22. ἔκεισο. 23. ἐδύνασο or ἐδύνω. 24. κείμεθα. 25. δύνασο. 26. ἐπίστασθε. 27. ἐδύναντο. 28. ἠπίστασο or ἠπίστω. 29. ἐκείμεθα. 30. δύναται.

Exercise 16θ

1. worthy (of). 2. peace treaty. 3. least of all, not at all. 4. river. 5. I besiege. 6. year.

Exercise 16ι

1. ὁ βίος. 2. ὁ θῡμός. 3. ὁ θάνατος. 4. λῡπέομαι. 5. λῡπέω. 6. ἡ σπονδή. 7. ἡ εἰρήνη.

Exercise 16κ

1. ἐπολιόρκουν, πολιορκήσω, ἐπολιόρκησα. 2. ἐλῡπουν, λῡπήσω, ἐλῡπησα.

Exercise 16λ

ODYSSEUS IS SAVED BY NAUSICAA

[1] Then for two days and two nights Odysseus was wandering, being carried by the wind. And on the third day, raised up on the top of a wave, he saw a certain island being not very far away. So leaving behind the wreckage of the raft, he was trying to swim to the island. But when he approached the island, everywhere there were huge rocks, so that it was not possible to go out of the sea there. So he was swimming along the shore, looking for a place where the shore was level. And finally he was being carried to the mouth of a river; so he swam there (to that place). So thus with difficulty he went out (of the sea) onto the land. And having suffered many terrible things, he was very tired; so for a long time he was resting on the shore. And finally he stood up and said, "Alas, what must I do? To whose land have I come? Are those living here friendly to men or (are they) barbarians and hostile to strangers? For I am very afraid, having arrived at a foreign land. So I will hide (myself)." So saying, he hurried to a certain woods being not far away and hiding himself in the bushes went to sleep.

[2] The city of the Phaeacians was not very far away, over whom Alcinous was ruling. And Alcinous had a certain very beautiful daughter, named Nausicaa. And Nausicaa was wanting to wash the clothes. So when the sun first rose, she hurried to Alcinous and said, "Father dear, I want to carry the clothes to the river and wash (them). For many are unwashed, both mine and those of my brothers. So are you willing to order the slaves to prepare a wagon for me? For the river is far away, and it is necessary to carry many clothes there."

[3] And Alcinous said, "Certainly, dearest daughter, I will immediately order the slaves to prepare a wagon for you." And the slaves, obeying Alcinous, led out a beautiful wagon. Then Nausicaa carried out the clothes, and her mother prepared food and wine. And Nausicaa called her handmaids and, having gotten upon the wagon, goaded the mules. And the mules, being goaded, were running quickly, carrying Nausicaa and the clothes, and the handmaids were following behind the wagon.

[4] And when they arrived at the river, having taken the clothes out of the wagon they washed them thoroughly in the river. And when they (had) washed (them) all thoroughly, they sat down on the shore and ate. And then Nausicaa, taking a ball, threw (it) to the handmaids; and they caught (took) the ball. So thus they were playing for a long (much) time, throwing the ball to one another. And finally Nausicaa threw the ball

toward a certain handmaid, but the ball missed the handmaid, and it fell into the river. Then all the handmaids shouted loudly and screamed.

[5] And in the meantime Odysseus sleeps in the bushes. And immediately he is awakened by the screaming girls. "Alas," he said, "to whose land have I come? Are there nymphs, who dwell in the mountains and the rivers, or human girls? But come on; I will leave the bushes and find out (learn) who they are."

[6] Then having said this (thus), he went out of the bushes and approached the girls. And they, seeing a man approaching who was (being) naked and a stranger, were afraid and all fled; only Nausicaa remained on the shore. And Odysseus, having seen Nausicaa remaining, slowly approached and said, "Are you some one of the gods or a mortal? For if you are some one of the gods who inhabit (have) heaven, you appear to me to be Artemis, the daughter of Zeus; but if (you are) some one of mortals, your father and mother are blessed/happy, and blessed/happy are your brothers, too. For I never saw such a man or woman (as you). Pity me, queen/lady, (me) who, having suffered many things, have come to your land. I beseech you to provide clothes for me and to take me to the city."

[7] And Nausicaa pitied him and said, "Do not be afraid, stranger; for I pity you, who, having suffered many things, have come to our land. And I will provide clothes for you and will lead (you) to the city." So saying, she called her handmaids and said, "Come here, handmaids; why did you flee having seen a man? Return and wash the stranger in the river."

[8] Then the handmaids, obeying Nausicaa, took Odysseus to the river and brought him very beautiful clothes and having left them near Odysseus went away. And Odysseus, having washed in the river and having put on the clothes, approached the girls.

[9] And Nausicaa having seen him approaching was amazed and said, "Handmaids, how handsome (beautiful) is the stranger; he is like a god. May I have such a husband! But provide food and wine for him!" Then the handmaids provided food and wine for him; and he ate up everything; for he was very hungry.

[10] Then Nausicaa said, "Come on, stranger, now I will lead you to the city." Then, having gotten onto the wagon, she goaded the mules. And the mules, being goaded, were running quickly, and Odysseus and the handmaids were following behind. Then soon they approached the city. And Nausicaa said to him, "Do not come into the city with me, stranger, but wait here. For if someone of the Phaeacians sees you following me, he will be amazed and will say, 'Who (is) this (who) follows Nausicaa, handsome (beautiful), great, and a stranger? Where did she find him? Will he be her husband (a husband for her)?' So I will hurry to the city, and you come in alone and seek the house of my father. And having found the house, go straight to the great hall. There you will see my mother. Go straightway to her and beg her to pity you and receive (you) kindly."

[11] Then Nausicaa hurried to the city, and Odysseus, having remained a short time, entered into the city and did all the things as many as Nausicaa ordered. Then, having found the house of Alcinous and having gone into the great hall, he saw Alcinous and many kings dining and the mother of Nausicaa sitting at the hearth. Then immediately he hurried to her and began to beg her to pity him and receive (him) kindly. Then all were amazed and fell silent. And finally Alcinous said, "Stranger, I pity you and will receive (you) kindly. Sit down beside me." Then he ordered a handmaid to provide food and wine to him. And to the kings he said, "Now all go away to your homes (to home); and tomorrow we will plan how we will send this stranger to his fatherland."

[12] Then all the kings went away to their homes (to home). And Alcinous said to Odysseus, "Tell me, stranger, how you have come to our land." And Odysseus told him

all the things as many as he suffered being held back by Calypso and how Nausicaa saved him when he was carried by the winds to Phaeacia. And Alcinous, having heard, was amazed and said: "Now you must sleep; for you are very tired. And tomorrow we will plan how we will send you away to your fatherland."

[13] And on the next day Alcinous called together all the kings to a feast. And Odysseus, having prepared himself to go to the feast, having washed and put on a very beautiful cloak, was hurrying to the great hall; but look, in his path Nausicaa was waiting, and she said, "Greetings, stranger; when you return to your fatherland, do not forget me; for I saved you." And he said, "Nausicaa, never will I forget you; for you speak the truth; you saved me." Having said this, he went into the great hall.

[14] There indeed all were rejoicing in the feast. And Odysseus related all the things to them as many as he (had) suffered fighting in Troy and all the things as many as he (had) suffered trying to return home from Troy; and they were rejoicing listening. And Alcinous said, "Tomorrow we will send the stranger home; so you all bring gifts to the ship! And now hurry home!"

[15] Then on the next day when first the sun rose, all went down to the sea, bringing gifts; then they put the gifts into the ship, and Odysseus, having bid Alcinous farewell, boarded the ship. And the sailors, having cast off (loosened) the ship, rowed (it) into the sea. Then they sailed quickly. And Odysseus was so tired that he went to sleep on the deck. And soon they arrived at Ithaca. And the sailors lifted him still sleeping and put him and the gifts down on the shore.